So
Each May
Soar

Also by Carol Ann Tomlinson

*How to Differentiate Instruction in Academically
Diverse Classrooms*, 3rd Edition

*The Differentiated Classroom: Responding to the Needs
of All Learners*, 2nd Edition

Fulfilling the Promise of the Differentiated Classroom

*Differentiation and the Brain: How Neuroscience
Supports the Learner-Friendly Classroom*, 2nd Edition
(with David Sousa)

*The Differentiated School: Making Revolutionary Changes
in Teaching and Learning*
(with Kay Brimijoin and Lane Narvaez)

Leading and Managing a Differentiated Classroom
(with Marcia B. Imbeau)

*Integrating Differentiated Instruction and Understanding by
Design: Connecting Content and Kids* (with Jay McTighe)

Assessment and Student Success in a Differentiated Classroom
(with Tonya Moon)

Leading for Differentiation: Growing Teachers Who Grow Kids
(with Michael Murphy)

Carol Ann
TOMLINSON

So Each May Soar

**The Principles
and Practices of
Learner-Centered
Classrooms**

Alexandria, Virginia USA

ascd

1703 N. Beauregard St. • Alexandria, VA 22311-1714 USA
Phone: 800-933-2723 or 703-578-9600 • Fax: 703-575-5400
Website: www.ascd.org • Email: member@ascd.org
Author guidelines: www.ascd.org/write

Ranjit Sidhu, *CEO & Executive Director*; Penny Reinart, *Chief Impact Officer*; Genny Ostertag, *Senior Director, Acquisitions and Editing*; Julie Houtz, *Director, Book Editing*; Katie Martin, *Editor*; Thomas Lytle, *Creative Director*; Donald Ely, *Art Director*; Georgia Park, *Senior Graphic Designer*; Valerie Younkin, *Senior Production Designer*; Kelly Marshall, *Production Manager*; Christopher Logan, *Senior Production Specialist*; Shajuan Martin, *E-Publishing Specialist*

All web links in this book are correct as of the publication date below but may have become inactive or otherwise modified since that time. If you notice a deactivated or changed link, please email books@ascd.org with the words "Link Update" in the subject line. In your message, please specify the web link, the book title, and the page number on which the link appears.

PAPERBACK ISBN: 978-1-4166-3029-6   ASCD product #118006   n6/21

PDF E-BOOK ISBN: 978-1-4166-3030-2; see Books in Print for other formats.

Quantity discounts are available: email programteam@ascd.org or call 800-933-2723, ext. 5773, or 703-575-5773. For desk copies, go to www.ascd.org/deskcopy.

Library of Congress Cataloging-in-Publication Data
Names: Tomlinson, Carol A., author.
Title: So each may soar : the principles and practices of learner-centered classrooms / Carol Ann Tomlinson.
Description: Alexandria, Virginia USA : ASCD, 2021. | Includes bibliographical references and index.
Identifiers: LCCN 2021007379 (print) | LCCN 2021007380 (ebook) | ISBN 9781416630296 (paperback) | ISBN 9781416630302 (pdf)
Subjects: LCSH: Student-centered learning. | Classroom environment.
Classification: LCC LB1027.23 .T656 2021 (print) | LCC LB1027.23 (ebook) | DDC 371.3--dc23
LC record available at https://lccn.loc.gov/2021007379
LC ebook record available at https://lccn.loc.gov/2021007380

30 29 28 27 26 25 24 23 22 21   1 2 3 4 5 6 7 8 9 10 11 12

For colleagues—teachers, administrative leaders,
authors, and researchers—who have been,
and continue to be, my mentors by word and example.

For students—from 3 years old to 80+ years old—
who have allowed me to teach them and,
in that exchange, have shown me what matters most
profoundly in teaching and learning.

For friends—past and present—
who give shape and meaning to everything.

And for Katie Martin, whose depth and artistry
as an editor and as a human being seem always to
lead her to understand what I'm trying to say more fully
than I do. Thank you for bringing light and lightness
to the solitude of writing over many years.

So Each May Soar

The Principles
and Practices of
Learner-Centered Classrooms

Preface

*To know how much there is to know is
the beginning of learning to live.*

—Dorothy West in *The Richer, The Poorer*

Writing has been central to my life for as long as I can remember.

I was an only child, and from early on, writing was a way to fill vacant time. It allowed me to create imaginary kingdoms that I might otherwise have conjured with a brother or sister in the backyard. It helped me figure out the world around me absent the kind of clarifying combat-and-condolence offered by siblings. By the time I reached high school and then college, writing was a way to test and refine my ideas through the filters of my teachers, with whom I was far too shy to carry on a face-to-face conversation.

For me, serious writing always has a pain-to-pleasure ratio. Sometimes the pleasure, or at least a kind of satisfaction, clearly outweighs the struggle. Sometimes, it's a wrestling match with words and ideas, with just enough faint rays of delight to keep me going. I never know at the outset, of course, what the pain-to-pleasure ratio will be.

The novelist George R. R. Martin has concluded that there are two kinds of writers of fiction—architects and gardeners. The architects plan everything ahead of time. They know how many rooms are going to be in the house, what kind of roof there's going to be, where the wires will run, what kind of plumbing they'll use. They have the whole thing designed and blueprinted out before the first board is nailed into place. The gardeners, by contrast, dig a hole, drop in a seed, water it, and wait. They kind of know what seed it is—if they planted a fantasy seed or mystery seed, or whatever. But as the plant comes up and they continue to water it, they don't know how many branches it's going to have; they find out as it grows (cited in Flood, 2011). Martin explains that he, himself, is a gardener.

There's a parallel in nonfiction writing, at least in my experience. Sometimes as I begin writing, I know the "punchline," the theme, the big idea—and I have a relatively clear sense of the steps that can lead to the big idea. That functions like a plotline for me. While there are absolutely fits and starts and changes of direction along the way, the theme and line of logic I envision act as a compass that generally keeps me on course. In those settings, I write as an architect, knowing what the structure needs to look like and crafting a blueprint that will get me where I was sure from the outset I needed to go. In other instances, I begin with a sort of idea—fuzzy, perhaps, but still promising—a seed that I plant and tend along the way. In those instances, I write more as a gardener, and I plow a lot of mud as I go. Over time, and in a generally stepwise fashion, however, I can see the seed sprout, grow, and ultimately appear worthy of harvest.

This book has turned out to be a different sort of writing journey. I began with what I thought was at least a seed and probably a line of logic as well. After many months and several drafts of the first few chapters of *three* different versions of a book, I realized the seeds were not seeds after all, and the line of logic wasn't actually logical. Here's a brief (at least relative to the length of the journey) history, which is only worth sharing because it brought me to the chapters that follow, and because it may be a thought journey that other educators take as well.

Round 1...

It all began about three years ago. My initial intent was to explore the similarities and differences between differentiation, which has been the focus of much of my career, and "personalization," which was just beginning to populate the literature of education. After months of reading, study, and reflective note taking, I was bogged down by the fact that personalization is defined in so many ways that it almost defies analysis. That was made more problematic by expert conclusions that (1) differentiation and personalization are the same, (2) differentiation is a kind of personalization, and (3) personalization is a kind of differentiation. To complicate things further, there was a body of writing on technology-based "personalization"—a whole different breed of animal. In the end, I found so many misconceptions about differentiation that, combined with the amorphous "consensus" on both human-centered and tech-driven personalization, I had neither a blueprint nor a garden.

Round 2...

My second foray into making a book happen was similar to the first in that I thought I had both a seed and a line of logic. By this point, I had decided that there was no meaningful difference between differentiation *rightly understood* and personalization, so long as I cast personalization as the *means* of generating greater student ownership of and agency in learning and excluded from consideration both the kind of personalization achieved through technology and iterations of personalization that seem more focused on "whatever the student wants" than on meaningful learning.

Once again, I was stymied by enormous variety in how personalization has been depicted. It's been cast as mastery learning, as a way to raise test scores, as "anything-anywhere-anytime" learning, and as the mechanism of small schools. It's been characterized as inquiry, as project-based, as Genius Hour, and as the outcome of community engagement. It's been explained as making sure all students have access to the same materials and as ensuring that students can select materials with which they want to work. I thought a great deal about the reality that differentiation looks quite different in a teacher-directed classroom than it does in a classroom where students are partners in design and decision making. I pondered how personalization would morph among project-based, mastery-based, inquiry-based, and test-focused classrooms. Maybe, I concluded, what I really wanted to write about was how our definition of curriculum necessarily shapes how we think about instruction.

Round 3...

By this time, I had concluded that it would be more useful to potential readers for me to abandon the differentiation/personalization comparison or alignment and instead write about what it might look like to create classrooms in which students not only have considerable voice in their learning but also find reliable support to grow in autonomy and agency. That was going reasonably well until I had a rather embarrassing epiphany, which might better be characterized as a grave lapse of awareness. I realized some distance into manuscript 3 that I was essentially the "blind man" describing one piece of the elephant.

I am a true believer in creating classrooms where students are at the hub of decision making, where students and teachers function as a team to make the classroom as effective as possible for as many members of the classroom as possible. I am a career-long, dues-paying subscriber to innovation in classrooms. And I believe fervently that making standardized test scores the measure of our effectiveness as educators was an uninformed, costly, and near-catastrophic mistake insofar as it reduced the realities of the young human beings in our classrooms to data points. But I also know in both my brain and my bones that we cannot be the educators we want to be, or help learners become the people they dream of being, by adding a new emphasis, a "new" strategy, to our current practice, which in the test-prep era, seems scarcely concerned with quality in the first place. We have to regain our sight, I finally realized, and deal with the whole elephant. And I needed to do that, too.

Version 3 of the book was moribund because I had developed a sort of myopia that enabled me to think about putting students at the center of classroom planning without remembering the elements that enable students to develop in ways that maximize their capacity cognitively, affectively, and socially. We know what these elements are from both research and examples of excellent classroom practice—or perhaps more accurately, we know *about* them. Over the two decades since test scores became the currency of success in schools (a currency that is quite scarce, as it happens), we have had little impetus or time to think about the nature of learning environments that make school safe and compelling for young people. In too many schools, we've had no opportunity to understand what it means to create meaningful curriculum because lists of standards and pacing guides have taken the place of actual curriculum. We have talked some about promising assessment practices that might inform instructional approaches, but we have been so busy with the standardized tests and the interim tests designed to result in better scores on the standardized tests that there seems to have been little heart for more assessment. Instructional quality has taken a back seat to covering curriculum, adhering to pacing guides, and teaching information and skills easily assessed by filling in bubbles. "In the interest of time," students' strengths, interests, needs, and dreams have too often remained invisible. I didn't want to write about pieces of the elephant. There are lots of sources for reading about elephant pieces.

Finally... This

And so, after a convoluted writing journey, there is this book.

Slightly editing a conclusion of poet, essayist, and educator Robert Hayden (1984), writing is a way of finding order in chaos. This is not the first time I've experienced this truth, but perhaps it's the clearest example of it in my own work. I'm also onboard with Alex Magnin, a very interesting thinker, creator of videos, and entrepreneur, who says, "Writing doesn't make the world how I want it to be. It makes me how I want to be for the world. It forces me to figure things out, as best I can, and to declare publicly who I am" (cited in Hodin, 2013).

This book *is* about creating classrooms that are intentionally and persistently designed with students at the center of thinking, planning, implementing plans, reflecting, and revising. It explores

• What it means to honor each learner;

• What it looks like and accomplishes when we create communities of learners that help young people to develop intellectual, affective, and social attributes that are likely key contributors to their own success and to the success of a free society;

• What it entails to envision curriculum that captures the imagination of learners and contributes to their willingness—even eagerness—to pursue content that reflects the wisdom and practicality of being human;

• What it looks like when assessment becomes a process for revealing a learner's growth to both the teacher and to that learner in ways that support each learner's growth; and

• What it means to create learning opportunities that develop the mind of each learner in accordance with that learner's unique circumstances.

The book is also about

• What it asks of teachers to lead classrooms that use our best knowledge of teaching and learning to shine the light of hope and promise on each young person in our care;

• Why equity of access to excellent learning opportunities is an imperative in our schools; and

• How each of the key classroom elements—learning environment, curriculum, assessment, and instruction—appropriately shaped, contributes to both an ethic and practice of equity and excellence.

I have written the book for teachers who understand that developing and maintaining professional excellence is a daily climb up a very tall mountain and who are ready to commit to that journey. They know that the backward slides and detours they encounter, and the accompanying soreness of spirit, are potentially instructive and that exhilaration will outweigh the discomfort. I hope this book will be helpful to all teachers who seek to build trust in themselves and in their students, who want to explore content for its significance, who want to develop systems that help clarify each student's learning trajectory as it evolves over the course of a school year, and who want to steadily increase students' voices in their own learning.

In sum, then, the book is about putting students at the center of classrooms where quality practice provides a trustworthy foundation for helping young people grow consistently toward a better understanding of themselves, others, and the world they are inheriting. It is about humanizing classrooms for every young soul who is more or less compelled to spend year after year in our company. I invite you to think along with me as I explore how high-quality, foundational classroom practices might be marshaled to increase student voice and agency in the classroom and in students' lives beyond the classroom. It's my hope that in doing so, you will extend your own agency and voice as well.

Learning to teach is mind-bendingly difficult. Learning to teach at a high level of proficiency affords not only a whole new level of possibility but also a whole new level of challenge. Developing excellence is never a one-and-done deal. With that in mind, and with the knowledge that the strengths and experiences of teachers are every bit as diverse as those of their students, the book offers explanations and examples of classroom applications designed to open the way to success for a very broad range of learners.

My greatest hope is that you will find the journey clarifying, as it has been for me—remembering that my journey to these understandings was neither quick nor smooth, even after 50 years of teaching. Figure things out. Then declare publicly what you have learned in the company of your students and, in so doing, declare who you are as an educator and a human being.

C3 C3 C3

1

From Standardized to Learner-Centered

While we are living in the 21st century, the institution of education started in the 19th or 20th century. It was built to meet the challenges of the past. It was built with resources we had before. And once it was built, society spent the last century perfecting it.... In essence, we are prisoners of the past. To create a modern institution of education we have to escape from the past first.

—Yong Zhao in *Leading Modern Learning*

I began my career as a K–12 teacher with no formal preparation to teach, little life preparation for the job, and more than a decade of declaring repeatedly that whatever I ended up doing with my life, it would unequivocally *not* be teaching. Two decades later, when I made the difficult decision to leave my role in public school to begin working at the University of Virginia, my passion for teaching defined not only my work but me as well. At the time, I did not realize that my colleagues and I were experiencing the end of a sort of "golden age" of teaching. In those days, teaching and learning seemed *alive*.

That statement doesn't imply that things were perfect. The rural district and school in which I worked for 20 years were, in the beginning, significantly underfinanced. I had 40 students in many of my classes. My classroom furniture was "rescued" from a warehouse of damaged and abandoned remains. The only classroom resource I did not purchase myself was copy paper, and even that was limited and rationed. For many years, I didn't know there were books about teaching—and, in fact, there weren't very many. We had virtually no "professional development" for at least my first decade in the classroom. Our technology was pencils. The idea of an instructional coach was three decades down the pike. The field of cognitive psychology was just beginning to emerge. We had no insights from neuroscience that could inform our work.

But we had things that mattered as much or more in terms of our development as teachers. We had a good degree of professional respect and autonomy, a culture of sharing, and a cohort of like-minded colleagues who were curious, determined, and fascinated with the possibilities of teaching. Not all faculty members signed on to that cohort, of course, but enough did so that there were always people around who were game for listening, sharing experiences, and asking, "What if?"

Early on, teachers whose experience had made them much wiser than I gifted me with four pieces of advice that shaped my instructional planning and continue to guide my work to this day:

- **Identify the non-negotiables for the lesson or unit.** "Make sure you know what's required for students to move forward successfully," they told me. "Make sure that sticks. Don't try to do everything."
- **Be sure students *understand* what they are learning.** "Memorization and mimicry have a short shelf-life," they stressed. "Conceptual understanding is durable and serviceable."
- **Always know where your students are in relation to the non-negotiables.** "It's how you'll be able to change whatever needs changing to help them move ahead when they are stalled."
- **Make learning joyful whenever possible—and satisfying always.** "Plan for engagement," they said. "If you lose students' attention and investment, you've lost the game."

My colleagues and I determined as a group what students needed to know and be able to do as a result of a segment of learning, but the *meaning* of that content was not prescribed. As individuals, we had to think deeply about why it mattered to teach what we were teaching and be able to help students discover the power in what they learned. Over time, we became adept at looking at our curriculum through multiple lenses in order to "mine" its significance. In turn, our students also began to look beneath the surface of the "what" in order to find the "why." And of course, we shared our thinking about larger meanings behind content and extended it in response to our colleagues' ponderings.

Critical content and its purpose became central in my thinking, but that was always accompanied by the search for a context, a "wrapper," a destination for the work my students and I did together that made it feel purposeful, exciting, fresh—and a little scary, because it seemed a bit beyond our grasp. At various points, my students and I took photographs of common objects around the school grounds or in classrooms or at home, selecting things that had personal meaning for us or evoked strong feelings. We talked about camera angles, backgrounds, light, depth of field, and color. We planned how to communicate the feeling we wanted to share. We made slide presentations of the photographs and selected background music that gave voice to the images we selected. Later, we'd assemble images that illuminated for ourselves the works of famous poets. We wrote "insta-poems" to instrumental music and came to understand the power of sound and words to capture meaning. And we polished our favorite works by using what we were learning about figures of speech, rhythm, grammar, and so on to make the poems "pop." Many of the 12-year-olds in my classroom became fast fans of a literary form they'd previously found off-putting or dismissed out of hand.

Sometimes, I created the "wrapper"—the context through which we would explore critical content. Sometimes I asked the students to develop an idea that seemed intriguing and challenging. One example of that happened in my fourth year as a junior high English teacher, when I asked them to think about what we could do to make literature come alive for them. They surprised (and terrified) me when, almost in unison, they said we should put on a play for the public. I knew only a little more than they did about how to make that happen, so we watched plays, studied criteria for excellent performances, set standards for our work, selected a play, cast it, figured out how to do make-up and lighting, rehearsed exhaustively, and invited the outside world to come see us. Throughout all of that, we had continual conversations about protagonists, antagonists, rising and falling action, themes, oral expression, and dozens of other "non-negotiables" for the year's curriculum. It wasn't necessary to underline or copy examples of literary terms from an anthology; these ideas became standard vocabulary for us—and the words took on a purpose as they helped us think about our work like professionals would. We surprised ourselves and our audiences with the strength of our work. That marked the beginning of about 15 years of dinner theater productions at our school. They grew in scope and quality every year, because every year, we set out to make that happen. As time went on, parents signed on to support us in varied ways, but students remained at the center of acting, set design, make-up, costuming, lighting, advertising, and all of the other roles it takes to make a high-quality drama unfold for audiences. That process did, in fact, make literature in varied forms live for us and in us.

Sometimes, I wanted to give students the chance to explore topics or issues they cared about deeply as individuals as a vehicle for applying skills and meeting criteria for quality that cut across the diverse topics the students selected. So, for several years, my students developed and carried out independent inquiries in a fascinating array of interests—building a computer, planting and growing a garden, learning calligraphy, writing songs, designing clothing, cooking meals for their families or invited guests, using an airbrush as a tool in drawing and painting, learning about family genealogy, writing and illustrating poetry, to name just a few. Students could determine how long they wanted to work on their chosen project (9, 12, or 18 weeks), depending on their goals and the complexity of the task they had defined for themselves. Classes, of course, continued while the independent work hummed along in the background. Students frequently shared insights and challenges from what they were discovering on their own as it connected to what we were doing in class. Common across the performance tasks was the requirement to demonstrate their proficiency with the skills of inquiry— gathering and analyzing background information, setting goals, defining task parameters, delineating criteria for success, establishing timelines, reflecting on progress and outcomes, getting input and guidance from knowledgeable individuals or sources, executing their plans, evaluating and learning from outcomes, and sharing their work with relevant audiences.

At other points, individual students would sometimes ask to develop a plan with me that allowed them to miss some class assignments in order to pursue an inquiry that held deep meaning for them. Geoff conducted research on theories of extinction of the dinosaurs using a computer program he developed (long before personal computers, laptops, tablets, smartphones, and coding were staples of everyday life) to test some of the current theories. His work challenged the knowledge of several professors who provided him support along the way. Scott created and sold comic books and said later that the opportunity provided him with the only K–12 learning experience that made him see school in a positive light. Amy wrote a good portion of a novel and benefitted in multiple ways from participation in a high school authors' group where older students served as both models and encouragers. In both single-student inquiries and class-based ones, students worked diligently to understand and employ skills like questioning, research, interpretation, presentation, and reflection. Opportunities for independent investigation provided an authentic and remarkably motivating manifestation of the skills in action.

Other Classrooms Where Teaching and Learning Seemed Alive

I was by no means the only teacher in my school or district who found ways to meet students where they were while expanding the "typical" parameters of learning. There was a tribe of us.

My middle school colleague, Mary Harrington, who was both an artist and a math teacher, continually looked for spaces in the community where math was more than a set of algorithms. One year, for example, her students studied the access route architects had planned for a new school that was being built in the district. Their work included looking at costs, materials, safety standards, building codes, and proposed designs—and they found some noteworthy concerns with the design under construction. Ultimately, they took their concerns and alternative plans to a local governing board, along with illustrative photos, charts, diagrams, and architectural sketches. The planning body listened attentively, asked questions, thanked the students for their thoughtful work, and promised to study the information the students had presented. That was affirming and exciting for the young adolescents—but not nearly as rewarding as it was when the new school opened the following year and the students saw that the initial access plan has been replaced with a safer one they had suggested.

Nancy Brittle, a high school colleague who taught English, brought relevance to her students' reading of *The Odyssey* by asking each of them to conduct their own personal odyssey in the county where we lived. Their job was to seek answers and understanding on a question they cared about, as it existed in the county. The question each chose, she stressed, needed to be one that did not have evident right answers or even any answer at all. Then she set her class free to grapple with uncertainty and make their way through the complex local geography when they did not yet drive independently and when resources for research were often slim—circumstances that helped the poem's struggle feel closer. In their own questions, insights, disappointments, and triumphs, they found remarkable parallels to those in the ancient text. Several decades later, Nancy's former students regularly comment on their personal odysseys on her Facebook page. At another point, she joined efforts with a science teacher to develop and teach a class called Bio-English. Students examined in impressive depth ways in which authors used setting, geography, scientific allusions, and detailed understanding of science to give meaning and substance to stories, novels, and poetry. As you might imagine, science-oriented students developed a far greater affinity for literature—and vice versa.

George Murphy, a high school biology teacher who was determined to teach science in a way that made its fundamental principles and practices feel vibrant, often had his students conduct an archeological dig on and off throughout the first semester. Initially, they couldn't figure out why they were doing the dig or how to determine what they should do with the curious artifacts they found. After a few weeks, the students began to ask much better questions about their newfound treasures, and they began to make much more thoughtful conjectures about the treasures' meaning. As the semester and the digs continued, the students began to have individual and group epiphanies about the process that had once seemed tangential and superfluous to them. They were doing the work of scientists. They were using the scientific process of inquiry to address an unknown. As the semester ended, they presented small-group hypotheses, inquiry processes, evidence, reasoning, and conclusions about the mystery culture buried in the ground outside their high school. Student attention, questions, and insights had the hallmarks of an important scientific conference. Then, during the second semester, George's students developed a new mystery culture and artifacts for students who would follow them in biology classes the next year. They took it as a badge of scientific honor to be sure there were no "leaks" or clues for incoming students. They wanted the experience to be as dynamic and revealing for their successors as it had been for them.

Mary Ann Smith has always been one of my elementary teacher heroes. She requested and received remarkably heterogeneous classes of 3rd graders every year. Many of them came with labels descriptive of learning differences. These labels were irrelevant in Mary Ann's class, however. She knew what her students needed to learn and had a clear sense of where they were in their development toward reaching those goals. She also understood that supporting the students in pursuing their own interests was important in helping them become competent and confident learners. Then, in a sort of instinctive Montessori-like approach, she worked with the students to figure out ways in which they might best be able to find success. The room was "busy." Students worked with reading in a variety of ways. They approached math reasoning and problem solving along many different paths. They found and developed their individual strengths and used those strengths to help them bridge weaker spots. The students also met as a whole class often, sharing their ideas, thinking, process, and progress. They felt capable and comfortable. Hard work was a core ethic in the class, but the work was designed to help students succeed in learning—and to grow as learners. There was no pacing guide, no mandate that every student had to learn in a certain sequence or common way. Every student who walked into Mary Ann's classroom each day did so eagerly—and so did I, whenever I had a chance to visit.

This is just a sampling of many examples of engaged and productive learning from that time period that are still quite alive in my memory. That sort of teaching and learning was not only feasible but also encouraged and supported by school leaders. It's important to note that at the end of each year, all students in the district took a standardized test. The appropriate people examined the test results and looked for and used insights about how we could modify our teaching in the coming year to better the learning of the students we taught. In most instances, student performance grew steadily over time.

Jay McTighe, a co-creator of the Understanding by Design model of curriculum development, uses an analogy I've long found useful. He points out that a person who cares to sustain good health takes care, over the span of a year, to eat wisely, exercise, sleep adequately, take necessary medicines, and so forth. Once a year, that person is likely to go to a physician to get a read on how his or her health is looking. If the physician has changes to recommend, the person is likely to listen to the recommendations, discuss them with the doctor, and implement the changes in a responsible way. Jay says that at some point in the relatively recent past, we turned that sequence on its head in schools. Instead of faithfully "living a healthy life" and "checking in with the doctor annually" to see how we're doing, we've begun practicing for the physical throughout the year—all but abandoning a day-to-day focus on what it means to live well. In other words, we have jettisoned "healthy" teaching and learning and are in a constant state of test prep. The two approaches are cataclysmically different.

Near the end of my 21-year tenure in K–12 classrooms, I was alternately surprised, confused, and incredulous as I saw a meteoric transition from classrooms where many teachers invested consistently in meaning-rich learning and innovative pathways to student success to classrooms in which many teachers felt their mission was to raise test scores. It was as if both the electricity of learning and the needs of the human beings in front of us had been erased as priorities.

It's instructive to examine the approximately 25 years between "then" and "now" before beginning our exploration of why student-centered instruction is worth serious consideration, why now seems like the time to invest in that consideration, and what well-grounded student-centeredness might look like. The nature of teaching and learning has changed dramatically during that time. If the "makeover" of education conducted over those years generated significantly positive results, we would be wise to exercise caution in charting a markedly new direction. If, on the other hand, we find that the metamorphosis K–12 education has undergone has produced significant "collateral damage," we should use this knowledge to chart pathways that will result in better outcomes for ourselves and the young people in our classrooms.

A Brief History of How We Got from Then to Now

Standardized tests have been used in U.S. schools for a variety of purposes for more than a century. The more recent buildup to obsession with those tests began in the early 1980s with the publication of *A Nation at Risk*: *The Imperative for Educational Reform*. Billed as "a report to the nation," the publication began with these words:

> Our Nation is at risk. Our once unchallenged preeminence in commerce, industry, science, and technological innovation is being overtaken by competitors throughout the world.... The educational foundations of our society are presently being eroded by a rising tide of mediocrity that threatens our very future as a Nation and a people. What was unimaginable a generation ago has begun to occur—others are matching and surpassing our educational attainments. If an unfriendly foreign power had attempted to impose on America the mediocre educational performance that exists today, we might well have viewed it as an act of war. As it stands, we have allowed this to happen to ourselves. (National Commission on Excellence in Education, 1983, p. 1)

In 1994, passage of the Elementary and Secondary Education Act (ESEA) required student testing in public schools. The mandate ramped up further in 2001 with the passage of No Child Left Behind (NCLB), which expanded student testing as a way to assess public school performance, tying federal funding of schools to results of standardized testing. This mandate required testing every student in math and reading every year from 3rd through 8th grade and once in high school. Schools that didn't make an adequate showing faced a series of consequences, which prompted those schools (and others) to add new standardized tests during the year to make sure their students would be ready for the mandated end-of-grade tests. As one policy analyst noted, "You prepare for the test to prepare for the test to prepare for the test" (Layton, 2015, para. 27).

Intended to give localities greater voice in educational decision making, the Race to the Top initiative, inaugurated in 2009, offered federal grants to localities that instituted specified policies, including use of performance-based assessments of teacher and principal effectiveness. Because standardized tests were currently mandated only in reading and math, and only in certain grades, states struggled to figure out how to evaluate teachers in untested subjects and teachers of very young learners (which is a problem since, together, those teachers constitute the majority of the teaching force). While many states focused on developing additional assessments for untested subjects and evaluation systems based on test scores, few focused on using the results of those evaluations to improve teaching (Weiss, 2013).

While all of these measures may have reflected a goal of incentivizing schools to improve their teaching practices and improve educational opportunities for students from groups that have chronically been poorly served in schools, their actual impact is more complex and a lot less positive. Over the past 35 years, the dominance of standardized testing has radically changed the educational landscape.

Paul France (2020) raises doubts about the entire premise. In his view, the movement reflected an obsession with governing, predicting, and comparing the outcomes of the U.S. education system with countries around the world; it was never really about bettering our education system. The mandates for standardized testing were generally enacted with a "fear of losing our perceived standing as the world's primary hegemonic power" (p. 16). By equating our success in education outcomes with our success as a nation, politicians and policymakers, France suggests, created a toxic culture that pervades the education system, generating anxiety and stunting our growth as a society.

Testing skeptics raise a number of additional points. Problems with test reliability and validity make scores relatively meaningless and their use in evaluation absurd. Inequities are inevitable when teachers are evaluated largely on student test scores with little regard to students' socioeconomic differences, racial inequities, language barriers, and both the identified and unidentified learning challenges many students bring to the classroom with them.

It is also, to say the least, a negative that teachers have had very little voice in educational decisions made during the 25-year reign of the standardized test. The emphasis on standardized testing has resulted in a de facto mandatory curriculum in schools rather than encouraging the more democratic ideal of localities shaping local teaching practices. A single-minded focus on standardized test scores has encouraged "teaching to the tests" at the cost of creativity and in-depth learning. Mandating standardized tests in certain subjects has diminished attention to and the importance of subjects that are not tested (K–12 Academics, n.d.).

Further, it is a difficult to assess the impact of the reality that while there has been a continual drumbeat for the importance of testing student outcomes, there has been little national or local conversation about the nature of knowledge that is most likely to appropriately serve students, their communities, and the nation. Thus, we have tended to teach shallow information and basic skills that often have little or no context to help young learners create meaning. We follow that path not because it results in the most robust curriculum we can envision to engage young minds and prepare them for a complex world, but because those things are most easily tested and, thus, most likely to appear on the year-end standardized test that has become the touchstone for what happens in the classroom.

To be sure, there are teachers in every school who have successfully resisted the teach-and-test approach to education, and there are many entire schools characterized by student-focused innovation. It is important to acknowledge, salute, and learn from those examples. On the whole, however, schooling in the United States and in many other parts of the world has yielded to the externally imposed mandate to "get those scores up," because it felt virtually impossible to do otherwise.

Where Are We Now?

If we accept that two key motivations of the emphasis on standardized testing were (1) to improve student achievement as measured by standardized tests and (2) to create more equitable outcomes for students who have persistently underperformed in and been underserved by public schools, it's appropriate to look at a snapshot of the sort of progress we have made toward those two goals over the three decades in which standardized testing has dominated schools, classrooms, and public discourse. Given the concern that the drafters of A Nation at Risk had about international competitiveness of U.S. education, it is also worthwhile to look at recent standings of U.S. test scores in comparison with those other countries.

In terms of test scores, there is not a great deal to celebrate. Analyzing trends in test results is a complex undertaking due to the varied nature of different tests, varying demographics and funding models of schools, changes in the numbers of students in various subpopulations over time, test revisions, and so on. Still, looking at some indicators of student performance over time is instructive in understanding what the dramatic shift in teaching and learning has or hasn't produced.

If NCLB and corresponding catalysts for change in classroom practice were successful in lifting the achievement of U.S. students as evidenced by standardized test scores, it would seem that SAT scores would have risen markedly in the 15 years between when NCLB became law and 2016. And yet, as Anna Aldric (2018) documents, mean math and reading scores on the SAT in 1994 and 2016 suggest otherwise, showing a very small increase in reading (from 504 to 509) and a parallel, very small decrease in math (from 499 to 494) over that time span. The SAT was revised in 2016, and scores from the new test were first reported 2017. Although SAT scores from 2017 and 2018 are comparable with each other, they cannot be compared with 2007 and 2016 scores. But we can see that since the revised test was first administered, mean scores for all SAT-takers have fallen slightly in both math (from 531 to 528) and reading (from 536 to 531). As shown in Figure 1.1, the mean composite SAT score of White students rose modestly during the nearly 10-year span between 2007 and 2016 and fell modestly between 2018 and 2019. During the same periods, mean SAT scores of Black/African American and Hispanic/Latino/Latin American students showed similar minor movement; however, for these traditionally underserved demographic groups, that movement was downward in both periods (National Center for Education Statistics, 2019; National Center for Fair & Open Testing, 2019).

Figure 1.1: Mean composite SAT scores for three demographic groups in 2007 and 2016 and in 2018 and 2019

Student Demographic	2007	2016	2018	2019
Hispanic, Latino, Latin American*	922	901	990	978
African American	862	855	946	933
White	1061	1077	1123	1114

Sources: National Center for Education Statistics, 2019; National Center for Fair & Open Testing, 2019.

*In 2007, scores were reported separately for Mexican/Mexican American, Puerto Rican, and other Hispanic, Latino, and Latin American students. In 2016, 2018, and 2019, the three categories are merged.

The data from a different test provide little more encouragement. The National Assessment of Educational Progress (NAEP) is often called the gold standard in measuring achievement of U.S. students. It is administered to students every four years in grades 4, 8, and 12. The chart you see in Figure 1.2 shows the percentage of students who scored at the "Proficient or Above" level (which is generally seen as a higher standard than "average" performance) on the 2014 NAEP in grades 4, 8, and 12 in seven content areas (The Nation's Report Card, n.d.). It would seem to be a reasonable hope that at least half of school-age students would be at least "Proficient" in the key content areas. However, the best performances in this graphic are in 4th grade math, reading, and science, where little more than a third of students perform at or above the Proficient level. Those figures provide *some* good news in the sense that math and reading are the two content areas targeted by standards associated with commonly administered standardized tests. Even in those instances, however, scores indicate that *fewer* than half of the students tested are proficient in those content areas. By 12th grade, there is only one subject (reading) in which more than a *quarter* of students met the "Proficient or Above" benchmark.

Figure 1.2:   Percentage of U.S. public school students performing at or above the Proficient level on the NAEP in 2018

Subject Area	Grade 4	Grade 8	Grade 12
Civics	26%	23%	23%
Geography	20%	24%	19%
Math	40%	33%	23%
Reading	34%	32%	36%
Science	37%	33%	21%
U.S. History	19%	14%	11%
Writing	27%	26%	25%

Source: The Nation's Report Card, n.d.

More recently, as NAEP began to release the 2018 scores, results of 8th graders' grasp of topics in history, civics, and geography were described as "disappointing," "pervasive," and "disturbing" (Sawchuk & Sparks, 2020). At least a quarter of students scored below "Basic" level, indicating they did not possess the skills to handle the content. In history, 34 percent of students fell below Basic, and in geography, the "Below Basic" showing was 29 percent. In the years between 2014 and 2018, scores in all categories tested fell, with the exception being civics, where scores have remained low over time, gaining only 3 points since the test was first administered in 1998. Less than a third of students tested scored at or above Proficient on the test—and in history, that number was just 15 percent. Further, the 2018 NAEP shows a highly concerning pattern—namely, a broad-based and growing gulf between top performers on the test and those who struggle most significantly. This disparity registers on virtually all standardized measures and should provide more than ample evidence that what we have been doing in U.S. schools for the last two decades is not working to reverse inequitable schooling and prepare students of all backgrounds to be productive, contributing, and fulfilled members of their communities and of the nation as a whole.

The low scores in civics and history may reflect a broad willingness by educational decision makers to drastically cut back learning time once devoted to subjects like history, science, and the arts—subjects not tested on most high-stakes tests. Whatever the cause, we should consider the implications of sending students forward to take on societal roles with little sense of history and citizenship, and, in a world that is increasingly interdependent and uncertain, the implications of sending them forward without the desire and skills necessary to make that world more hospitable and just for all its people.

Examining data from the NAEP specifically for "achievement gap" trends between 2003 and 2017, researchers at the Brookings Institution (Hansen, Levesque, Quintero, & Valant, 2018) noted ongoing, if slow, progress in closing racial and ethnic achievement gaps in grades 4 and 8—specifically, an approximately 13–25 precent reduction in the gaps between Hispanic and White and African American and White students. Progress in narrowing the Hispanic–White gap has been more evident than progress in shrinking the African American–White gap. At the same time, the "poverty gap" has remained stubbornly persistent and, in some cases, has increased. Overall, the authors say, large gaps remain, representing differences of approximately one and a half years of normal academic progress. They conclude, "Unless we rapidly increase the rates at which we close our race-, ethnicity-, and income-based gaps, unequal access to education and the consequences of this inequality will affect students today as well as subsequent generations" (para. 15).

The paucity of durable across-the-board increases in test scores should, on its own merit, provide cause for seeking a more promising vision of teaching and learning. Add to the generally disappointing test data the amount of school time spent on testing and test preparation, and "staying the course" seems even more destructive.

A comprehensive study of testing in the country's largest school districts conducted by the Council of the Great City Schools (Layton, 2015) finds that, on average, a student will take 112 mandated standardized tests between pre-K and high school graduation. In stark contrast, most countries that outperform the United States on standardized measures test their student three times during an entire school career. To make matters worse, the study found no correlation between the amount of testing in a district and the way its students perform on the NAEP exam, which is the only consistent measure of student achievement across state lines. The study describes the testing scene as "a-chock-a-block jumble" (para. 8), where tests have been layered upon tests as a result of mandates, further exacerbated by aggressive marketing of the tests by the companies that produce them. A spokesperson for an advocacy group *supportive* of standardized testing as a way of closing the achievement gap said, "For those of us who support annual assessments, it doesn't mean we support this craziness.... There's a clear problem here" (Layton, 2015, para. 19).

International measures of achievement are no more encouraging than U.S.-only measures. For example, in the most recent scores from the Trends in International Mathematics and Science Study (TIMSS) test administered to students in many countries across the globe, U.S. 4th graders ranked #14 in math of 49 participating countries. Students in five participating East Asian countries scored markedly higher than other countries. U.S. students were also bettered by students in Northern Ireland, the Russian Federation, Norway, Ireland, England, Belgium, Kazakhstan, and Portugal. Scores of U.S. students in 2015 remained at the same achievement level as in 2011. U.S. 8th graders ranked #11 of 39 countries taking the TIMSS in 2015, maintaining the same achievement level they had reached in 2011. Similarly, U.S. 12th graders who took the Advanced TIMSS showed the same achievement level in 2015 as in 1995, when the test was first administered. This was also the case for U.S. 12th graders who took the Advanced TIMSS in physics (TIMSS & PIRLS International Study Center, 2019).

Another well-regarded international measure of achievement, the Programme for International Student Achievement (PISA), administered in 2015 found U.S. 15-year-olds ranking #39 among 70 countries in math, #25 of 70 in science, and

#24 of 70 in reading. These scores reflect an 11-point drop for U.S. students since the previous administration of the PISA in math, with flat performance over the same time period in science and reading (Jackson & Kiersz, 2016). When PISA scores for the test administered in 2018 were released in 2019, students in the U.S. appeared to show a bit of improvement in reading and science while declining in math (OECD, 2019). In fact, notes Peggy Carr, associate commissioner for the National Center on Education Statistics, the scores remained flat from 2015 results, and U.S. student scores looked a little better only because scores in a few other countries slipped slightly. "We have remained steady and so our ranking has improved—not exactly the way you want to improve your ranking" (in Sparks, 2019, para. 3). The 2018 PISA results indicated that average U.S. scores hadn't changed significantly in reading or math since the test was first given in 2000 (Barshay, 2019).

Of interest in terms of U.S. competitiveness are the Organisation for Economic Co-operation and Development (OECD, 2019) rankings based on 2018 PISA combined average scores in reading, math, and science. These scores position 23 countries in a top-scoring group with the U.S. at the #4 position in a *mid-range* group of scorers. Regions bettering U.S. performance include Singapore, four large Chinese provinces, Macao, Hong Kong, Estonia, Canada, Slovenia, the United Kingdom, Japan, Germany, Czechia, Finland, Iceland, Korea, Poland, Sweden, and New Zealand. The list includes a mix of countries with varied profiles and means—including some that might seem less likely than the United States to be in a list of the highest scorers, some that have transformed their economies and schools in a short window of time, and some that would likely be of concern to the *A Nation at Risk* authors, who advocated more regulated curricula and more consequential testing to ensure the international competitiveness of U.S. students.

It's highly concerning that these PISA results offer evidence of widening disparities between top-performing students and those who perform at the lowest levels. While the highest-performing 10 percent of U.S. students show significant growth since 2012, scores of the lowest 10 percent of students have declined in that same time frame, "adding to a growing body of evidence showing worsening inequity in public schools" (Balingit & Van Dam, 2019, para. 2). Unlike many other countries, in the United States, only 20 percent of disparities between low- and high-performing students are attributable to between-school factors. This is worth stressing: 80 percent of the score differences are attributable to *within-*school disparities. These significant performance gaps within a school, experts hypothesize, are a result of the common practice of tracking students, which leads to students in lower-track classes typically encountering less-dynamic curriculum and instruction and less-experienced teachers. As Barshay (2019) observes, "If what students are learning in their classrooms is different, you'd expect the test scores to be different too" (para. 14).

There are many available iterations and interpretations of a myriad of standardized test scores for both current and past years. The examples here are not intended to be exhaustive. There are arguable ups and downs for varied groups in varied measures at varied times. All told, though, there are few, if any, analyses of test results over the last 20-plus years that are celebratory.

In general, scores on the tests that were supposed to be a catalyst for increased learning point to the real possibility that our fixation with test prep and standardized testing as the drivers of teaching and learning has cost us much more than it has benefitted us. The data, taken as a whole, seem to affirm the admonition of Alberto M. Carvahlho, superintendent of Miami-Dade Public Schools: "We can't assess our way to academic excellence" (in Layton, 2015, para. 25).

Adding to a persistently discouraging picture of our long fixation on standards and standardized test results, new research finds that seven years after most states adopted the Common Core standards in 2010 as a means to improve student achievement, "the standards appear to have led to modest declines in 4th grade reading and 8th grade math" (Barnum, 2019) as measured by the NAEP test. It is painfully difficult to find any evidence that standardized teaching and standardized testing are the path to student academic success.

Looking Back and Ahead

Nearly three decades ago, politicians raised the banner of a nation at risk, asserting that mediocre classrooms imperiled student learning. They proposed to address this problem by requiring annual student testing as a mechanism for improving the quality of teaching and learning.

We have persisted in that course ever since, subscribing to the idea that the only way to measure a child's knowledge is through prepackaged, high-stakes tests that, in the end, have undermined teachers' autonomy; de-professionalized the teaching field; and left students of color, students from low-income communities, and students with significant learning challenges in the crosshairs of projected inferiority (Love, 2020). These students persistently see themselves and their peers referenced as bottom-quartile scorers, regularly find themselves grouped with other low-scoring students, and experience curriculum that almost inevitably ensures that they will remain in the ranks of low test-scorers. Love (2020) poses a question that educators should not ignore: How does a student feel like he or she matters to a country and a system that measures knowledge against a gap it has created?

Intended or not, many if not most classrooms in the United States have also become standardized, low-level, and tense. We have not stopped the pursuit of better test scores long enough to ask whether we have any evidence that aiming our energies at better test results benefits learning, students, or teachers. Rather than expending resources to support teachers in designing and using curriculum and instruction that seem more likely to raise the sights of educators, learners, and the public, we have lowered our aspirations for student achievement and often for education resources as well.

It is not a leap to say that more than two generations after betting the future of our students on raising test scores, teaching is less stimulating, curriculum is shallower, learning is less engaging, fewer students find school satisfying, and teachers and students alike function at high levels of stress. Given that the promised pay-off from standardizing instruction to increase standardized test scores has not materialized—and perhaps even if it had—the cost of test-focused classrooms has been too high for students, teachers, and society.

So where do we go from here? One possibility, of course, is that we continue on this path that requires teachers to leave their professional judgment and ingenuity in the parking lot when they enter the school building and sprint through increasing mounds of often-meaningless content handed to them in teacher-proof formats and pacing guides designed for coverage rather than for student learning. Notably, it's a path that requires students to continue to measure their worth in test scores rather than in possibilities and dreams realized.

This book offers an alternative: refocusing our vision and energies to place students, rather than test scores, in the center of the work we do and working to ensure that the fundamental elements in student-centered classrooms *reflect our best knowledge of quality educational practice*. With those two goals to guide us, we would consistently grow our capacity to teach in ways most likely to humanize learning, to engage young people with the power of learning and their power as learners, and to prepare them for the world in which they live now and will live in the future. Toward that end, this book is a guide for creating learner-centered classrooms.

The chapters that follow present a framework for understanding learner-focused teaching and the principles of quality instructional planning that provide a compass for envisioning, crafting, and implementing education that puts students at the center.

Chapter 2 offers a rationale and descriptors that begin to answer the question *Why would we consider student-centered classrooms?* Chapter 3 invites a pause to consider the element in any classroom that is most pivotal in student success: the teacher. It explores the role of the teacher in learner-centeredness—a role that in many ways is a departure from the constricted role of teachers in test-focused classrooms. It also offers questions to prime your thinking for subsequent chapters. Chapter 4 considers what it means to honor students in learner-focused classrooms.

With this foundation established, Chapters 5 through 8 successively explore how honoring the learner, building community, honoring content, focusing on student growth, and crafting learner-centered instruction all contribute to consequential learner-centeredness. Each of these chapters recommends ways in which teachers can bring learner-centered practices into their own classroom, along with classroom illustrations for analysis. Because high-quality learner-centeredness can and should occur in schools and classrooms that use many different models of or approaches to teaching and learning, the examples in these chapters reflect a broad range of schools, classrooms, and models, including those that continue to value test-based evidence of student growth.

The book closes with Chapter 9's look at the overarching concepts of successful learner- and learning-centered classrooms, Chapter 10's "big picture" examples of teaching and learning in schools and classrooms where learner-centeredness is a way of life, and a final aspirational view of where this kind of work can take teachers and their students.

Yong Zhao (2019) points out that it is no longer meaningful to argue for or against changing the way we envision teaching and learning. Our current mindset about schooling is profoundly shaped by the nature of the schools we know, he says, which makes us prisoners of our past. And venturing out of that prison is not easy. However, the realities around us demand that we change, and we can't afford to wait for a new mindset to "happen." He urges us instead to take action—to act our way into new and more promising practices and beliefs.

This book is about understanding the past, escaping that past, and building better futures in our classrooms for *each* young person who comes our way. Every chapter is designed to help you move forward in concrete and observable ways toward more vibrant and promising practices that will enliven and extend the academic, affective, and social capacities of both you, the teacher, and the learners in your care.

ය ය ය

2

What Learner-Centeredness Is —and Is Not

Take a moment to reflect on the ephemeral nature of a classroom's tender moments: the quizzical conversations that bubble between engaged and curious learners, the moment a child's insightful comment changes the direction of a lesson, or even the frustrating interactions where you and your students struggle to understand one another. These cannot be controlled; in fact, the power of these moments lies within their ephemerality. They are powerful because they are unpredictable and undeniably *student-driven.*

—Paul France in *Reclaiming Personalized Learning*

The noted American naturalist Annie Dillard (1987) recalls the moment from childhood when she first understood the cost of restrictive environments:

At school I saw a searing sight. It was only a freshly hatched Polyphemus moth crippled because its mason jar was too small. The mason jar sat on the teacher's desk; the big moth emerged inside it. The moth had clawed out, as if agonizingly, over the course of an hour, one leg at a time; we children watched around the desk, transfixed. After it emerged, the wet, mashed thing turned around walking on the green jar's bottom, then painstakingly climbed the twig with which the jar was furnished. There, at the twig's top, the moth shook its sodden clumps of wings. When it spread those wings—those beautiful wings—blood would fill their veins, and the birth fluids on the wings' frail sheets would harden to make them though as sails. But the moth could not spread its wide wings at all; the jar was too small. The wings could not fill, so they hardened while they were still crumpled from the cocoon.

A smaller moth could have spread its wings to their utmost in that mason jar, but the Polyphemus moth was big. Its gold furred body was almost as big as a mouse. Its brown, yellow, pink, and blue wings would have extended six inches from tip to tip, if there had been no mason jar. It would have been as big as a wren. The teacher let the deformed creature go. We all left the classroom and paraded outside behind the teacher with pomp and circumstance. She bounced the moth from its jar and set it on the school's asphalt driveway. The moth set out walking. It could only heave the golden wrinkly clumps where its wings should have been; it could only crawl down the school driveway on its six frail legs. The moth crawled the driveway toward the rest of Shadyside. It crawled down the driveway because its shriveled wings were glued shut. I watched it go. I knew that this particular moth, the big walking moth, could not travel more than a few more yards before a bird or a cat began to eat it, or a car ran over it. Nevertheless, it was crawling with what seemed wonderful vigor, as if, I thought at the time, it was still excited from being born. I watched it go till the bell rang and I had to go in.

I have told this story before, and may yet tell it again, to lay to rest the moth's ghost, for I still see it crawl down the broad black driveway, and I still see its golden wing clumps heave. (pp. 160–161)

The image is a strong one—difficult to entertain, to consider. And yet, it is an apt analogy for both the student and teacher experience in a great number of classrooms since the press for raising standardized test scores established a chokehold on classroom practice. In those classrooms, students and teachers alike have too often lived out their school careers in jars that were too small to enable them to stretch their wings—to become their best selves, to thrive outside the jar, to soar. Curriculum constricted by test myopia has narrowed instructional options and, in many ways, dehumanized both learners and teachers. Even absent high-stakes testing and what it represents in terms of dehumanization and constriction of human potential, the classrooms many students enter each day are ones where educators and peers perceive them to be misaligned with schooling because of their race, language, exceptionality, culture, or economic status. For these students, the mason jar is even smaller and more injurious. As a nation, as members of a school faculty, and as individual educators, we have a defining need to do all we can—even against prevailing winds—to discard the jar and to release both the young people in our care and ourselves from its crippling confines. As the title of this book conveys, we do this so that each of us, all of us, may soar.

It is impossible to know how many students have spent their school days focused only on the mechanics of reading or writing without caring to read or write once the bell rang or how many of them learned to memorize math algorithms but not how to think mathematically. Similarly, how many young people and young adults today have no clear sense of our country's history or their roles in maintaining its legacy because this content was left off high-stakes tests and, thus, was deemed unworthy of instructional time and emphasis? How many young children have found it nearly impossible to pay attention throughout the school day because recess was abbreviated or eliminated to increase time for test prep?

Nor is there any way to know how many teachers have left the profession because they were required to follow tightly prescribed curricula that spoke neither to their experiences nor to those of their students, to follow pacing "guides" that were more like pacing straitjackets, to consign their own creativity to times and places outside school, or to jettison both their professional knowledge about and daily observation of student learning needs in deference to ill-fitting mandates in which they had no voice.

Recently, however, there is a promising, if still-small, shift in conversations around the nature of an education that could serve our diverse population of learners well. A variety of stakeholders and communities seem interested in broadening the discussion about the intent and shape of quality education. Certainly, there are many teachers who are ready to lead classrooms that are more generous than Annie Dillard's mason jar in making space to develop the varied and considerable capacities of their students. There are many teachers who reject the premise that numbers are proof of success and who already teach from the alternative belief that human flourishing is proof of success (C. Prather, personal communication, January 2, 2021). Rooted in the hope that this interest will endure, let's start our exploration of learner-focused instruction with a question: *What do students need from their 12-plus-year experience in classrooms in order to live meaningful, productive, and satisfying lives?*

A Good Place to Start (Over)—The "Why"

Simon Sinek (2009), noted for his study of what makes exceptional organizations stand out from the crowd, has found that the most successful ones begin by asking, *Why do we do what we do?* Most organizations, he observes, start by asking what they mean to do and then move on to ask how they will accomplish that "what." The great ones, by contrast, spend significant time in coming to understand their mission—the driver of their efforts, their "why." By understanding and working from a higher or deeper purpose, people in these organizations find meaning and long-term inspiration in their work.

Arguably, the "what-and-how" process has governed schools and schooling for the last quarter-century. The "what" clearly appeared to be raising standardized test scores. The "how" focused on things like teaching from scripted curricula, following rigid pacing guides, teaching to the test, taking time away from areas that would not be tested (for example, playtime for young students, science and history, the arts, and so on), and judging the worth of schools, teachers, and students on the rise and fall of scores. It's difficult to sense a higher purpose—a source of ongoing inspiration, a "why"—in that vision.

After much reflection, I'd like to offer this "why" for learner-centered classrooms: *Educators are obligated to ensure that each of the young people in their care is well-equipped for a meaningful, productive, and satisfying life, both during and after their "formal" education.* This statement does not imply preference for certain post-graduation pursuits, occupations, or lifestyles. (People find meaning, make contributions to the welfare of others, and feel fulfilled through a great variety of paths.) Instead, it asserts that educators bear responsibility for preparing young people to pursue and maintain the positive life they choose. The statement does not suggest that teachers and schools bear *full* responsibility for such an outcome. It does, however, represent the view that schools and teachers have significant opportunity and responsibility to support young people in acquiring the knowledge, skills, and other resources that will allow them to build healthy lives, strong families, and become responsible, contributing members of their community—to be (paraphrasing Jonathan Cohen, co-founder and president of the National School Climate Center) a good friend and a good partner, to be able to work, and to contribute to the well-being of the world (Love, 2020; Sloan, 2012).

Achieving this vision requires will on the part of the teacher—specifically, the will to place the student in the foreground of thinking about, planning for, carrying out, and reflecting on instruction, and the will to draw on an informed and growing understanding of the nature of learning environments, curriculum, assessment, and instruction in order to best serve the wide array of learners in today's classrooms. Take a few minutes to reflect on my "why" statement for learner-centered classrooms. Now is a good time to begin developing your own "why"—your own mission in considering student-focused teaching.

If we accept this idea that a teacher's work should help students develop in ways that will recognize and robustly advance their possibilities in both the short and long terms, it seems fundamental to consider another question: *What skills, competencies, attitudes and habits might we aim for as we plan, implement, and reflect on learning opportunities in order to actively support those possibilities?* Or, to put it another way, *What are the characteristics of people who live productively, meaningfully, and with a sense of satisfaction and fulfillment?*

A search for "attributes of educated people," "characteristics of successful people," "traits of self-actualization," "21st century skills," and related keywords generates a list that is simultaneously inspiring and daunting. In Figure 2.1, you'll see a selection of potential contributing factors to a productive and satisfying life that we might agree are important for young people (and older ones, for that matter) to develop and apply.

Multifaceted as the collection in the figure is, it's neither exhaustive nor intended to suggest a prescribed set of attributes that any particular educator should sign on to as targets to develop in the classroom. Still, it's useful to spend time thinking about which of these traits we value enough as individual teachers to want to support in our work with students. Certainly, it's worth considering that learner-centeredness implies creating learning opportunities that support each student in acquiring skills, attitudes, and habits of mind that enable that student to become the best version of him or herself. Take a few minutes to think about the connection between learner-centeredness and nurturing the attributes that seem most likely to benefit a student.

The teachers I know are likely to agree on numerous skills, attitudes, and habits of mind that most, if not all, students would benefit from understanding and developing. Being responsible, for example. Being self-aware would be on that list too, along with taking initiative, communicating effectively, and knowing how to make sound decisions. And, of course, students' varied strengths, dreams, experiences, and cultures will shape how they might develop these attributes and how they would apply them in daily life. But to me there is no question that helping the amazing array of students who come to us fully develop cognitively, affectively, and socially requires us to create classrooms that put the learner at the center of teaching and learning.

Learner-centered classrooms are—or should be—catalysts for breaking the mason jar and creating places where young people and their teachers have space and opportunity to spread their wings. These classrooms are—or should be—designed to increase voice, autonomy, and agency for young learners and for the people who teach them. This is the core of the "why" of learner-centeredness.

Figure 2.1: Some contributing factors to a productive and satisfying life

Listening, hearing, and seeking to understand	Establishing and maintaining lasting relationships	Making connections across ideas, cultures, disciplines	Understanding how a person's behavior affects others
Acquiring the knowledge necessary to live and contribute effectively in society	Being curious	Being flexible, adaptable	Caring—being empathetic
Knowing how to learn	Being self-reflective, self-critical	Demonstrating social responsibility	Embracing failure as an opportunity to learn
Making productive use of knowledge	Demonstrating enthusiasm for learning	Possessing cross-cultural understanding and appreciation	Taking initiative
Thinking and reasoning clearly	Communicating effectively	Being respectful, humble	Being a problem solver
Thinking creatively	Demonstrating accountability, responsibility	Appreciating and striving for quality	Tolerating ambiguity
Learning collaboratively and independently	Demonstrating ethical values, integrity	Persisting, being patient	Wanting to make a positive difference
Discerning truth from error	Understanding the connectedness of everything	Being self-aware (understanding one's values, goals, emotions)	Knowing how to make sound decisions
Demonstrating self-confidence	Exploring varied viewpoints	Being self-directed	Being aspirational
What else would you add?			

Giving Legs to a Vision—The "What"

If the "why" of learner-focused instruction is providing young people with opportunities, resources, and support necessary to help them build a sound foundation for meaningful and productive lives, both present and future, then what is the "what" of learner-centeredness?

Fundamentally, learner-centeredness encompasses beliefs about and approaches to instruction that place students and their needs at the heart of teaching and learning. Teachers who practice learner-centeredness ask themselves, *In what ways can I help each of my students most fully develop cognitively, affectively, and socially?* or, from a slightly different perspective, *How can I create an environment and learning opportunities through which my students and I can work together to help each of us, and all of us, build strong lives?*

Learner-centeredness is rooted in the reality that meaningful learning about any aspect of life generally results from the learner's active participation rather than passive receptivity. Thus, learner-centered classrooms are designed to engage students actively in their own growth and development and to ensure that what students learn endures and serves them well throughout their lives.

Figure 2.2 briefly outlines four essential and interdependent areas of focus in learner-centered teaching, each a critical element in ensuring that every student develops the knowledge, attitudes, and skills necessary for a satisfying, productive, and contributing life. The four elements in the figure—the learner, content, progress, and community—are adapted from the National Research Council's *How People Learn: Brain, Mind, Experience, and School* (2000), which is arguably the best digest of current understanding about the attributes of quality teaching and learning, based on research in cognitive psychology and neuroscience. Descriptors of the elements in the figure come from several sources, as noted in the figure's citation. As with most things in education, there is not a single list of characteristics for the four areas that will respond to all stages of teacher development, all ages of learners, or all school contexts. This graphic, however, offers a solid starting place.

The search for a "what" implies specificity. However, our goal for classrooms is not—or should not be—applying any particular instructional model, instructional strategy, or pedagogical approach. Those things are methods or tools that can be applied in ways that enliven student prospects or diminish them. They can be applied artfully or destructively. They can be used in ways that elicit student motivation or damp down its flames. They can be used to open the universe to young people or confine them in the mason jar. In the end, our goal is—or should be—creating classrooms designed to help students from all backgrounds and experiences soar: flourish cognitively, affectively, and socially in classrooms designed to guide each to reach and then push beyond what previously appeared to be the ceiling of possibilities. Learning opportunities in these classrooms should also enable each student to be the best possible member of the classroom community of learners and, ultimately, of all the broader communities in which the student participates.

Figure 2.2: Four essential and interdependent areas of focus in a learner-centered classroom

Focus on the Learner

- Learner's culture and language
- Learner's entry-level knowledge
- Learner's entry-level agency
- Learner's strengths, interests, and experiences
- Characteristics likely to influence a student's agency and success
- Learner's ongoing progress
- Student-appropriate challenge
- Focus on developing student voice

Focus on the Content

- Clarity about foundational elements of content
- Relevance to student experience
- Tools for deepening and broadening student interest
- Plans for student engagement
- Content organized to support application/transfer
- Active learning for student understanding and engagement
- Clear descriptors of quality work

Learner-Centered Classrooms

Focus on Progress

- Formative assessment as a vital information stream on learner progress
- Assessment that makes learner understanding and thinking visible to teacher and student
- Emphasis on feedback as a catalyst for growth
- Student use of assessment information as a tool for planning and development
- Classroom conversations and reporting that emphasize learner progress

Focus on Community

- Environment that supports student growth
- Student–teacher connectedness
- Student–student connectedness
- Learning as a collective endeavor
- Intellectual common ground
- Appreciation of diversity in culture, talent, and perspective
- Classroom–student connections to the broader community

Sources: Gay, 2018; Hattie, 2012; National Research Council, 2000; Schlechty, 2011; Sousa & Tomlinson, 2018; Wiggins & McTighe, 2005; Wiliam, 2011a.

Toward that end, I propose that learner-centered instruction be rooted in a focus on

- Understanding, responding to, and dignifying the learner;
- Developing a strong community of learners in the context of an empowering classroom environment;
- Developing and teaching content in ways that honor the power of the knowledge we commend and the capacities of the students who learn it; and
- Contributing to student growth cognitively, affectively, and socially.

The four components in Figure 2.2 are the "what" in learner-centered classrooms. We'll take an initial look at these components now and explore them in greater detail as the book continues.

Understanding, Responding to, and Dignifying the Learner

Learner-centered classrooms are, as noted previously, designed to support each learner's continual growth in cognitive, affective, and social domains. Growth in these three areas is interdependent, with development in each area affecting development in the other two, for better or worse.

As Duckworth points out, "teachers in learner-centered classrooms are aware that learners construct their own meanings, beginning with the beliefs, understandings, and cultural practices of each student. If teaching is building a bridge between the subject matter and the student, learner-centered teachers keep a constant eye on both ends of the bridge. The teachers attempt to get a sense of what each student knows, cares about, is able to do, and wants to do" (quoted in National Research Council, 2000, p. 136). Van Manen (1991) makes the same point in a similar way, asserting that in a student-focused classroom, the teacher works to develop a sense of who the learner is now as well as who the learner may become. The work of teaching, then, becomes collaborating with the young person to construct a sturdy and reliable bridge between "now" and "then."

Necessarily, classrooms that dignify each student and magnify each student's capacities are culturally responsive, equity oriented, and aspirational for every student in a class and for the class as a whole. All facets of learner-centered instruction reflect the teacher's intent to know a student well enough to guide his or her next steps in growth. Dignifying the learner includes the deeply rooted belief that each young person has the capacity to succeed and, therefore, should have full access to and full support in learning from the highest-quality curriculum and instruction a school has to offer.

Developing a Strong Community of Learners

While learning happens within an individual, the learning process is greatly enhanced when students work together as learners, much as a good athletic team draws on the strengths of each team member to better the outcome of the game and continually extend the abilities of each player.

Building a learning community, or a team of learners, requires a classroom environment that welcomes, challenges, and supports the success of each member—a place where students learn to listen carefully and respectfully to one another, develop empathy for peers, hold themselves and one another to high standards of work and interaction, seek and benefit from varied perspectives on topics and issues, give and receive feedback, address problems that arise among them positively and productively, and value the processes and outcomes of learning. In such communities, each student has ongoing opportunity for self-expression.

Teachers in learner-centered classrooms understand that how we present art, math, literature, social studies, science, or any of the other domains we teach will have much to do with a student's affinity for those content areas, and so they work to engage students with that content in energizing and thought-provoking ways. These teachers also understand that what they teach and how they teach can prompt a learner's affective and social growth—or erode it. Learner-centered environments link to community-centered environments as teachers model, teach, and call on students to practice mutual respect, develop their respective strengths, and work together from their varied entry points and experiences in these areas.

Crafting Curriculum and Instruction That Honors Both Content and Learner

Teaching as the transmission of information that is impersonal, uninspiring, and inert does little to benefit the quality of a student's life, either during their time in school or beyond. The human brain has at least two needs that must be met for durable learning to occur: (1) a need to *make meaning* of things and (2) a need to *understand* how things work (Sousa & Tomlinson, 2018).

To make meaning or make sense of the world around them, young people, like their older counterparts, begin with their current experiences and connect new experiences and ideas to the earlier foundational ones. A very young child who has a dog at home and has just begun to think of a dog as an animal that has four legs and a tail is likely to point to a horse in a field and proudly announce, "Dog!" It will take a while for that child to understand both the similarities and differences between dogs and other four-legged animals. That learning process likely has two preconditions. First, the child needs to care enough about the idea of "dog" and "animal" to want to continue trying to figure things out. If the dog continues to be important in the child's life, the motivation to persist is present. Second, the child will need to come to understand or make sense of the similarities and differences between "dog," "animal," "person," "kitten," and so on—not just memorize those labels.

Meaning suggests that a topic or idea feels both interesting and relevant to a learner. Meaningful learning evokes and grows from previous experiences and is relevant to those experiences. What we ask students to learn in any subject must directly reflect their experiences—what they already know and feel. This allows a learner to see what the learning is for, get the point of it, and identify its connection to the world outside the classroom.

Understanding indicates that a learner grasps how a topic, an idea, or a discipline works—how the parts come together to make a whole. Helping a student *understand* what's being studied (vs. remember and repeat it) empowers them to "learn their way around" the content (National Research Council, 2000, p. 127), to feel and begin to work like an "insider" in that area. Understanding, like meaning, builds from a student's prior experiences.

Meaning and understanding are fundamental to real learning. Without them, a student will struggle to recall what was "learned" even a modest distance into the future. Neither will that student be able to apply the learning to instances when it could be helpful in solving problems or use it to create something new and useful. Equally important, without meaning and understanding, students rarely feel an affinity for the content and thus have scant, if any, motivation to keep learning in that area.

Planning curriculum and instruction in learner-centered classrooms calls on teachers to teach from the "big ideas" or concepts of a discipline that are the building blocks of sense making. The teachers also seek to understand their students' prior experiences with those big ideas in order to connect present (and future) learning with past learning. Knowledge-centered environments first intersect with learner-centered environments when a teacher begins planning curriculum and instruction with an intent to know students' preconceptions about the new subject matter in order to ensure that learners can draw on prior knowledge and experience to construct new insights and understandings (National Research Council, 2000).

Using Assessment as a Vehicle to Benefit Learner Growth

The foundational premise of learner-centeredness is that teaching and learning should focus on developing those aspects of being human that enable young people to navigate their current and future lives with competence, confidence, productivity, and satisfaction. A corollary of that premise is that the myriad of ways in which our students vary, including race, culture, gender, experiences, confidence, hopes, and strengths, affects their learning. Therefore, learning opportunities are necessarily person-centered, because that is the only way that teachers can effectively mentor students who are at varied starting points in the multiple facets of being a learner. Formative assessment is a primary source of the information that builds teacher understanding of learners' strengths and needs.

John Hattie (2012) advises teachers to determine where each student is in relation to learning goals or intentions as a study begins and monitor the student's progress as the study continues. He goes on to talk about what he calls "+1 teaching" (p. 97)—helping each student move forward at least one step each day from his or her current point of development. This, he says, should be the aim of each lesson.

Learner-centeredness, then, relies heavily on the power of formative assessment to guide a teacher's understanding of a learner's current status in a particular trajectory of learning. Formative assessment can be indispensable in helping a teacher identify what a student's next steps should be in order to achieve the targeted learning goal. Teachers are also wise to integrate the examination of formative assessment information into students' learning experiences, as it can be a powerful way of boosting students' achievement and helping them develop "ownership" of their own learning.

For a teacher, thoughtful formative assessment practice draws on conversation, observation, and examination of student work. For students, it can include analyzing their own work in the light of a model, a rubric, or their own set of goals for a given time. In both cases, formative assessment requires reflection, careful thought, the intent to grow, and the conviction that humans can contribute to their own success as they understand their development more fully.

As teachers become more proficient in their own use of formative assessment, they become more skilled in assessing students' progress toward mastery of academic content and the learning processes that support critical thinking, understanding, and skill application. The skills of self-assessment will become a regular feature of instruction, ensuring that students learn to use what they discover from analysis of their work to revise their thinking and plan effectively to succeed in the "next steps" of their learning. Further, teachers skilled with formative assessment can ensure the feedback they provide students is growth-focused rather than comparative to a single norm or competitive against peers. They can also communicate to students that formative assessment is not a means of judgment but a method for refining skills and honing or expanding them. In classrooms like this, it's safe and smart to acknowledge errors and learn from them.

In time, formative assessment should be a seamless part of teaching and learning in student-centered classrooms, informing teaching and learning and dignifying the knowledge and experience students bring with them to the classroom as essential for taking the next steps in learning, Effective use of formative assessment *is* the bridge between teacher and learner, and between teaching and learning. Understood accurately and practiced effectively, it is the process through which teachers and students can determine whether what has taken place in the classroom is helping students grow and develop as intended (Wiliam, 2011a).

Because the four key components of learner-centered classrooms are interconnected and interdependent, it is useful to propose some principles of learner-centeredness that can guide our thinking as we explore the components in more detail and consider how they might work together to most fully benefit the development of each and every student. Figure 2.3 presents eight principles for that purpose, elaborating briefly on each and providing a short example of how the principle might play out in a classroom. If the four components launch our consideration of the "what" of learner-centered classroom, these eight principles distill it into particulars so that we can begin figuring out how to translate the ideas of learner-centeredness into classroom action.

Looking Ahead

John Hattie's (2102) often-cited meta-analysis of 50,000 studies uses effect sizes to report the relative impact of numerous approaches to increasing student learning. An approach with an effect size of 0.2 translates into about 9 months of growth for students—a result we might expect at the end of a 9-month school year. An effect size of 1.0 suggests 3 years of advancement at the end of a school year—an impact rarely demonstrated in research. Hattie identifies any approach or strategy

Figure 2.3: Key principles that guide the development of learner-centered classrooms

Principle	Implication	Example of the Principle Applied
Each learner is unique in ways that will impact learning.	The teacher should regularly observe and consult with each student and the whole class to better understand and respond to student interests, needs, and progress.	A 3rd grade teacher keeps quick notes on students' individual interests revealed during student talk so the teacher can help them connect their interests with what they study.
Teacher and student beliefs about intelligence influence learner success.	All students need "proof" that the teacher is confident in their capacity to succeed as well visible evidence of that success.	A middle school history teacher asks students to periodically record their "best shots" (a piece of work that represents their best effort toward achieving a goal) and explain the progress they have made in key goals.
The search for meaning is a critical component of learning that is durable and useful.	Learning experiences need to help students focus on the big ideas of a content area and understand how those ideas can help them make connections and transfer what they learn to unfamiliar settings.	Teachers in a high school agree to address a set of common concepts across content areas. In the spring, they work with students to create a giant concept-map mural in the foyer of the school showing connections they've discovered across subjects.
Curriculum and instruction have relevance for each learner.	What students study should capture their imagination and curiosity, and should connect with their experience and interests.	A high school science teacher uses "Dilemma Dialogues" in which students offer and respond to varied perspectives on how best to address science-related problems.
Learning is both personal and social.	Students need to learn how to succeed in both collaborative and independent work contexts.	A 1st grade teacher works with students to create and use guidelines for handling disagreements that arise in the course of group work.
Deep learning requires students to make sense of information, ideas, and skills—and this takes time.	Because learning happens *in* students, not *to* them, teachers should set timelines for learning that allow for variable pacing.	Students in a 9th grade world language class have voice in how much and what kind of practice they need, due dates for proficiency checks, and options for how to show what they have learned.

(continued)

**Figure 2.3:   Key principles that guide the development
of learner-centered classrooms—(*continued*)**

Principle	Implication	Example of the Principle Applied
Learning requires appropriate challenge and a support system that facilitates success with that challenge.	Teachers need to calibrate instruction so that the challenges each student faces are a little too hard, and calibrate support so that each student is ultimately able to meet the challenge.	A high school physics teacher provides links to websites that explain key concepts at varied levels of complexity and in different modes so that the ideas are accessible to students who possess varied levels of understanding.
Formative assessment is a critical catalyst for teacher and student insight into progress and the actions both take to pursue growth.	Teachers must study each student's work on an ongoing basis to understand that student's trajectory of learning and regularly involve all students in analysis of their work relative to learning goals to help them plan for and "own" their learning more fully.	An algebra teacher uses paper-and-pencil formative assessment as well as observation of students at work with algebra to understand their current development. The teacher also conferences with each student every week or two to hear how they feel they are progressing.

that results in an effect size of 0.4 as highly desirable—one worthy of attention as we try to create classrooms that build student capacity.

Student-centered instruction, he finds, yields an effect size of 0.64 in terms of cognitive outcomes, and 0.7 in terms of cognitive and behavioral outcomes. In other words, he found that effectively led learner-focused classrooms make a *very* positive difference for learners in those classrooms—among the highest effect sizes in his extensive review of research.

In the pages ahead, we will unpack what it means to create and guide learner-centered classrooms. They are a departure in significant ways from many classrooms of the last two decades. Learner-centered teaching is not about raising test scores, and it is not about adding a new thing to whatever exists now. It is about modifying our understanding of the intent and nature of teaching to be reaching each student equitably and then acting on that understanding to reshape what we do in the classroom. It is about a radical change in the role of teachers. It calls on us to do everything we can to put the student in the foreground of our planning and the execution of those plans in the context of an invitational learning environment characterized by a dynamic community of learners, high-quality curriculum, responsive instruction, informative assessment, and classroom routines that allow for both the flexibility and stability necessary first to meet each learner at their cognitive, affective, and social entry points and then to move each student forward in those areas.

Learner-centered classrooms rely on teachers who are willing to change and grow, and on school leaders who are willing to intelligently support that change. Change is never easy, but teaching has never been easy. Its goal is too grand for ease. While not easy, change is not only possible but also essential to address the needs of the young people we guide.

The chapters that follow will delve into the principles and practices of focusing on the learner, on content, on progress, and on community. I hope you will find *your* "why" as you read, reflect on, argue with, and try out ideas in your work, and that you'll also gain a deeper understanding of the "what" and "how" of learner-centeredness. If the book is successful in those ways, it should contribute to teaching and learning that are more humane, joyful, rigorous, and equitable.

Before we examine the four core elements of student-focused classrooms, however, we need to consider two obvious factors. The first is the teacher—the one non-negotiable required for meaningful learner-centeredness; Chapter 3 explores that topic. The second is the learner whom we seek to honor with our work, discussed in Chapter 4.

C03 CR C03

3

The Learner–Centered Teacher

The job of teaching is so difficult, so complex,
that one lifetime is not enough to master it.

—Dylan Wiliam in "How Do We Prepare Students for a World We Can't Imagine?"

During a conference several years ago, I sat at lunch with six or seven other educators who held a variety of professional roles and were based in various parts of the country. For much of the time we were together, we shared individual stories of the teachers who had been life-changers for us—the ones who believed in us more than we believed in ourselves, who helped us both dream and prepare to realize big dreams. The exchange was moving and occasionally funny, and it was far more nourishing than the food before us. Late in the conversation, someone at the table turned to the one person in the group who had not spoken and asked her if she was willing to share her experience of a teacher who had transformed her life in some way. The woman looked uncomfortable. "I never had a teacher like that," she said quietly. "Never. In nearly 20 years of school, I never had *one*." We need many more teachers who markedly change young lives for the better.

Teaching is devilishly difficult work. I'm not sure we prepare prospective teachers to understand how hard it is or help them understand that it *should be* hard work, because every teacher is a contributing author of every student's life story. Noted educator, child psychologist, and author Haim Ginott (1972) was still a young teacher when he made this observation:

I've come to the frightening conclusion that I am the decisive element in the classroom. It's my personal approach that creates the climate. It's my daily mood that makes the weather. As a teacher, I possess tremendous power to make a student's life miserable or joyous. I can be a tool of torture or an instrument of inspiration. I can humiliate or humor, hurt or heal. In all situations it is my response that decides whether a crisis will be escalated or de-escalated and a student humanized or de-humanized. (pp. 15–16)

On the one hand, Ginott's conclusion is daunting, even oppressive. On the other, it reveals a profound opportunity. Perhaps those among us who learn to teach from a sense of opportunity rather than oppression draw from that optimism both the direction and energy necessary to become the life-changing teachers. I am convinced that teachers who learn to develop and lead quality learner-centered classrooms are propelled by the opportunities far more often than they are depleted by the challenges. If teaching is hard and really good teaching is really hard, then really good learner-focused teaching is really, really hard. It is also exquisitely rewarding for both teacher and students.

Becoming a Learner-Centered Teacher

Placing the student at the core of classroom decisions and processes, which is the essence of learner-centered teaching, is challenging because it asks us to make a major shift in classroom roles and structures. We're asked to turn away from an arrangement in which we are the power source toward one in which we intentionally and widely share power with our students. Making that transition is perplexing for many teachers because it's so different from the idea of school most of us experienced in our own educational journeys, and because top-down mandates have provided teachers little opportunity to entertain student-centered philosophy and practice.

Figure 3.1 provides a visual overview of the power structure in a more "traditional" classroom, where a teacher is the predominant decision maker when it comes to learning environment, curriculum, assessment, instruction, and classroom leadership and management, along with descriptors of these five elements in a classroom with a high degree of teacher direction.

Clearly, the power structure in Figure 3.1 is relatively unidirectional, and the classroom elements function in ways that suggest preserving or protecting the teacher's dominance. That doesn't mean teachers in those classrooms are despots; most are caring, create positive environments, and are liked by their students. Rather, the unidirectionality points to the teacher as predominant decision maker and caller of the shots. The placement of the word *TEACHER* in the diagram relative to the placement of the word *Students*, as well as the use of uppercase letters for *TEACHER* and mostly lowercase letters for *Students*, are intentional representations of the power divide. In more extreme cases of teacher sovereignty, the word *Students* might lose its one capital letter and be written in plain text rather than boldface. In teacher-driven classrooms, decisions about the nature of the classroom elements emanate from the teacher and flow to students, whose role is generally to respond to what comes their way rather than initiate or collaborate on action.

Figure 3.1:   The power relationship in teacher-directed classrooms and the approach to various classroom elements

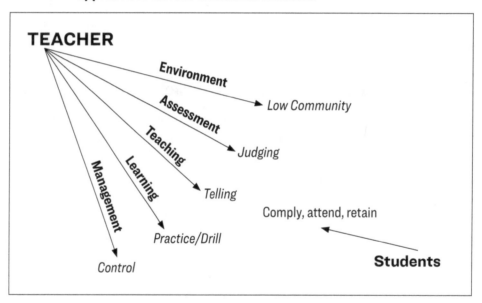

Figure 3.2 capsules the change in the power relationships in student-focused classrooms with corresponding descriptors of the resulting approach to curriculum, instruction, assessment, classroom management, and classroom environment. Here, the words *TEACHER* and *STUDENTS* appear at a similar height. In addition, both are capitalized and appear in boldface, which is meant to indicate the collaborative nature of learner-focused classrooms. Teachers in these classrooms are still charged by law, training, age, and experience with ensuring that students make appropriate academic progress. They still, of necessity, make many decisions about what will transpire in the classroom. However, because the

goals of student-centered classroom focus heavily on developing student voice, agency, collaboration, and decision making, the teacher involves the students in understanding and participating in the various decisions that bear on the five key classroom elements you see in the figure. Further, the teacher's decisions consistently include careful consideration of ways in which the progression of classroom events can help students mature in voice, agency, collaboration, and decision making, as well as the ways in which students can collaborate with the teacher on much of what transpires in daily classroom life. Thus, the teacher serves *at least* as much as a mentor, guide, and partner as a provider of information. As teachers become more comfortable with sharing responsibility with their students, the mentor/guide/partner role expands, and the role of teller-of-information lessens. As a result, the nature of the classroom elements is increasingly likely to reflect the students' perspectives, interests, and needs.

Figure 3.2: The power relationship in learner-centered classrooms and the approach to the elements in those classrooms

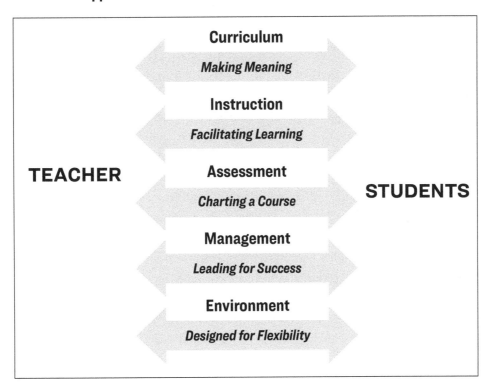

This is the shift that learner-centeredness requires of teachers. It happens neither quickly nor painlessly, but it can absolutely happen when, as Carol Steele (2009) suggests, inspired teachers are passionate about their work, believe they are responsible for their students' success as learners, and aim consistently to do a better job every day.

Working on the Most Significant Factor in the Classroom

Teachers affect learners and learning. There's no surprise in that statement. And sadly, there are as many teachers who have a significantly negative impact on students' learning as there are who have a significantly positive impact (Hattie, 2012). As it turns out, the school a student attends is not nearly as important a factor in that student's success as whose classroom the student is in. Wiliam (2011b) notes that of all the factors that might contribute to student growth, "the only thing that really matters is the quality of the teacher" (p. 7).

A central assumption in this book is that strong and effective student-centered classrooms will have the same fundamental attributes as effective classrooms in general *plus* the attributes necessary to support commendable learner-centeredness. Said a bit differently, classrooms in which the teacher supports student voice, choice, contribution, and agency but doesn't take equal care to ensure that his or her practices are strong in the areas of learning environment, curriculum, assessment, and instruction may see student growth—but that growth is not likely to be as robust as the teacher had envisioned.

The goal in this chapter is to explore teachers' personal and professional beliefs and practices that are foundational to effective student-centered planning and teaching. It's important to clarify that teacher-directedness and student-centeredness are not binary. It would be futile to attempt to classify every teacher solely into one or the other of those categories. Virtually every teacher at the helm of a largely teacher-directed classroom has moments of student-centeredness, and every leader of a highly learner-focused classroom has moments of teacher-directedness. We all fall along a continuum of practice at any given time, and our points on the continuum will shift for a variety of reasons as our careers play out. Nonetheless, student-centered practice calls for us to draw on these beliefs and practices in greater degrees or with a somewhat different focus than we are accustomed to doing.

Figure 3.3 (see p. 42) provides a reasonable framework for thinking about the needs of students in learner-centered classrooms and the traits the teachers of those classes would do well to continually develop in themselves in order to support as fully as possible the intellectual, affective, and social growth in each of their students. The side-by-side cells in the two columns of the graphic are not intended to align horizontally, and the descriptors in the two columns are intended not to be exhaustive but representative of the goals and attributes for students and teachers in learner-centered environments. I invite you to use the blank space in the figure to add to the student and teacher goals listed and make note of any goals you or your students are not pursuing at this time but might want to.

I want to stress that the goals and descriptors in the right-hand column of Figure 3.3 are *not dependent on teacher personality*. They apply to teachers who are outgoing or reserved, playful or serious, adventurous or cautious. They are not about how you tend to interact with the world but rather about *what you choose to do* and *what you represent* as you plan for work in the classroom, go about that work, and reflect on its outcomes.

While the goals for students and teachers represented in the figure are relevant to students and teachers in virtually all contexts, they have particular importance for teachers who elect to adopt and grow in learner-centered pedagogy. These are traits or goals that should help you work on the single most important factor in your student's growth—*you!* The work you do to continue growing yourself will very likely be the greatest contribution you make to your students and to the goal of an invigorated, student-focused classroom.

Before we begin a closer look at the goals for students in learner-centered classrooms and the teacher traits that support those goals, take some time to think about what you've read in this chapter so far and jot down a few thoughts and reflections.

Learner-Focused Classrooms as Human-Centered Design

"Human-centered design" is both a philosophy and a process used in many businesses, industries, and other settings where the primary goal is to serve customers or clients. The process of human-centered design begins by seeking to understand the people for whom you are working and the needs they have that the product or service you design must address (DC Design, 2017). Specifically, designers consider two topics: (1) "the needs and wants of product users" and (2) "how [to]

Figure 3.3: Example of goals for student development and teacher development in learner-centered classrooms

Goals for Student Development	Goals for Teacher Development
Develop voice, through ○ Self-understanding ○ Self-expression ○ Reasoning ○ Responsibility ○ Respect ○ Empathy	Model and support foundational attributes, such as ○ Respect ○ Equity ○ Empathy ○ Habits of mind and work ○ Community ○ Excellence
Partner in classroom effectiveness by ○ Exerting a positive influence ○ Demonstrating good citizenship ○ Contributing to and supporting classroom norms ○ Contributing to and supporting classroom processes and routines ○ Problem solving	Create an invitational environment that is ○ Positive ○ Accepting/affirming ○ Trusting ○ Challenging ○ Supporting ○ Enthusiastic ○ Organized
Acquire and use durable knowledge to enhance ○ Engagement ○ Joy/satisfaction ○ Understanding/meaning making ○ Application/transfer	Become a skilled student of students by focusing on ○ Observation ○ Teacher–student interactions ○ Teacher–class interactions ○ Use of formative assessment for student success
Identify as a learner in terms of ○ Skills, processes, habits of mind ○ Self-efficacy/agency ○ Personal connection with content ○ Satisfaction in learning ○ Using/transferring learning ○ Making connections with learning	Grow in curricular and instructional expertise such that you can ○ Teach by nature of the discipline(s) ○ Teach for meaning and understanding ○ Use multiple pathways to learning ○ Teach skills for successful learning, collaboration, and autonomy ○ Teach up/set high expectations
Participate in a meaningful community by ○ Listening in order to learn ○ Applying the skills of citizenship ○ Applying the skills of team building ○ Valuing diverse abilities and perspectives	Demonstrate flexibility through ○ Time, space, materials ○ Student working options ○ Student choice ○ Instructional approaches ○ Learning approaches
Aspire to grow continually by ○ Understanding academic, social, and affective targets and indicators of growth ○ Planning and working for growth ○ Reflecting on and learning from outcomes ○ Achieving satisfaction from growth	Grow professionally in terms of ○ Self-reflection ○ Decision making ○ Creativity ○ Leadership of students ○ Efficacy

satisfy those needs in both functional and emotionally meaningful ways" (Ruby Garage, 2017, para. 4). Groups that use human-centered design say that this little switch—looking first at needs and problems through the eyes of the people they serve rather than just saying, *Here's what we need to do, and now let's do it*—has resulted in solutions that are more creative, more effective, and more satisfying than those that typically emerged from traditional approaches. This early stage of the human-centered design process seems aligned with the counsel of Simon Sinek discussed in Chapter 2—start with the "why," move to the "what," and only then plan for the "how."

So another question that should be asked early on in a movement toward learner-centeredness is *What are the needs of the young people in our care that we can address through our work as teachers?* In student-focused teaching, our "product" or "solution" will be the sum of experiences our students have in our classroom. The nature of the content students learn and how they can learn it effectively are central concerns, of course (and we'll examine those elements in Chapters 6 and 8), but learning in student-centered classrooms includes affective and social goals as well as cognitive/intellectual ones. Whether we're focused on content, instruction, or affective and social outcomes, we can only address our learners' needs effectively if we understand those needs and plan accordingly. That stands in stark contrast to the common approach to planning, which begins with the questions *What do we have to teach here, how much time do we have to do it, and what materials will we need?* This is the "bottom up" curriculum design that Hattie (2012) cautions against—the one where we ask which standards we have to teach and what we'll do to cover them rather than asking what rich ideas are of central importance in a content area, building out those ideas, and incorporating standards that become a means to an important end. Think about all the ways in which that familiar approach restricts attention to affective and social needs and confines curriculum to a predetermined set of often-narrow outcomes that may have little to do with the great variety of needs, experiences, and interests of the learners who will be expected to "master" this content. Think about how little room that approach leaves for cognitive or intellectual development.

Figure 3.4 provides an organizer for the exploration we'll be doing. It suggests that the way to address the key development needs of students in learner-focused classrooms (drawn from Figure 3.3 and represented by the six boxes on the outside of the circle) is to understand and apply quality practices related to the four components of learner-centered classrooms reflected in the circle (drawn from Figure 2.2; see page 27). The arrows in the circle and between the outer boxes are there to indicate a continual interaction among the elements. In other words, as a teacher strives to become a better "student of his or her students," a goal of "Focus on the Learner" will likely have an impact on "Learning Environment and Community" and a strong connection with "Focus on Progress" and will produce insights for working with a student more successfully in "Curriculum and Instruction." Likewise, the teacher's focus on the learner at a given time may be intended to help that learner feel more confident in expressing ideas or opinions in class ("Developing Voice") but may simultaneously contribute to that student's comfort in "Participating in a Meaningful Community of Learners" and "Identifying as a Learner." Note that I have slightly modified the language in Figure 2.2 for use in Figure 3.4 to be a closer match for the vocabulary I'll use in this book.

Figure 3.4: A model for thinking about and addressing the needs of students in a learning-centered classroom

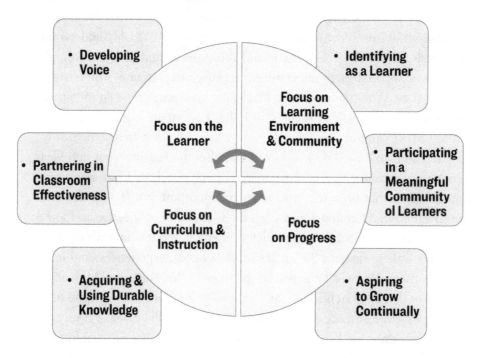

In upcoming chapters, we'll examine what it might look like for a teacher in in a learner-focused classroom to do the following:

- **Establish a positive learning environment** that leads to a strong team or community of learners and that operates with a balance of flexibility and stability necessary to foster students' cognitive, affective, and social development (Chapter 5).
- **Craft curriculum** that feels engaging and relevant to the full scope of learners in a classroom while building a solid understanding of the nature, intent, and fundamentals of the disciplines in which the curriculum is rooted (Chapter 6).
- **Use formative assessment,** both formal and informal, to understand the cognitive, affective, and social growth of each learner in order to plan for and support that learner's development in those three domains, and to help each learner understand and promote his or her own growth in those three areas as well (Chapter 7).
- **Craft instruction** that focuses students on the critical knowledge, understanding, and skill that characterize a topic and discipline, taps into student curiosity and interest, calls on students to use what they learn to address meaningful issues or problems, fosters deep thinking, and helps students develop a strong individual voice and a commitment to doing quality work (Chapter 8).

To prime your thinking for the fuller discussion of the "what" and "how" of learner-centered teaching in the chapters ahead, we'll spend the remainder of this one looking at five aspects of a teacher's practice that merit examination over the course of a career:

1. The ethics and values that ground teaching.
2. How the teacher sees, gets to know, and responds to students.
3. How the teacher thinks about the content that's taught.
4. How the teacher thinks about student growth and achievement.
5. How the teacher thinks about teaching and learning.

Growth in these five areas benefits virtually all teachers and the young people they teach.

The Ethics and Values That Ground Our Teaching: Which Way Is North?

Several years back, I asked students in one of my undergraduate classes to take a few minutes at the end of our first month together to identify something we'd covered so far that stood out to them as important. "It can be something you want to remember to carry into your own classroom next year," I told them. "It can be something that puzzles you and that you want to figure out… something you disagree with… whatever is occupying some of your mental space." It was early February, and nearly all the students would graduate with teaching credentials in May. In just over three months, their preservice teacher preparation would end, and they would officially be teachers.

The student response that jolted me was a brief one that came from a young woman who was passionate about teaching, insightful, and committed to learning and growing. Her paper said simply, "Until this class, I had never thought of teaching as having an ethical dimension."

I asked myself a hundred times that semester and still ask today how it could be that, in a strong university with a strong school of education, we had prepared an extraordinary young educator to handle scores of routines, diagnoses, procedures, policies, issues, and dilemmas without making it clear that teaching—much like medical practice, and for many of the same reasons—has to be rooted in and guided by ethical considerations. How was it that this young woman was so close to leaving us and had never before been prompted to consider her ethical compass—to determine her "ethical north"?

While a keen awareness of the ethical responsibilities of a teacher's work can't guarantee that no child in our care will ever suffer harm, that awareness certainly heightens our sensitivity to the possibility of harm and points our decision-making apparatus in a constructive direction. After all, our work with students should be about doing profoundly positive and impactful work, not just about avoiding damage.

Unlike some other professions, there is no single, definitive code of ethics for teachers in the United States, so consider the "ethical pillars" in Figure 3.5 as possibilities for ethically oriented learner-centered teaching. What other ones would you add to the list? Are there any you would strike off the list or reword?

A baseline principle of ethics is that people in positions of power must align their actions with the interests of stakeholders or anyone whose welfare is, to some degree, in the hands of the person who holds sway over them. Lorna Earl (2003), a noted Canadian educator, translates that principle directly into teaching when she says, "Teachers' overriding moral purpose is to meet the needs of students, even when it conflicts with personal preferences" (p. 120). That statement, in my opinion, applies to every teacher, but without question it applies to teachers who have signed on to put students at the center of their work. Whatever the orientation points on your particular ethical compass, let's take a moment to look at a few that merit close and ongoing attention as you grow in a student-centered approach to teaching: empathy, equity, fairness, accountability, and values.

Figure 3.5: Some concepts often associated with ethics

Accountability	Beneficence (doing good)	Citizenship
Empathy	Equity	Fairness
Humanity	Respect	Responsibility
What else would you add?		

Empathy

Empathy can be defined as seeking to *understand* a person's condition and needs from the perspective of that person with the aim of *acting* to make a difference in responding to those needs. To strive to meet the academic, affective, and social needs of each student and to create classrooms where all students have meaningful voice and choice seems out of reach unless the teacher can increasingly see the world through a student's eyes. When we feel genuine empathy for a person, that affects our sense of responsibility for the person's welfare, how we think of them, how we listen to them, how we speak to them, and how we interact with them. It also influences our willingness to learn from them and to invest in them. Action informed by the world a child sees and knows can be quite different from action based in our own experiences. It is certainly different from action directed by externally imposed mandates.

Geneva Gay (2018) distinguishes between "caring *about*" students and "caring *for*" them. Caring *about* the young people we teach suggests enjoying their company, thinking about them when we are away from them, enjoying their ideas, and so on. Most teachers I have known care *about* their students. Caring *for* them requires a whole different level of commitment. Caring *for* students suggests empathy—a caring deep enough and strong enough to compel us to act on their behalf and do what is necessary to make sure they have what they need to grow and thrive. Caring *about* students is an attitude; caring *for* them is an action.

A caution, though: It is often the case that the young person in greatest need of our empathy is the one with whom it is most challenging for us to empathize.

Equity

Equity and *equality* are not synonyms. Equality is about treating everyone alike, whereas equity is about responding to individuals based on their needs. Young people come to school with markedly different background experiences, support systems, degrees of economic stability, and views of what life holds for them. Schools have the opportunity (and, I would argue, the moral imperative) to meaningfully address and diminish the inequities that characterize the lives of many of the young people we serve. We contribute to the inequities when we see these young people as "less than," when we "remediate" them, when we lower expectations for them, when we "teach down" to them, when we allow them to fade into the background, and when we give up on them.

Chances are you're familiar with the cartoon drawing in which three children are trying to peer over a board fence to see a baseball game. In the first frame, which might be labeled "reality," one child is tall enough to see over the fence, a second child can almost see over if he stands on his tiptoes, and the third child's eyes align with the center of the fence. In a second frame, usually labeled "equality," all three children are standing on boxes of equal height. The box doesn't benefit the first child in any way; he could already see over the fence. And while it allows the second child to see over the fence, the shortest child is still looking at boards, not a baseball field. In the third frame, often labeled "equity," the first child is looking over the fence into the field without standing on a box. The second and third children stand on boxes of different heights sized so each can see into the field, too. In some versions of the cartoon, there is a fourth frame. Here, all three children are standing directly on the field looking at the game. The fence is gone. The boxes are no longer necessary, because the barrier has been removed. This frame is labeled "justice." Caring for students implies action on a teacher's part not just to "provide the right boxes" but also to contribute doggedly to removing the fences altogether.

Fairness

We can associate fairness with both equality and equity. Fairness in distributing cupcakes likely means each student will get the same number of cupcakes (equality). In matters related to learning success, teachers and students come to understand that fairness means each student getting the support he or she needs in order to succeed (equity)—*not* each student having to do the same number of math problems, spending the same amount of time completing an assignment, or even completing the same assignment (Tomlinson, 2017). Fairness doesn't even mean that the teacher will respond to each student in exactly the same way when a behavior-related response is required.

Accountability

Accountability does not mean we relentlessly pursue perfection, which is neither healthy nor attainable. What it does mean is that we accept responsibility for the growth of each student we teach, do our best to work with all students to set worthy goals for their growth, and are persistently mindful of what we want to represent and do in the classroom. It means that we honestly, faithfully, and regularly examine how each student is (or isn't) progressing and how we are (or are not) growing in our professional aspirations. It means that we adjust what we do and how we do it to maximize student growth and strengthen ourselves as professionals.

According to Hattie (2009), the fundamental task of teachers is to evaluate the effect our teaching has on student learning and growth. "Know thy impact," he advises (p. 192). In this sense, accountability becomes a manifestation of a growth mindset—the belief that by seeking to learn from both our successes and our failures, we become stronger, better, smarter, and more nearly self-actualized. The scope of accountability in a learner-focused classroom expands as our sense of the possibilities of student-centeredness expands and the classroom allows for increasing student voice and choice.

Values

The terms *ethics* and *values* are similar and overlapping. The distinction is that ethics tend to relate to a group or field and to focus on work in that field, while values are personal and shaped by family, culture, or religion. Take a look at the list of values in Figure 3.6, think about them, and revise the list so that it reflects the values you aspire to represent and encourage through your work. Cross out any values that you don't think are particularly pertinent or that you feel are inappropriate. Think about what other values you see or want to use to drive your decisions and actions in the classroom—and that you want to encourage students to consider in their decision making and actions as well.

Figure 3.6: Some concepts often associated with values

Calmness	Care	Collaboration
Curiosity	Diversity	Education
Enthusiasm	Excellence/quality	Flexibility
Generosity	Growth	Honor
Humility	Humor	Imagination
Joy	Kindness	Knowledge
Logic	Open-mindedness	Optimism
Originality	Passion	Patience
Perseverance	Reason	Respect
Teamwork	Trust	Well-being
What else would you add?		

Once, when I was walking my two very young puppies, a woman approached us and knelt to talk with the pups. In the course of our brief exchange, she made a comment that has stayed fresh in my mind. "You know," she said, "these pups will see the world through your hands." Our students see themselves, their learning, and the world through our words and actions. Think as often as you can about what you want them to see.

Seeing, Knowing, and Responding to the Learners We Teach

A friend was on outdoor duty at school one morning and began watching a colleague whose job was to stand by the buses as the young students got off, greet them, and make sure they seemed to be "good to go" for the day ahead. Knowing that, he had a good sense of what she was saying to the students as they exited the buses, but he was puzzled by the fact that she seemed to keep talking, head turned toward the departing student, as each one walked toward the school building. Later in the day, he asked her to explain to him what he had observed. "Oh, I do that with every student," she told him. "After I've spoken to a student, I say softly to myself, *There goes one more opportunity to make a difference.*" Sharing the story with me, my friend said, "I've long known she was an exceptional teacher. That morning, I learned why."

Noted educator and champion of underserved learners Bill Ayres (2010) reminds us that "the first and fundamental challenge for teachers is to embrace students as three-dimensional creatures, as distinct human beings with hearts and minds and skills and dreams and capacities of their own, as whole people much like ourselves" (p. 152). He cautions us against seeing young people through the prism of their deficits:

> A teacher needs a brain to break through the cotton wool smothering the mind, to break through the blizzard of labels to this specific child, trembling and whole, and to this one, and then to this one. And a teacher needs a heart to fully grasp the importance of that gesture, to recognize in the deepest core of your being that every child is precious, each induplicable, the only one who will ever trod this earth—deserving of the best a teacher can give— respect, awe, reverence, commitment. (p. 153)

Ayres is rightly advocating for students who carry heavy loads through life— those "who are put at the edges of the classroom and society" (Love, 2020, p. 2) and who, thus, have a profound need for our affirmation and belief. Still, we are better teachers as we become more and more able to say about *every* learner in our care, "There is so much potential in this young person that no one has yet seen. I am privileged to work with this child, first to help her realize whole new ceilings of possibility and then to help her push beyond *those* ceilings as well."

If you sometimes think of students as high achievers or low achievers, smart, average, or not smart, first quartile or bottom quartile, willing or unwilling, moti- vated or not motivated, this means you're normal. But keep pushing against this normal inclination. Believe in every student's strengths as a deliberate act of faith and then look for those strengths. Create opportunities for the student to push a little further than he or she thought possible. Put the student in a light that lets peers see the student shine in a new way. Remember that all students grow in stature, energy, and self-efficacy when we expect them to accomplish something that wasn't possible yesterday and when we provide a support system that turns yesterday's impossibility into next week's old news.

Here are some questions for your consideration, designed to help you build a personal foundation for the work of Chapter 4, which looks at honoring the learner in student-centered classrooms.

Points to Consider

- What percentage of time would you say you spending thinking about, planning for, and talking with "the class" compared to thinking about, planning for, and talking with students as individuals?

- How do you keep negative comments from colleagues or stereotypes that exist in and beyond the school from shaping your sense of who a student is and might become?

- How do you seek to understand your own biases? (We all have them. They are part of being human.) In what ways do you actively work against those biases?

- How do you continue to push yourself toward a deeper understanding of how race, poverty, language, physical or emotional weights, abusive homes, and housing and food insecurity might affect students' learning? How do you create opportunities to see and appreciate the unique strengths and capacities that accompany each student into the classroom?

- How do you hope to think and feel about your students as the school year begins? As it continues into the long "in between" that can challenge both students and teachers alike? As the year ends? What can you do to maintain, and even heighten, optimism and trust and investment over the course of a year?

- How do you try to ensure that each student leaves your room every day feeling as though the two of you shared a connection?

- How do you speak to students when they are being fingernails on your blackboard or someone else's? Why?

- How do you invest in getting to know your students better by the day, both in breadth and depth?

- How do you use new information and insights about a student to teach him or her more effectively? In what ways do you enable the student to be your partner in working for his or her growth?

- How do you ensure that students have a voice in all aspects of the classroom so that they understand themselves more fully and develop agency as learners?

- How does what you learn from studying your students and how you respond to them help you understand yourself more fully?

Thinking About the Content
We Ask Our Students to Learn

A colleague was observing in a 4th grade classroom where students were working on a writing assignment. Sitting down beside a student and hoping to gain some insight about the student's writing process, she said, "Tell me about what you're doing." With a heavy sigh, the child replied, "We're writing." "Yes," the observer responded, "I see that. I was hoping you could share with me what you're writing about." With a weary shake of her head and another fatalistic sigh, the child said, "In here, we don't write about anything. We just write." Not exactly a recipe for meaningful learning.

Apparently, this student's experience is relatively common. In a variety of surveys (e.g., Bryner, 2007; Stringer, 2019), high school students reported being bored as much as 70 percent of the time and being stressed 80 percent of the time. Two out of three students reported being bored in school every single day. The reasons these students gave for feeling bored are more concerning still. A third said they are bored because of a lack of interaction with their teachers. Three-quarters said they are bored because the material isn't interesting to them. The solution to a lack of interaction is addressed earlier in this chapter; the solution for uninteresting material is related to how we see and enact curriculum.

Here are a few things we know about how the brain learns—or doesn't—and some implications of that knowledge:

• The brain is a poor memorizing machine. A lot of energy is required to get information into the brain, and information leaves the brain with ease and speed.

• Envisioning curriculum as information that we as teachers need to "cover" so that our students will retain what they've heard creates a swampy ground for learning. Many students will forget much of the information they "learned" within a very short time.

• The brain seeks organization in order to make sense of, store, retain, retrieve, and be able to use information.

• As teachers, we need to understand the concepts, or big ideas, that connect knowledge within and across content areas, times, places, and contexts, and then we need to help students identify and understand those connectors so that they will be able to make sense of, store, retain, retrieve, and use what they learn.

• Students need to see knowledge connected to their own lives and experiences in order to make meaning from what they learn. When the brain's owner makes those connections, the brain is able to store them and make them available for future use in meaning making, connections making, and application.

• When a student finds learning engaging, relevant, and interesting, that student is more motivated to devote energy and intentionality to the kind of work that leads to success.

• We would do well to begin planning both curriculum as a whole and individual lessons or learning experiences by asking, *Where is the spark in this content that can ignite learning in this student—and in these students?* Remember that students with widely diverse backgrounds and experiences won't always have their interest sparked by the same thing. In learner-focused classrooms, the goal is always to reach each learner, not simply to generalize to the group.

Here are some questions related to how you think about curriculum. As with the questions in the previous section, they are intended to prime your thinking on this topic in preparation for a discussion in an upcoming chapter—in this case, Chapter 6's look at quality curriculum in a learner-centered classroom.

 Points to Consider

• To what degree do you think of a textbook in the subject(s) you teach as your curriculum? What are the upsides and downsides to your answer?

• To what degree do you think of a set of standards as your curriculum? What are the upsides and downsides to your answer?

• To what degree does a pacing guide become the curriculum in your classroom? What are the upsides and downsides to your answer?

• How do you go about finding deep meaning in what you teach so that you can help students see that meaning as well? (A student asking, "How come we gotta do this?" is seeking meaning and relevance. If the best answer we can offer is "Because it will be on the standardized test at the end of the year," or "Because it will help you when you get older," or "Because it's in the pacing guide," we need to keep searching for meaning until we find something the young people in our class will value.)

• How do you help students *understand* how the content or subject or discipline makes sense, how the parts make a whole, and how the whole is useful to them? How do you keep *understanding* in the foreground of what you and your students do every day?

• How do you connect what the students are learning to the lives they lead both inside and outside school? How do you know what's relevant to a given student, and which students are not likely to find those same things relevant?

• What is a recent example of an assignment you gave that not only allowed students to do something they found individually meaningful and engaging but also required them to apply essential knowledge, understanding, and skills they were learning in class?

• What do you do to help yourself understand the content you teach more deeply and broadly each year? How prepared do you feel to help your students learn more deeply and broadly than you were able to in the past? Why do you answer as you do?

• How do you feel about including affective and social goals in what you teach and how you teach it? Why do you answer as you do?

• How do you ensure that students have a significant voice in the curriculum they study?

As you see, the principle of "starting with why" is a theme in this book. It applies to curriculum design too. Often in school, someone hands us "a curriculum," which is sadly likely to be a list of standards or a textbook or (even worse) a pacing guide, and says or implies, *This is what you need to teach. Here's how you teach it. Go!* If we want to honor the learner, the learner's brain, the power of the discipline, and our own potential to positively impact the people we teach, it's incumbent that we first ask ourselves three questions: *Why am I teaching this? Why is it important for who these kids are and who they will become for them to learn this? How can my students and I work together to make this content relevant, engaging, and enlightening?* Our *Go!* should come only after we answer these questions, with periodic pauses thereafter to take stock, consult our students, and recalibrate our approach as needed.

Thinking About the Instruction We Use

A middle school student whom I interviewed for a research project clearly felt valued and affirmed by her teacher. "Not everybody always 'gets' me," she explained. "This teacher gets me. She has since the first day of school." When I asked to her to explain why she liked the class so much, the middle schooler responded, "I like this class because there is something different going on in here every day. In my other classes, it's like peanut butter for lunch every single day. In this class, it's like my teacher runs a really good restaurant with a big menu and all." That's a winning combination—a teacher who gets you and instruction that is lively and varied.

Dylan Wiliam (2011a) observes, "The greatest impact on learning is the daily lived experiences of students in classrooms, and that has much more to do with how [teachers] teach than with what they teach" (p. 29). I am a staunch believer in the power of rich curriculum to shape brains and lives, but I have seen many an instance in which a teacher (including myself) drained every last ounce of life out of good curriculum by teaching it poorly.

Here are some questions related to how you think about instruction, intended to prime you for Chapter 8's discussion of quality instruction in a learner-centered classroom.

Points to Consider

- If you could be an impartial observer in your own classroom, would you conclude that learning is more valued than teaching—or the other way around? Why do you answer as you do?

- What steps do you take to engage each of your students in learning? How do you monitor each student's engagement with the assigned work and associated ideas?

- As your students work, is each of them clear on what they need to know, understand, and be able to do in order to succeed? How do you know? Do they directly connect those requirements with the work they are doing? How do you know?

- How often is understanding (vs. information and skills) in the foreground of your teaching in the work students do and in class discussions?

- How often do students collaborate meaningfully and successfully in your class(es)?

- What proportion of student work calls on *every* student to understand, apply, solve problems, and make connections with the content?

- How often do you model and teach the skills students must internalize to grow academically, affectively, and socially? What evidence do you look for to help you understand each student's comfort with those skills and the effectiveness of their skill application?

- How do you ensure that your instruction consistently reflects student voice and helps further the development of student voice and learning agency?

The goal of these questions is not for you to grade yourself or to boost or erode your confidence. As with the questions in the other sections of the chapter, they should help you think about your strengths as well as areas in which you'd like to continue to develop. In fact, sometimes your strengths are the most fruitful areas for further investment. My aim here is twofold: to help you focus on where you are, and to invite you to consider your willingness or eagerness to continue to think and grow in the various aspects of your teaching—both in general and in regard to learner-focused teaching. As a teacher in a book for young readers explains, you can't get where you want to go without being where you are (Graff, 2015). It also highly unlikely that you'll get there without a keen desire to grow from your current point of development.

Thinking About Student Growth and Achievement

Schools often operate from an achievement orientation rather than a growth orientation. That tends to communicate to students that they need to arrive at a specific point by a given time with a predetermined set of criteria in order to see themselves as successful and in order for *others* to see them successful.

A sad-faced boy explained to me once that he was bad at school. "I can't finish my work as fast as teachers need me to finish it," he said. "I think if I could finish faster, I would be OK at school. But I can't. I just get more behind all the time. So… I'm bad at school."

By contrast, one of my middle school students once asked me, with apprehension, if I would mind *not* grading her writing assignments going forward. She explained, "Every piece I've written this marking period I did either on the bus on the way home or in the cafeteria before school started. On every one of them, you gave me an A, and that ought not to be what an A represents."

If growth were our focus, the sad-faced boy might have drawn a very different conclusion about himself. The truly stellar young writer might have encountered the need to grow in my class much sooner than she did. (Still, I understood her message, and we walked a very different path going forward—a path that she helped me carve out and that permanently revised my thinking.)

Here are a few questions to help you consider the relative role of achievement and growth in your work.

Points to Consider

- Which would your students say you value more, achievement or growth? How do *you* feel about the balance of those two elements in your work with students?

- How do your assessment and grading practices help students see themselves as worthy learners?

- In what ways do you help students analyze, reflect on, and plan from current work so they know how to move forward as more successful learners?

- When you prepare formal assessments of student learning, what do you do to ensure that the assessment enables each student to show you all that he or she knows about the topic? What steps do you take to remove barriers that might inhibit or limit the ability to do that?

- What proportion of the formal assessments you administer asks students to demonstrate understanding of important concepts and ideas? What proportion of them asks students to supply knowledge or demonstrate skills?

- When your students are working, what do you do to better understand how they are progressing with key knowledge, understanding, and skills? How do you keep track of what you see? How do you use what you learn to ensure their continuing growth?

- How do you use formative assessment to help students develop agency as learners?

- How do you assess students' social and affective development? How do you communicate your insights about those areas to students? How does what you observe about their affective and social development inform your planning and teaching?

- What choice and voice do students have in the nature and use of assessment?

Learner-centeredness doesn't require that we exhibit all of these beliefs and practices in our work next week, or even that we ever exhibit them all at the highest possible degree. What it does ask us to do is turn away from inhospitable, inequitable, and indefensible practices and turn toward purposes and practices that center on dignifying and tending to the flourishing of each learner in our care.

The title of this book, *So Each May Soar*, reminds us to focus on *students*. After all, they are (or should be) the reason we do the work we do. Strong learner-centered teaching is a sort of a "call and response" enterprise. The teacher presents an idea or exploration to students, and as they respond, the teacher watches, alert to their thinking, emotions, and behaviors. The watching will shape the teacher's own next response. The call-and-response chain is long, running throughout a class period, a day, an entire school year.

The premise of this chapter, and much of the book, is that the student can't flourish without a teacher who fully engages in learning how to teach responsively—both to the individual and to the group. In every classroom, every day, teachers misjudge, utter a poorly crafted sentence that wounds, lose patience, and preside over a mundane lesson; that is the nature of being human. What makes a learning-centered teacher, however, is a persistent drive to know better, to do better, to reach out better in order to lift up better.

Teaching allows for a certain transformative synergy in that, as a teacher helps a student extend his or her capacities, the teacher's capacities extend further as well. In that way, teacher and student flourish together—or are diminished together. For a student to soar, he or she must have a teacher who soars.

Looking Ahead

As noted, the next four chapters expand on the nature of quality practice in each of the four key components of learner-centered classrooms. They also provide some important indicators of quality practice that reflect both the art and science of teaching and illustrate how the principles and practices spotlighted might look in a classroom and benefit student and teacher alike.

4

Honoring the Learner

When we understand that everyone wants to be cared for and that there is no recipe for caring, we see how important engrossment (or attention) is. In order to respond as a genuine carer... one cannot say, "Aha! This fellow needs care. Now let's see—here are the seven steps I must follow." Caring is a way of being in relation, not a specific set of behaviors.

—Nell Noddings in *The Challenge to Care in Schools*

All aspects of learner-centered instruction begin with a *teacher* whose attention is focused not on himself or herself, or even on the content, but on the *student*.

Due to external pressures or personal habit, the planning sequence in classrooms often begins with "What do I have to cover tomorrow?" or "What work will I need to have ready for the students tomorrow?" Learner-centered thinking calls on teachers to begin with a different set of questions: *What are the needs and nature of this class as a whole?* and *What are the needs and nature of the individuals who make up the class at this point in our work?* The answers to those two questions drive everything that comes next, including how teachers plan the learning environment, curriculum, assessment, and instruction. This chapter focuses on what it means to honor the learner and all the implications of doing so: how it shapes the teacher's mindset, how it positions the student to assume increasing ownership of his or her own learning, and how it contributes to a classroom environment that helps each learner recognize and work to develop his or her full potential.

Let's start with some reflection. Have you ever been in a meeting or at a party where it seemed like everyone else had people to talk with, while you felt essentially alone? Have you spent time in a place where virtually everyone spoke a language you didn't know, leaving you to navigate through the day with only hand signals and a plaintive face? Now think about a colleague or friend who is a great listener and always makes you feel that what you're saying is important enough to merit his or her full attention. Take a step back and consider which life moments have made you feel less than, invisible, incapable, demeaned. Which have made you feel valuable, worthy, stronger, validated, more determined? Why do you think those experiences affected you as they did?

Young people's self-concept is informed in large measure by the environments in which they spend their time. An environment that is affirming, encouraging, challenging, and supportive is likely to help a young person come to believe in his or her capacity, make productive decisions about engaging with learning, develop skills and resources that support success, and ultimately identify as a learner. Conversely, environments in which young people feel unseen, devalued, judged, awkward, or socially isolated diminish their optimism, energy, focus, and attention.

Neuroscience reminds us that the primary job of the brain is to protect its owner from harm. Negative emotions, like feeling judged, devalued, and so on, trigger the limbic system (the part of the brain that is charged with protection) to shut down processing in the cortex (the part of the brain in which cognition largely occurs) in order to focus the brain's energy on protection. Learners who feel threatened, uncomfortable, or anxious in the classroom are thus less likely to be able to function at a cognitive level necessary to do what is required for learning at that point in time (Sousa & Tomlinson, 2018).

In learner-centered classrooms, the goal of maximizing student capacity is paramount. While fully recognizing that no teacher is, or should try to be, Superman, T'Challa, or Wonder Woman, a learner-focused teacher aspires to help young people become their best selves cognitively, socially, and emotionally, and works persistently to be a predictable catalyst for positive student development. It is simply the teacher's goal to do whatever he or she can do as often as possible to make sure the classroom is an incubator for individual development rather than a deterrent to it.

Toward that end, teachers in learner-centered classrooms honor or dignify their students in at least the following ways:

- By accepting and affirming each student as they are,
- By believing in each student's capacity to grow and to succeed,

- By expanding their multidimensional knowledge about each student, and
- By acting, planning, and responding in a way that maximizes each student's growth.

Let's take a closer look at these ways of honoring the learner.

Accepting and Affirming Each Student as They Are

Here is a great exercise. Before meeting a group of students for the first time, look at the class roster and imagine the variety of faces, backgrounds, fears, hopes, talents, and dreams that will be entering the classroom. The students will represent some degree of a cross-section of the world. If you find yourself excited to meet these students, eager to discover both their similarities and their differences, and ready to greet each one with actions and words that convey your pleasure in learning about *and* from them, you are solidly positioned at the starting block.

Recall what Ayres (2010) said about teachers needing to not just recognize students as whole, complex, and distinct human beings with unique motivators, dreams, and minds but also embrace each one's individuality. Each student we teach needs to have an ongoing sense that we are happy to see them, pleased with their presence, interested in what makes them unique, and excited to be their partner in learning. For some of us, these feelings are almost instinctive. For others, there are habits to break, biases to overcome, and past experiences to grapple with before eager anticipation is likely. If positive anticipation is not yet a reality for you, it can be learned; it's simply an alternative lens for seeing.

Figure 4.1 provides some practical ways that teachers might demonstrate student acceptance and affirmation. Use the blank space at the end of the figure to add your own ways of communicating to your students that you accept them just as they are, or ideas for new ways you might do this.

Believing in Each Student's Capacity to Grow and Succeed

Continuing his thoughts about teachers' challenge of embracing young learners who are initially strangers to them, Ayres (2010) reflects that it is "initially an act of faith. We must assume capacity even when it is not immediately apparent or visible" (p. 152)—and even, it's wise to add, when some students seem to provide evidence to the contrary.

Figure 4.1: Strategies for affirming each learner

- Be aware of your own habits, tendencies, strengths, and biases; work to build on the strengths and to temper inclinations that might inhibit your ability to accept and affirm students as they are.
- Watch your words; try to use language that is affirming and constructive in all interactions with each student and all students.
- Avoid language, labels, materials, groupings, and other indicators that might convey the message that some students are better or more worthy than others.
- Do the preparation work so that you can pronounce each student's name correctly and confidently from Day 1.
- Use strengths-based assessments to convey the message that students' "positives" are important to you.
- Use information about student positives to create work that will draw on their strengths and demonstrate to them, their peers, and yourself the power of these positives in action.
- Find opportunities to talk with each student as close to daily as possible.
- Understand that every learner needs you in both similar and unique ways. Look for the similarities and differences in students' needs. Make a consistent effort to "be there" for each of them.
- Practice listening, observing, and noticing.
- Practice empathy.
- Give students considerable voice in making decisions about classroom agreements and classroom operation, in determining how those processes are working, and in modifying them as needed.
- Stand at the classroom door each day as students enter and exit and use this time to speak briefly but directly to each student.
- Let students know you are eagerly learning about them as individuals so that you can understand how to be the best possible teacher for them.
- Invite students to share with you (privately) their interests, past experiences, and classroom preferences, so you can plan with that knowledge in mind.
- Talk with students about your desire to make the classroom a place where everyone can find partnership for success and where everyone can contribute to the success of others. Ask students how they can help you make that happen—then plan, implement, and reflect together.
- Share with students things you are learning about them by talking with them and observing their work; explain to them how what you're learning is helping you plan instruction and activities.
- Learn about students' values (holidays, traditions, music, hobbies, etc.) and apply what you're learning to individual conversations, class discussions, and decisions about curriculum and instruction.
- Encourage English learners to work in their first language whenever feasible.
- Teach in ways that honor a student's first language (including language shaped by race, country of origin, and/or language spoken primarily at home).
- Build connections with families, letting parents and other caregivers know that you are pleased to be working with their child and that you'd appreciate their help in knowing more about how their child is feeling about the class and how you can help their child grow throughout the year.
- Pursue greater understanding of the ways in which race and culture shape learning and school experience—including how long-term discrimination and bias erode students' prospects and how attention to cultural strengths extends learning.
- Teach in ways that enable a student to affiliate with their dual cultures and languages.

(continued)

Figure 4.1: Strategies for affirming each learner—(*continued*)

- Include everyone's history, literature, stories, heroes, art, music, science, and math as an integral part of the curriculum throughout the year. Be sure students see themselves and their cultures in what they study.
- Schedule open room time before and after school or during lunch, which gives you an opportunity to be with students informally and help them produce quality work.
- Conduct structured observations of students and their work while they work independently and collaboratively, and use what you see to strengthen your teaching and their learning.
- Make use of student/teacher dialogue journals online or on paper.
- Attend events that are important to students, being certain to go to a wide range of events that are representative of the students you teach.
- Ask every student regularly (in person, online, on paper) what is working in class and what could be changed to make the class a better fit.
- Regularly ask students to help make the classroom run more smoothly and effectively, being sure to include students who others might see as "unlikely" choices in the invitations to leadership.
- Seek and present multiple perspectives on issues, controversies, or problems that need solving.
- Understand that some students must live in and navigate between two worlds. Be sensitive to both, and help them be better navigators.

What else would you add?

Sending the same message through a lens that's more scientific than philosophical, Dweck (2006) provides strong evidence that a teacher with a growth mindset is more likely to invite and support student success than is a teacher with a fixed mindset. A fixed mindset orientation reflects the premise that heredity and early environment determine the reach of an individual's ability. In a worst-case (but not uncommon) scenario, that orientation leads to stereotyping and dismissing the likelihood that "those kids" can succeed or that they even care to. A growth mindset orientation rejects that premise and proposes instead that the human brain is quite malleable; with appropriate encouragement and support, a person can appreciably grow their intellectual capacity just as they can grow their physical capacity. As we'll see in a later chapter, the mindset of a teacher is predictive of that teacher's current pedagogy. It is also a likely predictor of a teacher's current success in extending the reach of every learner and leading a learner-centered classroom.

Of course, teachers are aware of the challenges some students face—aware that geography, physical or emotional development, economic circumstance, racism, and a host of other factors can present children with an array of seemingly insurmountable challenges to learning. A teacher with a growth mindset sees each child as something of an iceberg: a small portion of the child's potential is visible above the surface, but the majority of it is hidden from view. That teacher sees his or her role as working wisely, empathetically, and consistently with the learner to ensure that more of what's beneath the surface rises into view each day. The message that teacher strives to deliver in words and actions to each student on a regular basis is "I am excited to welcome and work with the person you are today, and I am eager to help you discover horizons you have not yet dreamed of."

When it comes to developing a growth mindset in students, the teacher's task is akin to the work a skilled trainer might do to guide an athlete toward greater physical performance. There's a method to it—a three-step cycle of challenge and support, repeated consistently over time (see Figure 4.2).

Figure 4.2: Three key aspects of fostering a growth mindset

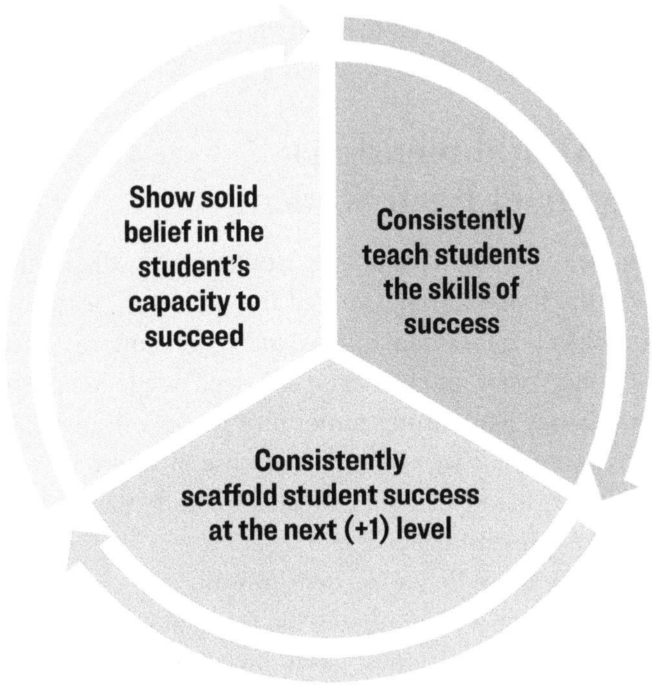

Having embraced the idea that much of human ability is hidden, the teacher manifests this conviction in the classroom. This means guiding all students to develop the skills and attitudes necessary for academic success—how to read directions with care, ask questions when needed, persist in the face of difficulty, study for understanding, set goals and monitor progress to those goals, contribute to the success of a group, aim for quality products, and so on. At the same time, the teacher uses observations and formative assessment data to provide work that is slightly beyond each student's current reach and scaffolds learning tasks in a variety of ways so the student can succeed with work that might have seemed impossible at the outset.

The process has dual benefits. Each student's progress demonstrates to the teacher that belief in that student is warranted, further energizing the teacher's efforts on the student's behalf. Simultaneously, it proves to all students who are succeeding at levels they had not imagined that their reach is greater than their assumptions, further energizing their efforts on their own behalf. In this way, all students continue to grow in agency and academic self-concept—crucial goals in learner-centered pedagogy. It is important to remember that this process is pivotal to the growth of every learner, no matter where the learner might fall in a learning progression at a given time.

Figure 4.3 offers some practical ways for teachers to demonstrate belief in the capacity of their students. Use the blank space at the end of the figure to add other ways in which you work—or could work—to accomplish those goals.

Expanding Multidimensional Knowledge About Each Student

How would we assume to teach a particular student well without knowing about her dreams, how she feels about school and the subject we teach, and what has brought her to that feeling? Without understanding her culture or her peer-group identity and how they factor into her sense of herself as a learner? Similarly, how could we plan in a way that ensures tomorrow's lesson will move a student forward with critical content if we don't have a sense of where his understanding was last week, or how what we did today affected his understanding? And yet, how often do we attempt to do just that?

Still driven by the sense that a teacher's mission is to ensure students make progress in reading, 'riting, and 'rithmetic, too many of us don't understand that there are three additional Rs that must be in the foreground of our thinking and

Figure 4.3: Strategies for demonstrating belief in each student's capacity to succeed

- Look consistently for student strengths and interests.
- Place those strengths and interests in the foreground of instructional planning.
- Set high academic, affective, and social expectations for students, then scaffold their success so that they regularly see themselves succeeding and growing.
- Have students perform as many classroom tasks as possible, teaching them how to carry out those roles successfully.
- Teach students about the concept of a growth mindset—how and why they can improve their brains just as they can improve their physical strength.
- Regularly remind students of the growth mindset cycle: *If you work hard and work wisely, you will grow. If you continue to work wisely and persistently, you will continue to grow and eventually achieve success.*
- Make the importance of growth a regular topic of discussions with the class and with individuals, stressing that competing against yourself is more productive than competing against others.
- Monitor student growth in key areas and respond in ways that support the individual student's next steps in growth; do not assume that all students share the same next step.
- Be sure each student typically works at a level of content and skill challenge that is slightly ahead of his or her current proficiency.
- Reject use of tracking or "fixed" instructional groupings that convey to students that some learners are "better learners" than others.
- Teach students various ways to monitor their progress toward short- and longer-term goals, including using checklists, following timelines, and comparing samples of their work over time.
- Work with students individually to set goals that are personally meaningful to them.
- Use brief student conferences to talk with individuals about their goals and their growth toward those goals. Include evidence of academic, social, and affective progress.
- Encourage students to acknowledge both their own growth and growth in their peers.
- Engage individual students and the whole class in metacognitive conversations to model thinking that guides success.
- Realize that "challenge" is a highly individual concept and respond accordingly.
- Understand that every student will need mentoring, coaching, and support when working at a challenge level appropriate for that student.
- Use time flexibly so students can have additional time to master content or take on tasks that are more complex.
- Look daily for small (and larger) cognitive, social, and affective successes for the class as a group and for individuals. Share what you observe with students when useful.
- Send brief communications to parents or other caregivers about student growth and what that growth suggests.
- Have students text, write, or dictate messages to parents or other caregivers to let these adults know about their progress in significant areas.

What else would you add?

planning: *relationships, relevance,* and *rigor.* Until we establish trust with each student, know each student well enough to know what's relevant to him or her, and have a sense of what rigor looks like for that student at the moment, our attempts to boost students' prospects with the content we commend to them is likely to fail (Littky & Grabelle, 2004).

The quest to know each student in a meaningful way begins on Day 1 of the school year, or possibly before, and it ends on the final day of the school year (though, for many teachers who are centered on the growth of each of their learners, teacher–student relationships continue well past the last day a student is "in residence" in a particular classroom or school). The quest is destined to be imperfect. To know and understand a young person in the myriad ways that could *fully* inform teaching is, of course, impossible. Accomplishing that degree of insight about 30 or 150 students is beyond reach. Nonetheless, succumbing to "there are just too many of them" shuts down a remarkably fruitful process. Persisting in the quest to know each student equips us, each day better than the day before, to support that student's development. It also continues to secure our ownership of each student's success and strengthens student–teacher relationships. Over time, it teaches us how to be more observant and listen beyond words for meaning. It elevates our practice and our capacity for empathy.

Figure 4.4 offers some practical ways in which you can come to understand each of your students more fully in order to teach them more effectively. Use the blank space at the end of the figure to add other strategies you use or might use.

Acting, Planning, and Responding to Maximize Each Student's Growth

The primary goal of understanding our students in meaningful ways is to improve our ability to plan for all aspects of the classroom in order to contribute most significantly to student development. Understanding our students increases the likelihood that we'll be able to address their learning needs, enlist their contribution to their own success and to the success of others in the classroom, and maximize their academic, affective, and social growth. Figure 4.5 illustrates the continual, interconnected cycle of studying students' needs, using what we learn to plan, carrying out our plan, reflecting on the plan's impact, and using what we learn to adapt our approach for greater effectiveness.

The plans we make and enact range widely in terms of scope, duration of implementation, and how much time we devote to reflecting on lessons and units

Figure 4.4: Strategies for building your knowledge of students

- Use strength-based surveys and interest inventories.
- Use parent/caregiver surveys to ask what the respondent likes best about the young person and what you need to know in order to teach the student well. Ask the respondent to share a positive school experience in the student's past, a negative experience, and something he/she would like for the student to learn or be able to do in the class this year.
- Expand and deepen your understanding of your students' home cultures.
- Ask students to bring in and share artifacts that represent them in some way.
- Learn about both the cultural richness of your African American students and the persistent challenges of growing up Black in the United States.
- Learn to listen with your full attention.
- Observe how students conduct themselves with peers—at lunch, on the playground, waiting for buses, in small groups, and in the halls.
- Observe how students conduct themselves during extracurricular activities.
- Ask students to share their goals for the class.
- Ask students about their dreams and aspirations for themselves.
- Ask students to tell you what they were like as young children, how they see themselves currently, and how they imagine themselves in 10 years.
- Use class meetings, morning meetings, idea jams, and other "gatherings" to provide time for students to share ideas and perspectives on a range of topics.
- Join students for lunch or invite them to have lunch with you in your classroom.
- Pay attention to the choices student make when you give them options about how to work, where to sit, how to express what they are learning. Underscore for the class the value of presenting an idea in varied modes and formats.
- Share your hobbies and interests (music, sports, etc.) as ways to open conversations with students about those same topics.
- Talk with students regularly as a whole class.
- Talk with individual students regularly, making sure those conversations happen with every student.
- Use notes or shared journals to talk with students who are shy or unlikely to speak in class for a variety of reasons.
- Start each class or day with small talk to reconnect and set a friendly tone.
- Talk with students individually and in small groups as you walk around the room—briefly, but often.
- Notice students' personality, degree of inclusion with peers, leadership qualities, and expressions of concern for others.
- Schedule regular mini-conferences with each student focused on feedback and planning.
- Use an annotated class list to remind yourself of things you want to look for related to individual students during a lesson, unit, week, or grading period.
- Include independent inquiries of varied lengths as part of your instructional plans to learn about things that matter to students, how they use resources, and how they choose to share what they learn.
- Create a record-keeping system to record insights, examples, reflections (spreadsheets, notebooks, sticky notes placed in a file folder) for each learner.

(continued)

Figure 4.4:   Strategies for building your knowledge of students—(*continued*)

- Track who answers questions in class, who contributes to discussion, and who does not. Use what you learn to create more inclusive patterns.
- When a student is clearly anxious about responding orally in class, offer alternatives such as writing answers in a journal or notebook and sharing them with the teacher.
- When students seem sad or tense or discouraged, take time to ask if they are OK. Listen. Let them know you are there for them. Show interest in their well-being.
- Treat challenging students as you would treat a friend or family member.
- Do "checks" that indicate your progress in learning about each student. For example, create a three-column grid. In Column 1, jot the name of students in the order you recall them. In Column 2, write something interesting or valuable you've learned about each student. In Column 3, note how you've used the information in Column 2 to work more effectively with each student.

What else would you add?

we have implemented. For example, planning a new unit of study is time intensive. Its implementation is not a unitary act but a series of implementations—each of which allows for reflection and invites us to adjust original plans based on how previous lessons have affected student engagement, understanding, quality of work, and so on.

Within a single lesson, by contrast, a teacher who is attuned to student body language may, in the moment, ask Vonda (a child who is fidgeting) to work with Lea (a classmate who has been absent for several days) to help bring Lea up to speed. Vonda, the student cast in the helper role, generally engages with and understands the work but struggles to sit still when feeling anxious. She also communicates well with peers in calmer times. The teacher knows that she is likely to enjoy mentoring Lea and likely to be effective in that role.

By picking up on Vonda's anxiety and asking her to help Lea, a classmate who needs assistance, the teacher has taken positive action on behalf of two learners, yet the decision to take that action was not preplanned in the way that sculpting a curriculum or planning a lesson necessarily is. This action was spontaneous, informed by the teacher's evolving understanding of the student cast in the role of helper, and it was enacted in a matter of seconds. Based on how both students fare in the new collaboration, the teacher will determine how to follow up with one or both students later in the day.

Figure 4.5: The iterative planning cycle to maximize student growth

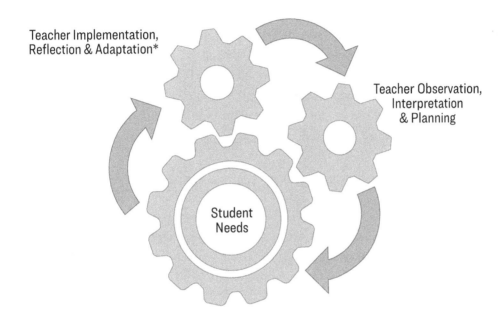

*Vehicles for response include adaptations of environment, curriculum, assessment, and classroom leadership and routines.

In short, learner-centeredness has much to do with making the best long- and short-term decisions we can in order to maximize student growth and success in every aspect of classroom life. It is about taking care to create long-term plans that account for the range of strengths and needs our learners bring to the classroom with them and also about knowing how and when to adapt those long-term plans in the moment as we observe a student's continuing academic, affective, and social development. This is not about becoming "perfect teachers"; it's about committing to grow ourselves as observers, thinkers, planners, and responders. It asks of us what we ask of students—that we take our own next steps in development as often as we can. As we come to know each of our students in more multidimensional ways, we become more skilled at creating curriculum that is more likely to support engagement and understanding for the individuals we teach and for entire classes of individuals. We learn to speak with greater awareness of the implications of what we say and how we say it. We understand assessment's value as a means to help students develop agency as learners rather than as a method of judging them. We seek opportunities to elicit student voice in more aspects of the work we share and in ways likely to help students develop and trust their own voices.

Figure 4.6 offers some practical ways in which teachers act, plan, and respond to enhance student success and growth. Once again, use the space at the end of the figure to add strategies of your own. As the book continues, we will focus on ways that student-centered teachers can use their growing understanding of their learners to shape learning environments, curriculum, formative assessment, and instruction. In Figure 4.6, you'll find a preview of that broader exploration.

Analyzing Examples of Teachers Honoring Learners

To help solidify understanding of the concepts we've discussed in this chapter, I'd like to share some examples of how teachers honor their students through inter-actions, curriculum design, and instruction. Each is followed by a few questions to highlight important ideas for your consideration.

In a High School Honors English Classroom

I observed a high school honors English class in which there were several African American female students who had never taken an advanced class prior to this one. These young women were predictably anxious about their prospects in the class, and they were anxious about whether the other students in the class, accustomed to advanced-level courses, would see them as "belonging there."

The teacher, Mrs. Wilkerson, began the year with a whole-class study of *The Color Purple*. The novel was challenging reading for some of the first-time honors students, but so compelling to them that they came to class excited and eager to contribute to discussions every day. These African American learners were not able to summon similar enthusiasm for *The Scarlet Letter*, which the class read later in the year. They were not alone in this respect.

One day, about a quarter of the way through the study of the Hawthorne novel, Mrs. Wilkerson began class by telling everyone that she'd heard a news story on the radio on the drive in that day that she thought would interest them—a report on the 100 most compelling heroines in American literature, as generated through a poll of readers. She told the class that Celie, from *The Color Purple*, was number 8 on the list. The African American students clapped enthusiastically.

Figure 4.6: Strategies for applying knowledge about students to honor them and help them grow

- Develop affective and physical environments that feel safe, affirming, challenging, and supportive to students with a range of learning needs, strengths, cultures, races, prior school experiences, and degrees of home security and support.
- Develop classroom routines with the flexibility required to address students' varied strengths and learning needs.
- Create curriculum that is likely to be relevant to students with varied interests, cultures, and experiences.
- Develop and learn from a variety of pre-assessments designed to locate students' varied possible entry points into an upcoming unit of study.
- Use formative (ongoing) assessment information to consistently monitor student progress toward mastery of the knowledge, understanding, and skill designated as essential for a given sequence of learning.
- Use formative assessment information to help students better understand their progress toward targeted goals and to plan more effectively for their own continuing growth toward those goals.
- Provide actionable, student-specific feedback and work with students to create their own plans for next steps in learning.
- Use formative assessment information to create instructional plans designed to meet students where they currently are in an instruction sequence and to provide support for helping them move forward.
- Mentor students in developing the skills and habits of mind that support success both in and beyond the classroom.
- Use information from observation and conversation to link instruction with student interests.
- Find and/or help students find resources likely to support their growth in a learning sequence.
- Differentiate all assessments to maximize students' opportunities to show what they have learned.
- Provide periodic feedback to students and caregivers that clearly explains a student's status with designated learning goals, habits of mind and work (agency) during the learning cycle, and growth during the learning cycle.
- Create a variety of instructional groupings that change frequently to enable students to work productively with a broad range of peers and for a variety of purposes related to academic, affective, and social growth.
- Create student work that positions all students as thinkers and problem solvers, and provide a variety of scaffolds to support individual growth and success with the work.

What else would you add?

"I have an idea," the teacher said spontaneously. "I'd like everyone who just clapped for Celie to come up front and form a line facing the class." Once the young women, looking puzzled and uncertain, were in place, she asked them to share, one at a time, a reason why Celie was a more compelling heroine than *The Scarlet Letter*'s Hester Prynne. She added, "When you get to the end of the line, go back to the other end, start again, and see how many times you can go all the way up and down the line without stopping."

After about three and a half trips up and down the line, one of the students furrowed her brow and asked the teacher, "How did you do that?"

"How did I do what?" Mrs. Wilkerson replied, equally puzzled.

The student shook her head and laughed. "Don't you hear us? Everything we're saying about Celie—all the things we admire in her—are also present in Hester Prynne. We just never saw it until now."

 ## Points to Consider

- Take a moment now to review the variety of ways in which teachers can demonstrate acceptance and affirmation of students (Figure 4.1); show that they believe in students' capacity (Figure 4.3); build multifaceted knowledge of each learner (Figure 4.4); and act, plan, and respond in ways that extend individual students' prospects (Figure 4.6). Which of those categories of action do you see represented in this example? What specific actions do you see that represent the intent of any of those categories?

- This unplanned moment in the class was a significant event for the young African American women, for other students in the class, and for Mrs. Wilkerson. What benefits might each of them have derived from that 10-minute impromptu activity? Why?

In a 3rd Grade Classroom

Prompted to come up with an activity that would use some of the writing practices they had been introduced to, Ms. Chu's 3rd graders decided to write a note of gratitude to someone important to them. Sam, who found writing difficult and unpleasant, asked if he could write to his dog. Ms. Chu said, "Tell us why you would like to choose your dog, Sam."

Sam replied, "His name is Alfie. He listens to me and he is always glad to see me when I get home."

Ms. Chu smiled and said to the class, "Does that seem to be a good reason to express gratitude?"

The students nodded, and several shared examples of how much they cared about their dogs or cats. "Well, Sam," Ms. Chu said, "the class seems to agree with your choice."

As the students worked on their drafts, Sam wiggled in his chair and rolled his pencil on the desktop. Ms. Chu knelt by his side and said quietly, "Tell me again why you love Alfie so much."

Sam repeated his original responses. "Are there other reasons?" Ms. Chu prompted. Sam nodded his head and said, "He watches TV with me, and he plays with me outside."

Ms. Chu smiled and said, "Those seem like important reasons to love him, too. How about writing your list of four reasons to love Alfie on this piece of paper? I'll be back in a minute to ask you another question."

When she returned, she looked at Sam's list and said, "Now, tell me *why* you like it when Alfie listens to you." Sam thought a minute and responded, "He looks like he wants to hear what I'm telling him."

Ms. Chu wrote that sentence beside the reason Sam had written. She could see how much effort it had taken him to get all the letters on the page. "What if you pick two or three of the reasons you appreciate Alfie and tell him in your note why each one matters to you? Would that be a way to explain your gratitude to him?"

Sam nodded and, with great effort, completed his note to his pal, Alfie. When he finished, he took it to his teacher and said, "Whew! That was hard." Ms. Chu read the note with her full attention and then asked Sam, "How does it make you feel to have written this whole note?"

Sam thought a minute and said, "I guess I'm proud of myself."

 ## Points to Consider

- Think again about the proposed four categories through which teachers can honor their students: accepting and affirming students as they are; believing in each student's capacity to succeed; growing in knowledge and understanding of each learner; and acting, planning, and responding to maximize student growth. Which of those do you see at work in this example?

- Why do you feel Ms. Chu spoke to Sam as she did? In what ways did her language and actions extend Sam's possibilities during the class and thereafter?

• Can you point to any evidence that this interaction was representative of the nature and tone of the classroom on most days?

In a Middle School History Classroom

On the first day of school, Mr. Alvarez told his 8th graders that history is often the story of people struggling—even fighting—for what mattered most to them in life. He led the students in a discussion about what things might be of such value that people would be willing to go to great lengths to preserve them. As they offered suggestions (e.g., faith, freedom, other people, wealth, education, health), Mr. Alvarez would occasionally share a historical example of people protesting, fighting, or otherwise struggling to preserve these things. He also shared what he himself believed in strongly enough to stand up for, even when there might be a significant cost.

Next, Mr. Alvarez gave the students a sheet of drawing paper with the outline of a shield on it. "I want you to think very carefully about the things, people, ideas, and values in your life that matter so much to you that you are, or might become, a warrior for them," he said. "I'm not suggesting you'd literally fight or go to war to defend or protect them, but you would stand up for them if they were ridiculed, demeaned, or threatened in some way."

He went on to explain that the paper he had just given them was meant to help them generate ideas. Their job was to divide the shield outline printed there into the number of sections they'd need to portray the ideas, people, causes, or things they decided mattered most to them and to sketch into each section colors, symbols, or other images that would represent their choices. He also asked them to incorporate a picture or other image of themselves. "We'll have time for each of you to share with the class what you've created," Mr. Alvarez said. "This is a way for us to understand one another better as the year begins. We'll build on that understanding throughout the year. I'll post the shields in the room and in the hallway as you finish your presentations. And we'll refer to them to connect with what we're studying as the course progresses."

Mr. Alvarez told the students they could turn in their shields on any of the first four days of the following week. He gave them a checklist of key qualities of graphics that communicate effectively. He also gave them approximate dimensions for the shields so that there would be space for all of them to be displayed, and he told them he had cardboard, poster board, and some art materials students could take home to use for their work if that would be helpful.

Points to Consider

- How do you feel Mr. Alvarez honored or dignified his students both individually and as a group?

- What do you think he is hoping to learn from the students' shields—via the content they choose to depict and the explanations they provide?

- Note as many things as you can find that tell you something about the way this teacher views his students and how he strives to work with them. In other words, in what ways do his thinking and work suggest a learner-centered classroom?

Looking Ahead

The chapter that follows explores what it means and how it looks to guide the creation of a learning environment that addresses students' varied learning needs, strengths, interests, and approaches to learning and to create a community of learners. As you'll see, this work is about fostering collaboration as well as independence and building a "team" in which all the "players" work together to reach shared goals and in which individual players have the opportunity to work on their specialties and personal goals as well.

As you have probably realized, there is a firm link between the emphasis in this chapter and the next. In learner-centered classrooms, honoring students is the intent of everything the teacher does, and that's certainly the intent of creating a dynamic and productive classroom environment as well. On to Chapter 5!

5

Creating the
Learning Environment

Our greatest contribution is to be sure there is a teacher in every classroom who cares that every student, every day, learns and grows and feels like a real human being.

—Don Clifton, in "How to Improve Student and Educator Wellbeing"

To create a learning environment is to erect an invisible architecture—one that calls on teachers to manifest their ideals, beliefs, and intentions in concert with their students. While the learning environment itself is not visible to the eye, you can see it daily in teachers' actions and reactions. It shapes every classroom element, for better or worse. It affirms or erodes learner self-confidence, builds or diminishes trust in the teacher, fosters or undercuts community, invites or damps intellectual risk taking, commends or disparages learning. It's an intangible entity that's powerful to a degree we can scarcely imagine. The truth is, the learning environment largely determines the degree to which a teacher can realize the vision of students developing their own unique voices, working as partners in success, acquiring and using durable knowledge, identifying as learners, participating in a meaningful community, and aspiring to grow continually (see Figure 3.3, p. 42).

To be sure, the nature and quality of curriculum, fruitfulness of formative assessment practices, efficacy of instruction, and classroom organization are key to achieving the goals of meaningful student-centeredness. But the learning environment is the context in which all of these classroom elements play out—the

78

"weather" in which they exist, the culture that will shape them. If you're in a dark parking lot at night, one that feels lonely and threatening, how eager are you to linger there? If you're in a space where others seem to view you as "less than" because of your clothes or language or race or physical difference or sexual orientation, how likely are you to sign up to be a member of that "team"? If you work in a place where the people around you signal that your work is inferior or lacks value for the organization, how long would you continue to give your best efforts?

By contrast, think about being in a setting that offers you a kind of "home" where you always feel welcome, where the people around you encourage and support your growth, where it's agreed that making mistakes not only is part of being human but also offers exciting opportunities to do better. Think about a place where people value you in part because you *do* bring different experiences, talents, and perspectives—and because they understand that everyone is enriched by these differences. Consider a place where it's possible to be fully yourself and still be fully included. How would you say these contexts or environments position you as a learner of math or history or organizational dynamics?

Chapter 3's focus on the power of the teacher foreshadowed the foundation of a positive and productive learning environment with students at the center. It is the *teacher's* vision and the *teacher's* will and skill in enacting that vision in partnership with students that drive a learning environment to be invitational to each individual student and to the students as a group.

Yet neither this vision nor the skill and will to give it "legs" come automatically or easily. As in most aspects of teaching, our vision and skill mature as we mature professionally and personally. The expectation is not that you will launch and maintain an ideal, student-focused learning environment on Day 1. Rather, it is that you will reflectively articulate a few elements you feel are centrally important to students' cognitive, affective, and social development, then plan how you will influence the climate and direction in the class toward these elements.

As you begin carrying out those plans, observe as carefully as you can the impact of what you are doing. What seems to have the effect you were hoping for—and for whom? In what ways and for whom does an approach seem less effective? Think about why you might be seeing positive and negative consequences. What might you do differently or more skillfully? Getting it "right" is a long, slow process, much like trying to guide the kind of environment wise parents want to foster in their home. Some things work; some don't. Generally, some things work for some students under certain circumstances. Over time, however, as you reflect on your goals and your efforts to reach those goals, you manage to become a bit wiser, a bit more insightful, and a bit closer to being the teacher you strive to be. Be patient—and persistent—in becoming an architect of the invisible for, and with, your students.

There are at least four pathways through which teachers can lay the foundation for an environment that enlists student commitment to the hard work of learning, cultivates student voice, builds student agency, and contributes significantly to student academic, affective, and social growth. Those pathways are (1) forging trust, (2) building community, (3) establishing partnerships, and (4) modeling and teaching. They will be our focus in this chapter.

Forging Trust with Students

Most students arrive at the classroom door on the first day of each school year asking themselves the same question: *How is it going to be for me in this place this year?* Because the teacher is the adult in the room, students look first to him or her for clues to answer that question. Other questions follow. *Does she know my name, pronounce it correctly, seem interested in getting to know me? Does he seem to understand kids my age and know how to keep the day running smoothly? Is he a good listener? Does he appear to prefer some kids over others? How does she handle it when someone makes a mistake or crosses a line? Is she enthusiastic about what we are going to learn, and does she make me excited too?* These questions are almost never asked aloud. Still, the answers will come in time, with every student in the class acting as an expert observer, considering the data, and arriving at a personal conclusion.

Forging trust is an incremental process established (or eroded) through ongoing snippets of conversation, shared experiences and opportunities, tones of voice, body language, and responses to the thousand interactions that go on in classrooms daily. In my experience, young people are adept at figuring out which teachers are trustworthy and which are not. While students are willing to give teachers a second chance—and probably a third and fourth one—they are not generally willing to invest fully in the risks associated with academic learning or affective growth when they sense that the teacher, and therefore the learning environment, cannot be trusted.

The decision to withhold trust is actually made by the student's brain, whose first job, as noted earlier, is always to protect its owner. When anything, including a classroom environment, appears to threaten its human's physical or emotional well-being, the limbic system takes control. It employs its only two defenses against the danger—fight or flight—and essentially shuts down the thinking and reasoning part of the brain (Sousa & Tomlinson, 2018). In fact, the human brain is wired so strongly to connect with others that it often experiences what others are experiencing as though it were happening to them. So, when a teacher is positive and encouraging to one student, others feel that encouragement as well. When a teacher speaks or acts in a way that devalues a student, others are likely to feel diminished as well (DiSalvo, 2013). The mission of a *learning* environment—that is, a student-focused environment dedicated to the fullest possible academic, intellectual, affective, and social development of each learner—is to establish trust, lower risk, and then do what's necessary to support students in taking risks that better their prospects. In such an environment, the teacher is continually seeking to understand each learner more fully in order to make adaptations that will both reduce barriers to learning and open doors to even more learning.

Earning student trust is rooted in the teacher's awareness of the importance of developing and honoring that trust. It requires the ability to create a sense of welcoming support in the classroom; sensitivity to students' academic, social, and emotional needs; respect for student diversity and diversity of perspectives; and other teacher attributes discussed in Chapter 3. Student trust is earned via the ways in which teachers plan for and enact curriculum, assessment, instruction, and classroom organization practices, all of which we'll examine later in the book. For purposes of this chapter, it is a useful reminder that creating a positive emotional climate, showing sensitivity to student needs, supporting the development of student voice and agency, and creating meaningful opportunity for productive peer interaction are associated with significantly higher gains in student achievement than in comparison classrooms where those characteristics are less evident (Allen et al., n.d.)

These words from van Manen (1991) capture the message that learner-centered teachers seek to convey to their students—and then to enact—in order to establish trust:

> Leading means going first, and in going first, you can trust me, for I have tested the ice. I have lived. I now know something of the rewards as well as the trappings of growing toward adulthood and making a world for yourself. Although the going first is no guarantee of success (because the world is not without risks and dangers), in the pedagogical relationship, there is a more fundamental guarantee: No matter what, I am here. And you can count on me. (p. 38)

The message here is simple, direct, compelling: *You matter to me. I know learning about academics and life is hard and sometimes dangerous. I can't promise you there will never be a rough spot in the road we share, but I can guarantee you that I'm here for you and you can trust me to do whatever I can to help you navigate even the rough spots as you grow your way to success.*

Figure 5.1 presents some teacher actions that can build trust. There are many others, and I invite you to use the blank space at the bottom of the figure to add anything you do or can think of that's not included. Also, note that this pathway (forging trust) is tightly interwoven with the other pathways for developing a student-centered learning environment (building community, establishing partnerships, and modeling and teaching) so that strategies in this category are likely to be relevant for the other categories as well, and vice versa.

Figure 5.1: Strategies for building trust with students

- Learn students' names and the correct pronunciation of their names—before students arrive at school, if possible, and certainly within the first day or two.
- Make certain that the first few days of class allow time and space for the students to share their hopes and needs and begin to know one another; don't just forge ahead with content coverage.
- Learn about students' families, and let students know why that's important to you.
- Make talking with students one on one a high priority for each day.
- Acknowledge holidays and special occasions for all cultural and racial groups in the class.
- Make personal and content connections with students' personal and cultural interests.
- Recognize and encourage students to value the richness in the languages they bring to class with them from home, the neighborhood, and other geographies.
- Use teacher–student dialogue journals (on paper or online) that exist only for the purpose of providing a place for you and a student to communicate.
- Involve students heavily in planning for the success of the class.
- Share your stories and experiences with the students and invite them to do the same.
- As you learn about students, let them know ways in which you find them unique or interesting.
- Talk regularly with students about how you plan a lesson and what you have done to try to make it meaningful and successful for them.
- Let students know that you value each student in the class, have high hopes for each student, and plan to be part of the success of each student.
- Demonstrate to each student consistently that he or she can grow and succeed at doing challenging things.
- Plan ways you might respond to negative student behavior so that you are prepared to speak and act in ways that show respect and hope.
- Avoid blaming students. Instead, try to understand ways in which they need your help in order to make better choices and decisions.

- Be sure the directions provided for student work are clear and that they are written in a way that guides students toward success.
- Continually move among students as they work, taking every opportunity to talk with students individually and in working groups to help them function more successfully and plan for continuing growth.
- Create a plan for switching gears when a segment of class is going poorly so that you and the students can smoothly transition to work that is likely to be more successful. Talk with them about your reasons for the transition.
- Let the students know when you make mistakes and let them see you learning from them. Apologize when your words or actions are hurtful.
- Be respectful to all students, taking special care to be respectful to those students whose peers may expect to see them disrespected.
- Let students see when you do something incorrectly or awkwardly—laugh at yourself when appropriate to show that teachers are imperfect too, and it's just part of being human.
- Use positive humor to defuse tense situations.
- Help students find joy in learning.
- Demonstrate high expectations for all students, and make sure students are continually aware of the supports available to enable each learner to reach those expectations.
- Let students continue working with important skills or concepts until they "get it," so they come to understand that with persistence and practice they can do things they once thought they could not do.
- Throughout the year, make it possible for students to see multiple manifestations of your care and concern.
- Celebrate successes for each student and for the class as a whole.
- Be mindful of the varied levels of support and access to technology, transportation, materials, and supplies students have at home as you create and/or work with them to create assignments.

What else would you add?

Building Community

Throughout the year in which I completed writing this book, students across the United States and much of the world experienced unprecedented and unnatural isolation as a result of the COVID-19 pandemic. While great numbers of teachers worked heroically and tirelessly, in the face of their own isolation and fears, to develop online learning experiences that could nurture their students' minds and souls, the great aloneness persisted for many students. Returning them to schools and classrooms became a priority, with the expectation that life would be richer and students would feel more fully human when that goal was realized. Yet even when students are once again able to spend most of every school day in the company of peers, many of them find themselves "alone in a crowd." It's far too common, especially at the secondary level, for students to sit side by side in a classroom with little opportunity for meaningful peer interaction. At all grade levels there are also students who feel isolated because of race, language barriers, social immaturity, sexual orientation, learning challenges, home trauma, the clothes they wear, or even because they seem to know too much.

There are other classrooms where students regularly work together in groups but only occasionally find that experience to be positive. It's common in group work for some members of the group to have the skill and will to complete assigned tasks quickly and successfully while others in the group lack the skill, confidence, or opportunity to contribute. In those settings, students who are grade-focused and ready for the challenge often co-opt the process and complete the work while the others in the group watch or become frustrated and restless. In the end, the students who did the work are unhappy because the noncontributors "got credit" for work they didn't do, and the students who were "shut out" of the process feel invisible, judged, rejected, angry, or any one of a host of other negative emotions that are unlikely to draw them to future group collaborations.

Community is not a given. It grows only as its members learn to listen carefully to one another, respond with respect, plan together, work together to accomplish plans, draw on the strengths of each member to solve problems, monitor outcomes and relationships, celebrate successes when warranted, and revise plans and processes when that would benefit growth and success. Figure 5.2 shows the cycle through which community evolves over time.

This is a point worth stressing: being in a group and even working in a group is quite a different matter from being a contributing member of a positive and productive community. Strong, learner-centered classroom communities function like strong teams. Their members do the following:

• Develop a shared vision about the nature and purpose of the class;
• Develop a common understanding of the nature and purpose of the work they are doing;
• Realize that the members of a team have complementary skills and that the absence of any member lessens the effectiveness of the whole;

- Develop a sense of responsibility for self, others, and all;
- Draw on and extend the varied strengths and contributions of members;
- Generate synergy through a coordinated effort that allows each member to maximize personal strengths and minimize personal weaknesses;
- Know they will have to learn how to help one another reach their potential while also functioning as a whole;
- Practice and hone both their individual skills and group skills;
- Share responsibility for effective classroom operation; and
- Emphasize and celebrate growth within the group rather than competition within and among groups.

Figure 5.2: The cycle of constructing a classroom community

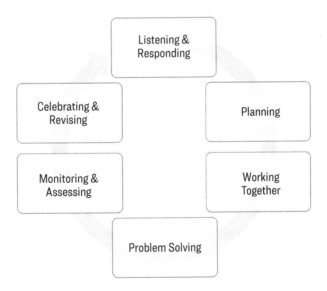

Classroom communities are environments in which students feel connected to the teacher, to one another, and to meaningful work that lifts the prospects of each member of the community. And while classroom communities share common characteristics, each one is necessarily unique. As Steele (2009) says, "Each classroom is a collection of individuals; each student brings unique experiences, talents, perspectives, and needs. They have different assumptions about meaning and proper behavior" (p. 116). It's up to the teacher, Steele points out, to be mindful of these subtleties. Gay (2018) reminds us that culture is at the heart of whatever we do in schools. Developing a classroom culture that honors and draws from the cultures each student brings to school creates a community that is richer for its complexity and supports the following:

- A sense of safety and belonging;
- The human need to bond;
- Shared ownership and partnership in learning;
- Engagement in learning;
- Identification as a learner;
- Appreciation of the diversity of perspectives;
- Inclusiveness;
- The development of individual strengths;
- Empathy;
- The development of social skills;
- The development of student voice and agency;
- Learner self-confidence; and
- A sense of accomplishment.

In learner-centered classrooms, teachers work with their students to build a sound, trustworthy community whose members try to enhance the growth of each member and bolster the success of the whole team. When a teacher helps students learn to rely on and trust one another, the group's resources expand, and everyone gains from the partnership (DiSalvo, 2013). As is the case with forging trust, the goal of building community is to create a context in which students are likely to invest in cognitive, social, and affective learning and maximize their growth and success in those domains. Further, community becomes a proxy for the larger world and provides a place for students to learn to be informed and active citizens working together for the common good—which is key to a democracy (Love, 2020). Experiencing many years of successful citizenship in classroom communities helps young people develop attitudes, skills, and a sense of responsibility that will serve them and their communities well for years to come.

Figure 5.3 provides some steps teachers can take to develop community in the classroom. There's space at the end of the figure for you to record additional ideas of your own.

Figure 5.3: Strategies for building community in the classroom

- Focus on developing relationships from Day 1.
- Emphasize "morning meetings" or class meetings.
- Involve the students in creating a shared vision and shared goals for the class.
- Begin the year with numerous, brief activities that encourage students to learn about one another. Continue these activities as the year goes on.
- Shortly after the start of school, begin to add opportunities for students to engage in teamwork, share ideas, and work respectfully together.
- As the year progresses, add regular opportunities for students to collaborate on long-term work that is meaningful to them.
- Help students think about themselves as citizens of the classroom community, and provide ongoing opportunity for conversations about what it means to be a good citizen, the benefits of shared citizenship, and the responsibility citizens share to better the lives of others in a community.
- Link collaborative and individual work in the classroom with roles and responsibilities of citizens in their neighborhoods, towns, states, nations, and the world.
- Make problem solving a regular feature in the classroom, casting students as teams of problem solvers.
- Emphasize inclusiveness, helping students think about and understand its power.
- Make sure everyone has a role in welcoming newcomers, integrating them into the classroom, and mentoring their success.
- Work with students to create a classroom narrative that recurs as the year unfolds (e.g., this is who we are and here are examples; here's how we demonstrate that we matter to one another; this is how we're growing; these are some challenges we conquered as we've continued on together).
- Emphasize both individual and group identity.
- Point out and discuss student and group strengths and accomplishments in academic, affective, and social domains.
- Ask student photographers to capture pictures of collaborative work and post them in the classroom.
- Seek regular input from students on what is going well and what isn't during their collaborative work, including their suggestions to make that work more satisfying and successful.
- Assign classroom tasks to students and teams of students.
- Talk about what you appreciate in the group.
- Create (or work with students to create) assignments that draw on multiple strengths and interests in collaborative groups.
- Be sure room arrangement(s) are hospitable to dialogue, flexible grouping, and collaboration.
- Create opportunities for students to address needs that exist beyond the classroom walls.
- Give students a strong voice in designing work and the processes of doing that work.
- Encourage students to suggest new avenues for collaboration.
- If possible, go places together—a museum, a play, a discovery walk around the neighborhood or the school grounds, and so on.

What else would you add?

Establishing Student–Teacher Partnerships

K–12 classrooms are busy places. Among synonyms for *busy* are *hectic, energetic, exacting, eventful, vibrant,* and *tiring.* Depending on the moment, several of those adjectives are likely to provide apt descriptions of classroom action! Although teachers often assume responsibility for most of what needs attention in a classroom, it's wiser and healthier to have reliable partners in making the classroom work effectively.

Creating student–teacher partnerships does help teachers manage classroom details, but its value extends far beyond that. These partnerships are an indispensable element of student-centered education, accomplishing at least three purposes: (1) making the vision of learner-centeredness clear, (2) making success a shared endeavor, and (3) getting the job done.

Making the Vision Clear

For many young people, the role of student is largely passive, dependent, and subservient. Teachers set the rules, determine what happens when a rule is broken, make decisions about curriculum and instruction (which can result in lockstep and solitary working arrangements), and mete out grades that are—at least to a good number of students—something of a mystery.

The vision for learner-centeredness is quite different. While classrooms that place learners at the center differ in look and operational details (depending on the age of the students, the content area, the teacher's degree of confidence in enacting this approach, school and community culture, and so on), teachers in all truly learner-centered classrooms communicate some fundamental core messages to students. The statements that follow, or similar ones, should be spoken directly to students—often and over time:

• Each of you shares some important traits and needs with your classmates, and each of you is unique in important and valuable ways.

• The collective goal in this classroom is to help each of you more fully understand and build on your commonalities with others as you also come to better understand and build on your particular strengths.

• I am eager to know you well both individually and as a group so that I can teach you well both individually and as a group.

• Your voice in this classroom matters. The development of your voice is core to our success.

• We will be stronger individuals as we grow into a group in which each of us respects and supports the success of the other members of our community.

• I intend this classroom to be a place where you can grow significantly in understanding yourself, understanding those around you, and understanding how to do the work we undertake in ways that support your own success and the success of your classmates.

• I have every confidence that each of you can grow and succeed in ways you have not yet imagined.

• I trust you to grow and succeed, and I am here to support you in making sure it happens, but it will take more than my hopes and energy to make the classroom work well. We need to be a team to make that happen.

It is important for those you teach to hear you say these things, and it's more important still that they come to believe them. Some students may never before have encountered these ideas. Even students who have had home and school experiences that make self-confidence, a growth mindset, inclusion, and positive interdependence familiar concepts instead of foreign ones begin every school year unsure how these factors will play out in this place, with this teacher.

Therefore, a key element in building a sense of community or team is to involve students in thinking about and discussing questions such as the following early in your relationship with them:

• What would it take for this class to be a good place for you—and for each of us?

• Have you ever tried to learn something new and hard in a place that didn't work well for you? How did you feel there? What made it a poor fit for you?

• Think about times when you were learning a lot and learning confidently. How did you feel in those times? What circumstances helped you learn?

• Do you think it's possible for us to create a class that encourages every student to develop and use his or her voice effectively and to grow academically, personally, and in relationships with peers?

• What does it mean to create an inclusive classroom? Why is that important? What challenges might we encounter in trying to be inclusive?

• What does it mean to be a good citizen? Why is being a good citizen worth the effort it requires?

• What traits would we need to draw on in ourselves to address the challenges of inclusion and citizenship effectively?

- What sorts of agreements could we develop that would remind us of what we must do to make this a class that works like a good team and helps all of us become more responsible citizens?

- What would it look like if we aimed to do high-quality work—work that would make us proud and even benefit those around us?

- What does "fair" look like in this classroom, given that our goal is to help each student develop his or her talents and interests rather than always do the same things in the same way or always be on the same page with everyone else?

- How do we remain a team during those times when some of us are doing different work?

- In the long run, which benefits us most: competing with other people or competing with ourselves?

- What's *my* responsibility for your learning growth and success? What's *your* responsibility for your learning growth and success? What's your responsibility for the growth and success of others in the class? What is mine?

Spaced appropriately over time, addressing and revisiting these and similar questions in age-appropriate language prepares students to work with the teacher and with one another to contribute meaningfully to the vision of student-centeredness. The shared conversations also help students begin to construct a narrative about "who we are in here" and "what makes us unique."

Making Success a Shared Endeavor

As the discussions of the vision of the learning community evolve, it's important to get students involved as early as possible in figuring out their role in bringing that vision to life. In that way, achieving the vision becomes not only an ideal but also a common endeavor.

So, as the school year kicks off in a student-centered classroom, it's also time to begin working with students to

- Describe what a classroom that works well for both individual and collective growth will look like.

- Establish the classroom agreements or norms that provide broad indicators of productive and respectful behavior.

- Decide on the routines that will enable various aspects of the class to run smoothly and effectively (e.g., routines for starting class, stopping class, getting materials, using technology, working in centers or stations).

- Establish guidelines for successful collaboration and successful citizenship.
- Decide on classroom jobs that will need attention (e.g., making sure the room is in good order at the end of a learning session, making sure materials and equipment are in the right place and in working order, distributing and collecting student work folders, greeting visitors to the classroom, feeding the classroom fish or gerbils—whatever needs doing on a regular basis).

These deliberations must always address the topic of shared responsibility. What roles will individual students play? What roles reside with small working groups or with the whole class? What is the teacher's responsibility in each instance? How will everyone work together to determine what's working well in the classroom and change something when the consensus is that it's not working as it should?

When we explore the various ways of thinking about curriculum in Chapter 6, it will be clearer how the nature and focus of your curriculum can shape the nature and degree of student voice in your classroom and, thus, affect the degree to which responsibility can be shared between teacher and student. In instances where curriculum is designed largely or solely to prepare students for standardized tests, student voice and choice will necessarily play a more limited role in determining content, approaches to demonstrating knowledge and skills, working formats, and so on than would be the case with curricula intentionally designed to incorporate student input. In both cases, however, there *is* opportunity for students to express their ideas and preferences, and those opportunities should begin in the very early segments of instruction in a classroom. Eliciting student voice as early as possible in the year is always a powerful way to manifest the vision of student-centered learning and reinforce shared responsibility for that vision.

Getting the Job Done

As the teacher and students consider the "why" of their classroom (the vision) and the "what" (everyone's role in making that vision a reality), it's also important to figure out the "how"—and get the many moving parts of the classroom turning toward those ends. In other words, building a dream is valuable, but that plane still has to fly. Getting the job done means actually *handling* the myriad of details that are a reality in classrooms at all levels.

Figure 5.4 provides examples of some classroom routines, processes, and mechanics that can go a long way to create a classroom that operates smoothly, fosters student ownership of the classroom, builds community, and provides a support system for the teacher. Items on the list would, of course, change with the age of the students, content area, student needs, and the teacher's personality. Add to the list other examples that are important in your classroom.

Figure 5.4: Some examples of classroom routines, processes, and mechanics

Checking in homework	Using classroom reminders to support your work	Asking for a time extension for work
Distributing materials and supplies	Signaling the teacher that you or your group need the teacher's help	Redoing work to demonstrate mastery
Getting materials and supplies on your own	Setting up and taking down equipment in the lab	Making transitions within a class period
Moving around the room	Starting class	Reflecting on your progress and next steps
Moving furniture	Working on experiments/in the lab	Preparing to end the class or class segment
Monitoring noise level	Storing work that's in progress	Returning materials, supplies, and technology
Monitoring time	Using classroom reminders to support your work	Leaving class or changing subjects in the same classroom
Getting help from a classmate	Submitting completed work	Storing completed work
Helping a classmate	Finishing an assignment or task early	
	What else would you add?	

Establishing routines, processes, and mechanics is about making learning more effective and efficient as well as creating a caring classroom culture (Rimm-Kaufman, 2020). Conversation about those elements with students should not only communicate a sense of trust in them but also address the support that they'll receive to ensure that they are prepared to carry out their responsibilities successfully. In other words, classroom routines and related practices should not be viewed by either the teacher or students as control mechanisms. They are co-constructed plans, designed to enhance learning for each member of the learning community. It's important to create plans and teach routines in "doses" that are appropriate to the developmental stages and attention spans of students in the class, always making sure that language is accessible to English learners.

When discussing the hows of creating your learning community, be efficient with detail and language. For example, I am a fan of making classrooms rules, guidelines, and agreements brief, memorable, and comprehensive. There's one particular set of guidelines that I've long admired for its capacity to cover virtually all classroom actions and behaviors in all grade levels: *Take care of yourself; take care of this place; take care of one another.* I also recall a middle school classroom that operated under two guidelines: *I will be the student I need to be in order to become the person I ought to be* and *I will practice the Platinum Rule* ("Treat others as they want to be treated"). For further illustration, here is a set of agreements crafted by a grades 3–4 classroom:

> We agree to give **respect** to people, feelings, space, property, and ideas.
> We agree to be **responsible** for our actions, words, and choices.
> We agree to show **appreciation:** no put-downs, be inclusive, be friendly
> We agree to be **X-Factor Learners:** positive role models, working for excellence, with can-do attitudes, and striving for our personal best!

All these example agreements display a sense of optimism and trust and speak to an invitational learning environment far more readily than a long list of dos and don'ts that seem to be aimed at anticipating every possible infraction a young person might devise.

It's also a good idea to introduce and map out new routines and procedures as they are needed, taking care not to overload student capacity. Practice routines before expecting students to carry them out (Rimm-Kaufman, 2020). In the early years of school, that likely means practicing most routines, perhaps multiple times. In later grades, it may only be necessary to actually practice (vs. talk through) more complex routines, like re-arranging the classroom furniture quickly and without noise or confusion.

Finally, early in the year, be sure to invest time in discussing what each routine is, why it matters to have the routine, and how you'll carry it out. (The gist of this discussion will generally be "We're doing this so we all can work effectively in a variety of ways that will benefit our growth.") Throughout the year, take time to ask students to recall the purpose of a routine, how the class decided it would work, and how it seems to be going. Then look together at ways the process or procedure might be improved to support learning more effectively.

There are, we are told, three kinds of classrooms: dysfunctional ones, in which a lack of order and predictability significantly undermines learning; adequate ones, in which order often prevails but is periodically and unpredictably disrupted in ways that restrict learning from time to time; and orderly ones, in which student behavior and classroom flow are rarely problematic (Policy Studies Associates, 1992). Interestingly, however, experts go on to say that there are two kinds of orderly classrooms: orderly *restrictive* classrooms (tight ships) and orderly *flexible* classrooms. It is only in this latter category of classroom that student voice, autonomy, complex thinking, and creativity thrive. These are "smoothly run classrooms, with an often looser (though not loose) structure, and a wider range of routines and instructional strategies in evidence" (p. 11).

We sometimes fall prey to the notion that creative production lies somewhere between loosey-goosey and willy-nilly. In fact, as Lucy Calkins (1983) reminds us, "the most creative environments in our society are not the ever-changing ones. The artist's studio, the researcher's laboratory, and the scholar's library are each kept deliberately simple so as to support the complexities of the work in progress. They are deliberately kept predictable so the unpredictable can happen" (p. 32). Said somewhat differently, there is a strong relationship between a teacher's facility in guiding a set of complex activities in a classroom and that teacher's ability to teach the kind of intellectually challenging ideas and skills that are at the heart of a classroom where meaning, relevance, and collaboration are the non-negotiables (Darling-Hammond & Bransford, 2007). They are also essential anytime it's important to focus on the needs of individuals or clusters of individuals rather than on "the class."

Guiding students in the work of answering three questions—*Who are we and what do we stand for? How will we share responsibility for our own growth and success and the growth and success of our classmates?* and *How do we get the job done?*—lays the groundwork for teacher–student partnerships. It begins to unite students and their teacher in co-creating an environment of respect, responsiveness, shared effort, flexibility, stability, and reflection.

Modeling and Teaching the Skills of Success

Classrooms aren't containers; they're networks of relationships. At their best, classrooms are communities of human beings working to enact the principles and practices that foster mutual respect, harmony, and productivity. Of course, the impediments to achieving this ideal state are innumerable. Few young people of any age enter the classroom demonstrating cognitive, social, and affective maturity. Few have already developed a strong and grounded voice. Few are wholly confident in their agency. Acknowledging that most young people have much to learn in all those areas, a teacher who holds these attributes in high regard acts as a mentor to the whole learner, teaching and modeling the skills, attitudes, and habits of mind each student needs to grow in the various dimensions of life.

So we remind ourselves that kids are people, not test scores (Duckworth in McKibben, 2018) and that learning should always be about more than academic performance (Gay, 2018). Academics may be central in the mission of schools, but even academic brilliance is likely to fall short of its potential in the absence of affective and social competencies. Accordingly, our job is to teach the whole child—the academic *and* social *and* moral being.

The ninth president of the University of Virginia, James Ryan, noted in his 2018 inaugural address that UVa is widely known to be a great university. He spoke about its greatness, but he also referred to the school as "an unfinished project." Ryan pointed out that it's imperative in our world that individuals and institutions strive to be both great *and* good—to make the world around us better for all those with whom we share time and space. This calls to mind Martin Luther King Jr.'s emphasis that the goal of education is intelligence plus character. I believe that to live up to our possibilities as educators, to lift the young people we serve, and to do justice to our profession, we need to be about "nurturing the whole human condition" of the very diverse students in our care (Gay, 2018, p. 241). To do those things, teachers must be free, supported, and encouraged to both teach and model the skills and attitudes that can lead students to cognitive, affective, and social success. In this way, we help them acquire the tools they need to better the world.

Duckworth (in McKibben, 2018) provides a useful, research-based framework for thinking about what it means to teach and model those attributes most likely to support students' present and future growth. She speaks of three families of character strengths that she and her colleagues see in their data:

- **Interpersonal character**—or strength of the heart—is what helps us get along in the world and make a positive difference in the lives of others. Among traits of interpersonal character are gratitude, empathy, honesty, joy, and social and emotional intelligence.
- **Intrapersonal character**—or strength of will—is what helps us "do the work" and move toward our own goals. Examples of interpersonal character traits are academic self-control, delay of gratification, perseverance in the face of challenge or adversity, and optimism, which Duckworth associates with a growth mindset.
- **Intellectual character**—or strength of mind or intellect—is what propels us to learn, to understand, and to pursue wisdom. Among traits of intellectual character are curiosity, open-mindedness, intellectual humility, imagination, creativity, challenge seeking, and openness to feedback.

Noting that there is a higher correlation between strength of will and grades than between strength of heart and grades, Duckworth stresses that strength of heart is nonetheless a social or moral imperative. It is also instructive to ponder the possibility that our grading system (and emphasis on standardized test scores) may also value will over intellect, even though the traits of intellectual character speak of evolving wisdom, which would evidence judicious application of knowledge and experience rather than mere reproduction of information.

Duckworth proposes that strength of heart + mind + will = character. It seems evident that a classroom, which by definition seeks to maximize the possibilities of each student, would make room for students to consistently encounter and engage with all three of the character families.

Look again at Figure 2.1's list of attributes that contribute to productive lives (see p. 25) and the goals for student development in learner-centered classrooms included in Figure 3.3 (see p. 42). Which of these descriptors do you believe are particularly important for your students to develop, remembering that not all students will have the same developmental needs in the same areas at the same time? Make a list of these, and then go ahead and add them to the appropriate character family in Figure 5.5. Then, as you review the examples of modeling and teaching in the figure, think of examples from your work where you model and teach about traits from a particular character family—or ways you *might* teach about those traits in the future.

Figure 5.5: Teaching and modeling the traits that support learners' academic, social, and affective growth

Interpersonal Character: "Strength of Heart"

Associated Traits: gratitude, empathy, honesty, social/emotional intelligence

Your Additions:

Example of Modeling Interpersonal Character
A high school history teacher tells his students each year that the most important thing he will do is to get to know them well enough to see the class through their eyes. He makes it a point to be in the hall to talk with students every day as students come and go, and to begin and end each class with an opportunity for students to respond to an idea or question about why a current event or movie or song does or doesn't relate to their lives. He finds opportunities to check on a student who doesn't seem to be in a good place during class. He uses what he learns to connect their experiences with what he teaches.

Example of Teaching Interpersonal Character
A middle school math teacher takes notes as students work on a complex problem in small groups. She is looking to see how groups were applying the rules for group success they had developed as a class the previous week. When the class comes back together, she posts two lists: "Things I heard you say" and "Things I didn't hear you say." She leads the group in a whole-class discussion interspersed with small-group deliberations. Then she asks students to talk about the sentence "Not doing something helpful can be as problematic as doing the wrong thing." From there, students meet with their work groups to set goals for their next day of collaborative work.

Intrapersonal Character: "Strength of Will"

Associated Traits: academic self-control, delay of gratification, persistence in the face of difficulty, optimism (growth mindset)

Your Additions:

Example of Modeling Intrapersonal Character
An elementary teacher says to her students on a Monday, "I was in a rotten mood when I left school on Friday because I realized that activity I asked you to do in science confused most of you instead of making things clear to you. I had worked on that activity every night for a week to be sure I had it right, and then it didn't work at all like I had hoped. I gave myself a break Friday night and watched a movie with my family, but on Saturday and Sunday, I spent several hours redoing the activity. I hope it will work better for you today. If it doesn't, I'll go back and try again. It matters to me that this makes sense to each of you."

Example of Teaching Intrapersonal Character
A teacher who has many English learners in her class shows the class a video each year focusing on how people get stronger when they persist in difficult tasks because they believe that with hard work, they can most often succeed. She also uses Road Runner cartoons to talk about the difference between working hard and "working smart." She and the students talk about times when they kept doing the same thing over and over when a piece of technology wasn't performing right, and how that's both a natural thing to do and an unhelpful approach. The students began compiling and illustrating a list of what working smart looks like and what it doesn't look like. The teacher continued that discussion throughout the year to help students understand specific ways they could improve their work by being smart about how they worked on it.

(continued)

Figure 5.5: Teaching and modeling the traits that support learners' academic, social, and affective growth—(*continued*)

Intellectual Character: "Strength of Mind/Intellect"

Associated Traits: curiosity, open-mindedness, intellectual humility, imagination, creativity, challenge seeking, openness to feedback

Your Additions:

Example of Modeling Intellectual Character
Once or twice during each unit, Mr. Alcero asks his students to complete a "Watch Us Grow" chart with the goal of helping everyone in the class think about how they and others (including the teacher) can work more effectively. In the left column, students suggest things the teacher might do differently to support their learning. In the middle column, they generate similar suggestions for the class as a whole. In the final column, they point to ways they can personally work more effectively. Mr. Alcero synthesizes the lists and presents them to the class, one column at a time, for discussion. He is careful to share ideas he is already putting into practice or planning to use as a result of their feedback and thanks them for helping him grow. Students eagerly discuss the whole-class column and share suggestions they will implement. Finally, students consider their own lists and ideas gained from discussion, generating one or two goals they will set for themselves in the short term.

Example of Teaching Intellectual Character
A banner over the whiteboard in a middle school science class says, "Feed the creativity that's in you!" The students learn about four stages that creators often go through in their work (von Oech, 1986), and the teacher supports the students in thinking about, trying out, and reflecting on the stages in the products they create in their science class. The Explorer looks long and hard and in many places for ideas related to a topic—for big picture ideas and details. The Artist uses many tools to create something new and useful with the ideas they have gleaned, looking through varied lenses, making connections, connecting, making analogies. The Judge critiques his or her ideas for effectiveness, focus, and blind spots while being open to new ideas. The Warrior does what's necessary to move ideas into action. Students use the model to discuss inventions and breakthroughs of scientists from many times and cultures throughout the year. In addition to applying the model to major science products, they talk about how understanding the stages helps them in other ways both in and out of school.

Source: Duckworth in McKibben, 2018.

When students lack the traits or attitudes that would likely benefit their growth and development, it's important—for both our sake and theirs—to recall that it's a teacher's duty to silence the instinct to blame them. We must instead seek to understand each student's ineffective behavior as an indicator of need— for additional support, for better instruction, or for more opportunities of a kind that will provide both direction and hope (Duckworth in McKibben, 2018). The job of educators is to create circumstances under which character can grow (Gay, 2018). That is, in essence, the rationale for investing heavily in a learning environment where vision, trust, community, and partnerships prepare the way for and nurture those circumstances and the students who will benefit from them.

Analyzing Examples of Teachers Working to Create a Learning Environment

To solidify understanding of the principles discussed in this chapter, let's look at some examples of teachers working to apply them. The prompts following each example are provided to kick off your own analysis.

In a Kindergarten Classroom

"Huddle up, everyone," Ms. Bowman called to her students, who were working in their school's outdoor space.

"What does 'huddle up' mean?" one of the children asked.

"It's when you get together and share great ideas," she responded.

A moment or two later, these kindergartners, who had never huddled up before, were gently holding on to one another's shoulders. When they discovered that one of their class friends was missing, they un-huddled and searched the outdoor area, getting back into their huddle when the missing student was found.

Ms. Bowman gave some directions about what they were going to do next and asked them if they would be OK staying in place for a minute so she could take a picture of the group huddle. After the picture was taken, one of the friends asked to see the photo on the teacher's phone, and one by one, the children began to surround Ms. Bowman so they could see too. As they gathered, one child looked around at the configuration of her peers and said, "Hey, this is like a huddle up again!"

 Points to Consider

• In this example, do you feel like Ms. Bowman was making the vision clear, building community, establishing partnerships, or teaching and modeling? Why do you respond as you do?

• What do you suppose she might have done during the first day and week of the year to set the stage for what you see here?

• How do you imagine Ms. Bowman readies herself to maintain the course she has set for herself in her work with students each day?

In a High School English Classroom

At the beginning of the school year, Ms. Horne, an English teacher, explained to her 10th grade students that their study of literature would be a year-long conversation about the richness diversity brings to our awareness of life. So that the "conversation" aspect would be more than just a metaphor, their work together would involve lots of discussion, the uncovering and elevation of everyone's expertise, and students making connections between course content and their own lives and experiences.

A unit on American literature from the mid-1950s through the early 1970s involved using writing and music by nonwhite creators as lead-ins to several activities. All students read Martin Luther King Jr.'s "Letter from a Birmingham Jail," with Ms. Horne providing a variety of supports for students whose first language was not English and those who had difficulty with reading for a variety of other reasons. At several points in the unit, the teacher deployed the Four Corners instructional strategy to expose students to multiple perspectives. After reading an excerpt from a text and posing a question about it, she asked students to gather in small groups (in designated corners of the classroom) with others who had a similar reaction or response. In these like-minded groups, they talked about their thoughts and feelings for a while, then at an appointed time the students were shuffled into small groups containing representatives from all four corners to talk about their different takes. Finally, students reassembled as a whole class, at which time the teacher reread the originating quote and question. Once again, she asked the students to assemble in the corner corresponding to their current thinking. There, they shared with others the change of perspective they'd had as a result of their group conversations.

As the year continued, students read a variety of news articles from varied sources, poems, stories, and excerpts from canonical plays that typically appear in literary anthologies (like their textbook). They also read Angie Thomas's novel *The Hate U Give* (about a police murder of an unarmed Black teenager), *Narrative of the Life of Frederick Douglass*, and *In Darkness* by Nick Lake (a novel that weaves together events in present-day Haiti and the life of Toussaint L'Ouverture). They wrote about these works and their own reactions to them, but they didn't always use traditional essay forms; sometimes they used rap songs, which was a way of recentering expertise. As Ms. Horne explained, "Using the word-smithing genius of great rap songs as writing models gives a new set of learners [in this classroom] advanced background knowledge. Having a new group of experts who can enrich discussions of these texts for everyone in the room often completely changes the class dynamic."

The strategy of flipping the expert was a go-to throughout the year. In a later unit on time periods in the United States that were strongly shaped by immigration, students had a choice of reading *The Kite Runner* by Khaled Hosseini or *One Hundred Years of Solitude* by Gabriel García Márquez, as well as pieces reflecting the experiences of other non-Western writers from ethnic groups present in their school and classes. The focus on content from outside the traditional Western canon was designed to draw in students whose family roots were in Asia and South America, extend to them greater ownership of classroom content, and position them as experts. The outcome was greater empowerment for these students and learning that was more textured, accessible, and interesting for the entire classroom community.

 ## Points to Consider

- Do you think Ms. Horne is more focused on developing students' interpersonal character, intrapersonal character, or intellectual character?
- Which attributes under any of these character categories are at play in the scenario? What other attributes do you think might come into play in this scenario? Which other attributes do you feel you could effectively spotlight by adding to or changing the scenario in some way?

In a 2nd Grade Classroom

Mrs. Navarro used a variety of activities to build her 2nd grade students' respect for and trust in one another. For example, there was "Classroom Kudos," which asked students to look for peers being kind or helpful and place the names of those students on slips of paper to put in the Classroom Kudos box. Mrs. Navarro shared both their kudos and hers with the class from time to time. To help students become more comfortable working with all of their classmates, she presented group "escape room" challenges, in which groups with constantly changing members were tasked with solving dilemmas in a set amount of time. She also encouraged students to nominate their literature circle or math circle as an example of "Wise Workers" and provide specific evidence of how using their class guidelines for effective group work helped them do a good job. She could see that students in her class were becoming more respectful and more of a team with each passing week.

Still, Mrs. Navarro worried about Ben, a boy with significant emotional challenges, and about how Ben's peers seemed to feel about him. When Ben got angry or frustrated—common occurrences—he became combative, often flailing or tossing objects that were nearby. With assistance from both the school counselor and special education staff, Mrs. Navarro was learning to provide Ben with better support and help him integrate more smoothly with his peers. But she noticed that Ben's name was not showing up in the Classroom Kudos box. Groups that Ben was a member of were not self-nominating for Wise Worker recognition or finishing escape room challenges.

Then, when Ben had been sick and out of school for two days, a student said to Mrs. Navarro, "Did you notice how everything seems calm when Ben is gone?" She had noticed. And this signaled to her a need to enlist the understanding and partnership of her students in helping Ben have a better school experience.

During the next day's Morning Meeting, with Ben still absent, she asked the students if they could share a time when they got so angry at a brother or sister or friend that they said something they wouldn't normally say, or yelled at the person, or maybe even threw something. Lots of students came forward to share their stories. She asked them how they felt after they had calmed down. All of them agreed they were sorry. Many said they felt bad afterward or ashamed. Then Mrs. Navarro said, "You know, all of us have those moments. Ben does too. He just has more of them right now than some of us do. What do you think we might do to help Ben when he has a moment like that?" In the end, following a thoughtful conversation, they decided they wanted to be sure to be kind to Ben when he was feeling good and to keep on working on their assignments when he got really frustrated so he didn't feel like they were staring at him.

The students seemed to feel better once they had this plan in place. "They were remarkably consistent with both parts of their suggestion," Mrs. Navarro said. "They made an effort to include Ben in his better moments and more or less ignored his outbursts." She noted that she knew the road ahead with Ben would be long and bumpy, but the plan was helping in at least two ways. "Ben's classmates see him now as a friend who needs their support. And it makes things so much easier for Ben, for me, and for them when they keep on working during an outburst so I can attend to him without losing them."

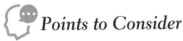 *Points to Consider*

- Where do you see evidence of Mrs. Navarro's trustworthiness in this scenario? Push your thinking a bit beyond the first answer that comes to mind.

- It's likely that Ben's most critical need for growth and the needs of the class as a whole at the time of the scenario would fall in different "character families" (interpersonal character, intrapersonal character, intellectual character). How do you (or how would you like to) think about attending to both the common needs of the class and the specific needs of individuals in terms of supporting their growth in one or more of these areas?

Looking Ahead

A classroom designed to nurture learners and learning is fundamental to the success of those learners. It is, in some ways, like the seed shell that houses incipient life. Alexs Pate (2020) writes compellingly about the many young people who come to school feeling guilty, "less than," or "wrong" because of negative stereotypes and narratives that are omnipresent in our society. They are "terrorists," "illegals," "aliens." They are "dangerous," "thugs," "criminal," "freeloaders." They are the kids in the low-level classes at school, the causes of the "achievement gap." As early as kindergarten, Pate says, these students are already trying to scale a mountain of guilt that they are unprepared to climb, and the one person who steps forward to help them (their teacher) is someone who's hard for them to trust. The driver of this distrust is the guilt they carry with them.

Pate envisions a context that he calls the "innocent classroom." Here, the student lives and works without the weight of stereotypes and guilt, because here, the teacher embraces the idea that innocence is an imperative for academic, social, and emotional growth. Here, the teacher sees the child as an individual, not a stereotype or a statistic. Here, the teacher sees the good in the child and teaches the child *from* that good. Here, the teacher teaches children how to learn successfully, shows them that they are worthy of high expectations, that they are achievers of high expectations, and that learning can change their lives. In this way, over time, the teacher becomes trustworthy. Each child, at least in that classroom, is free from imposed limits and free to accept his or her own good, become an active and curious learner, and become fulfilled.

We cannot really aspire to be learner-centered teachers without working tirelessly to understand and attempt to ameliorate the weight many of our students carry because of race, skin color, or the geography of birth. We can, and should, simultaneously see student-borne weight resulting from stereotypes that surround mental illness, abuse, neglect, poverty, sexual orientation, bullying, physical differences, and a host of other realities that are too big for the young to bear. Learner-centeredness asks teachers to do their best to create an "innocent classroom" so that each learner and the class as a whole are liberated to learn—to *become*. This is a fundamental goal of learner-centeredness as I understand it. This is the ground from which the other ideas in this book must grow.

Still, however, schools and classrooms are about encouraging the development of intellect. And so, what we select as intellectual fare for students is of great consequence. How we think about what is most important in a content area, how we give students voice in what they learn, and how we craft plans that will open the world to young people—all these things matter profoundly. In the next chapter, we'll consider what it means to honor, dignify, and enliven important content so that each of our students can feel animated by the human gift of learning.

6

Curriculum That Honors the Learner and Learning

The development of common curriculum... and most importantly the debates about desirable curricula in a democratic society are often presumed to be answered by... test-outcome-based questions rather than based on a debate about what is worth preserving in our society, and what is worth knowing in order to live the desired "good life."

—John Hattie in *Visible Learning for Teachers*

John Keating, the English teacher portrayed by Robin Williams in the movie *Dead Poets Society*, was onto something big about teaching. He really knew the content he signed on to teach. It's probably not an overstatement to say he was in love with it. He also, however, deeply understood the young people he was charged with teaching. He probably loved them too. One of the memorable moments from the movie is a scene in which Mr. Keating unites these two loves, speaking to his students with a passion that both puzzles and captivates them:

> We don't read and write poetry because it's cute. We read and write poetry because we are members of the human race. And the human race is filled with passion. And medicine, law, business, engineering—these are noble pursuits and necessary to sustain life. But poetry, beauty, romance, love, these are what we stay alive for. To quote from Whitman, "O me! O life!... of the questions of these recurring; of the endless trains of the faithless... of cities filled with the foolish; what good amid these, O me, O life?" Answer? That you are here—that life exists, and identity; that the powerful play goes

105

on, and you may contribute a verse. *That the powerful play goes on, and you may contribute a verse.* What will your verse be? (Weir, 1989)

People who truly love the law or medicine or art or acting would probably beg to differ with Keating. They would be equally as convinced, and convincing, that those pursuits are *also* ways to understand what makes life worth living and ways to participate in and contribute to a meaningful existence. Great teachers of medicine, law, business, engineering—and all other fields—teach with Keating-like passion. They bring together content and meaning for their students so that those two elements become one. "I will help you explore," they say to their students, "how this field can make us more fully human and how it will deepen and extend the talents you bring to it." In this chapter, we turn our focus to curriculum— what we teach and what we ask our students to learn to fuel their quests to explore and develop their humanity.

The word "curriculum" stems from Old Latin, and its initial referent was a racecourse that might be run by a chariot. In the field of education, curriculum has come to mean a planned sequence of study or a set of courses that comprise a domain specialization. While the history of the word is interesting (and a bit ironic, given our recent tendency to race through content so that students can take a high-stakes test by the end of the school year), the definition doesn't provide much of a match for the "course" John Keating has in mind. Current concepts of curriculum leave little room for his passion for connecting students with meaning and purpose, and it seems to me that this is a result of our losing track of what curriculum is and is not.

What Curriculum Is Not

In my early days at the University of Virginia, my colleagues and I would often ask the doctoral students on our research team to contact the schools where we would be working the following year and ask them to send us copies of their curriculum so we could incorporate the questions we wanted to study into that curriculum. Already several courses deep into their graduate studies, and consequently well versed in some "new" ways of thinking about curriculum, our students were bewildered when the "curriculum documents" arrived. "Why did they send us a box of textbooks?" they would ask. "We asked them for their curriculum!" That scene played out repeatedly over a period of five or six years, then abruptly shifted into a similar scenario that held for nearly two decades: "Why did they send us a set of standards? We asked them for their curriculum!"

Those scenarios from the research lab were not aberrations but indicators of the nature of curriculum in many schools. The common misconception that a textbook or a set of standards is synonymous with a curriculum reflects a misunderstanding of what a curriculum should be. And it contributes to under-educating a substantial portion of the students who come our way.

The Textbook Is Not a Curriculum

Educators are so habituated to using the term *curriculum* as synonymous for *textbook* (or *standards*) that many of us have lost sight of the real meaning and intent of curriculum. Many of us—but not all.

As part of my dissertation research, I observed a middle school history teacher and her students. In one of the first student interviews I conducted, a boy said something very surprising in a tone that told me he was checking me out to make sure I understand how things were: "You know, don't you, that in our class, we hate the textbook?"

"That's interesting," I said. "Why is that?"

"Because," he said, sounding wiser than his years, "the textbook is shallow. It just teaches us at a surface level. It's not real history!"

"So what do you do about that in your class?" I asked, thinking perhaps he would say they didn't use the text.

"Oh," he replied confidently, "we read the text as we get started on a new unit. It gives us common background and vocabulary to build on, but then we put the book aside and do the *real* history."

The surprise I felt at this student's comments turned to intrigue as I conducted more interviews and found that the majority of students raised the issue of the textbook without my prompting. They told me the history book didn't make history feel real for them, that it was mostly about names and dates and places, that it never told the whole story, that it left out the history of a whole lot of people, that it wasn't interesting, that they didn't learn anything useful from it, and so on.

The "real" history in this teacher's classes included doing interviews with experts and with people who had lived through events the textbook noted. It included analysis of music, literature, and art, and comparison of primary and secondary sources and accounts in varied media that differed wildly from one another. It involved looking at the lives of teenagers in different time periods. It involved drawing connections between science and the events in history and how fabric in clothing speaks of culture. It meant discussing human contributions to culture and technology. For these students, "real history" was a reason to get up in the morning and go off to school; the textbook was not. The difference between the textbook and the curriculum was perhaps best captured by a 12-year-old who explained to me why so many students in the class saw it as the best class they had ever taken. "Well," he said, "it's because in most other classes, teachers tell us what to think and what to learn. In this class, the teacher helps us learn to think on our own and figure out how to know what's worth learning." In this teacher's class, the textbook played a useful role, but no one made the mistake of thinking the textbook was the curriculum. The *real* curriculum was a plan to engage students in exploring, thinking, discussing, figuring out, and connecting their lives with lives that came before them. To be sure, they learned names, events, and dates that were central in the times and events they were learning about, but repeating names and dates was most definitely not what made this the "best class" they had ever taken.

A Set of Standards Is Not a Curriculum

I watched as students in an elementary classroom cut out strips of paper from a worksheet and taped them together to form a paper chain. When I asked one of the students to explain to me what he was doing, he replied, "We're studying penguins."

"Oh," I said. "So the thing you're making is about penguins?"

Still cutting and taping, he furrowed his brow and said, "I don't think so."

"Well, what's the name of this thing you're making?" I asked.

"It's a food chain, I think," he said, pointing to a label at the top of the paper from which he was cutting the strips.

Realizing the task probably *did* relate to penguins in some way, I asked, "How do you know which order to paste the strips to make the chain?"

"It's easy," he said, pointing to a strip. "This one has a 1 at the top, so you start there. Then you tape number 2 to number 1, and number 3 hooks to number 2. Like that."

"Do you like learning about penguins?" I asked.

"It's OK. I like the way they walk." He paused, then added, "I saw penguins at the beach last summer." Another pause. "But they were swimming."

A little more conversation revealed that this beach was in North Carolina—a spot not known for penguins. The student, striving to connect personally to the content, was confusing penguins and pelicans. He had no sense that the "chain" activity related to penguins or any other animals. They had been learning about penguins for three weeks.

The teacher in this classroom had given the students directions for their work, including an explanation of a science standard related to ecosystems and food chains. She explained to me that she preferred to cover a lot of standards in each unit—in this case, a unit on penguins—rather than cover each standard separately. She found that these combinations helped to increase student engagement. For the student I spoke with, however, even if the work was interesting and engaging, it had no meaning. He was not making sense of the science he was "learning." He only knew it had something to do with penguins, who sometimes swim in North Carolina and sometimes walk funny.

Standards themselves are not enemies of learning. Used correctly, they are guideposts in a world characterized by information overload. They help us ensure that the learning experiences we create with and for our students are on an acceptable path. They enable us to understand more specifically the various ways in which individual students are advanced or advancing and the areas in which their current performance has "potholes" that we need to help patch. The problem with standards is not inherent in standards; the problem is our misuse of them (France, 2020).

Standards ought never to be seen as a list of skills to be "covered" and "checked off." As France (2020) puts it, they "should not be used as a bar we hold over students' and teachers' heads.... They should not be created as an unreasonable performance indicator, used to punish learners for opportunity gaps and obstacles outside of their control" (p. 122). Standards-based teaching does not mean that the standards must be presented and applied in the same prescriptive way to all students in a class or grade level. In short, standards should not imply *standardization*, which is currently too often the case.

When they are appropriately used, standards can provide meaningful reference points for the "real" reason-to-get-up-in-the-morning-and-come-to-school curriculum that we create for and with our students. But like textbooks, they are tools; they are not curriculum and *cannot* be adequate curriculum. Standards are to curriculum what ingredients are to dinner. We fall short of the aims of student-centeredness when we settle for ingredients as a proxy for dinner. Instead of nourishing students so they can grow to their full potential, we are complicit in their malnourishment when we fail to actually put dinner on the table. Instead of creating *high-opportunity* curriculum that would support students' intellectual, affective, and social growth, we settle for *low-opportunity* curriculum. For example:

- When curriculum is focused on right answers and easily scorable responses, teachers tend to emphasize practice focused on fact recitation and basic skill mastery over practice of the complex thinking required for intellectual development.
- When standardized tests largely dictate the curriculum and are the measure of both student and teacher success, there is little impetus to provide instruction that centers on solving high-relevance problems through application of understanding, which supports intellectual growth and powers student joy and satisfaction in learning.
- When we value, support, and even mandate coverage of a long list of content standards, instruction will most often call on students to remember and repeat information rather than think deeply about what they are learning. Dylan Wiliam (in Lough, 2020) asserts that our failure to determine what is truly essential for students to learn, along with our annual race against time to cover far more information than most students can possibly remember, is immoral. It privileges shallow, surface learning over deeper, substantive learning because it robs most learners of opportunities to make meaning, reason, use what they learn in consequential ways, and receive and learn from feedback. Further, when we present acquisition of a standard set of knowledge as synonymous with real learning, many students see what we ask them to learn as unrelated to how they live or to the dreams they have. In one way or another, we lose those students as a result (Love, 2020).
- When we subscribe to standardized curriculum and delivery of that curriculum, we make the teacher's job of understanding and addressing student differences in learning, culture, language, disposition, and interests exponentially more challenging, if not impossible. Honoring students' varied cultures, languages, talents, developmental rates, approaches to learning, and affective needs is foundational to learner-centered classrooms. Too often we find that "standardization [is] the enemy of diversity" (Gay, 2018, p. 141).
- When curriculum is rigid, prescribed, and standardized, there is typically little opportunity for students to have a meaningful voice in shaping their learning or other aspects of classroom life. They cannot find room to explore their interests, ask their questions, and extend their talents.
- Because of the interdependence of curriculum, assessment, and instruction, low-opportunity "curriculum" typically results in low-opportunity assessment and instruction. Narrowing the parameters of the content we ask students to

engage with also restricts the ways in which we might measure their learning and ask them to interact with the content and with one another.

Now let's turn our attention to the other option: high-opportunity curriculum.

What Curriculum Is—Or Should Be

Curriculum, this book proposes, is—or should be—a design plan to maximize the cognitive/intellectual, affective, and social capacity of learners. It should help them encounter and engage with the most significant information, ideas, and skills that a discipline or content area affords. As a wise colleague reflected, curriculum is something students use, not something teachers present or cover. It's less the road map or mile markers on a journey to a test or to college and career readiness than the shoes students journey in. Curriculum is not a labyrinth to be navigated but a lantern that students hold aloft to find their way to a richer experience of life.

The two concepts at the heart of quality curriculum (and, therefore, at the heart of quality instructional and assessment practices) are engagement and understanding. They are central to quality curriculum because they are central to learning.

Cognitive psychologists have long contended that quality curriculum can be identified by the degree to which it supports student *engagement* and student *understanding* (see Erickson, Lanning, & French, 2017; National Research Council, 2000; Wiggins & McTighe, 2005). This aligns with more recent insight from neuroscience, which suggests that the brain needs two conditions in order to learn—*meaning* and *sense* (see Sousa & Tomlinson, 2018).

Essentially, both fields are making the same point in different terms. *Engagement* and *meaning* both refer to a feeling of personal relevance or personal significance—a state experienced when a student thinks, *I see myself in that. That's like something I know. This interests me; it matters to me.* And *understanding* and *sense* both refer to the *a-ha!* feeling of grasping how something works, why it works that way, and how parts operate together to make wholes—a state experienced when a student thinks, *I get it!* In the absence of engagement (or meaning), it's unlikely a student will invest in learning content deeply. Why bother with something that has no personal relevance? In the absence of understanding (or sense), students can't retain, retrieve, apply, transfer, or create with what they have "learned." In other words, they have not learned in a way that gives them agency and power in the classroom and in life.

It's important, then, that teachers think carefully about ways in which *what* they teach and *how* they teach can lead each learner in the classroom to engagement and understanding. This is a foundational aspiration for student-centered classrooms—something to aim for every day. Let's consider a few ways to go about this.

Pursuing Engagement

According to Schlechty (2011), the primary business of schools is "engaging students in work that results in their need to learn material that is essential to the education of citizens in a democracy and to their right to claim to be well-educated human beings," (p. 8). It's an assertion that clearly aligns with the goals of student-centeredness. For that sort of learning to occur, it's not enough for students to be compliant and "receive" knowledge; they must be fully engaged, which requires that the work they do has inherent meaning for them. With engagement, students are committed enough to persevere with tasks, even when they stumble and get stuck along the way.

Schlechty digs into what makes work engaging and identifies the following attributes:

• **A product focus**—Students work toward a product or performance that they find meaningful and that connects them to others (rather than demonstrating knowledge on a test, for example).

• **Content that is core to the discipline**—Teachers shape content to make available to students the understandings, facts, and propositions that experts in the field would likely agree best represent the field or discipline.

• **Organizing instruction for engagement, meaning, and access**—The content is embedded in high-interest activities and products that incorporate a range of materials, presentation formats, media, and technologies to maximize its appeal to students. Students have choices about how to work on assignments, and teachers ensure that students know how to succeed with the choices they make. Students are also asked to use what they are learning in relevant contexts and to connect what they are learning in one class to what they are learning in others.

• **Clear and compelling standards for quality**—Students are aware of what success will look like, and those indicators of success, or "success criteria," seem relevant, challenging, and attainable to each student.

• **Protection from adverse consequences**—Challenging work is inherently risky work; failure is always a possibility. Students know that there is support for the work and that they will not be "punished" for mistakes or shortcomings when they are working diligently in the right direction.

- **Opportunities for affiliation**—Students learn best when they are working collaboratively with others (in school or in the wider community) or creating something that they perceive will contribute to the betterment of others. In other words, learning flourishes when students "engage the world and change the world" (Fullan, Quinn, & McEachen, 2018, p. 156).

- **Opportunities for affirmation**—Students receive not only honest, positive feedback but also the guidance they need to understand that the work they are doing is important and that they are important in that work.

- **Novelty and variety**—Work that is fresh, surprising, or curiosity-evoking to students is a strong energizer and motivator.

- **Choice**—Students are typically motivated by having a voice in how they will proceed with their work and opportunities to shape the nature of the products through which they demonstrate and share their learning.

- **Authenticity**—Students recognize in the work they are asked to do the world as they see it. It's important to remember that students in most classrooms come to us from markedly different "worlds." This means teachers need to consider multiple avenues that will likely engage students in a given unit or inquiry, rather than just one.

As we design curriculum and ultimately teach it, we should continue to revisit these elements with the goal of incorporating them into the curriculum design plan whenever they can serve students well. We take it as a given that schools provide curriculum as a catalyst for student development. However, personal experience, classroom observation, and research indicate that not all curriculum results in durable and consequential learning. To contribute to student understanding of the world, stimulate intellectual growth, forge the ability to meaningfully address complex problems, and spark a keen desire to be a continual learner requires something far grander than the word *Curriculum* stamped on the cover of a notebook. As the chapter continues, so will our examination of curriculum that honors both the discipline it represents and the students who will engage with it.

Pursuing Understanding

When writing about student learning goals, authors often speak in terms of what students should *know* and be able to *do* as a result of a lesson or unit or year or K–12 sequence in a content area. Those two categories of learning would be adequate if the authors and their readers had a shared conviction that *knowing* is more than accumulating facts or information, and that *doing* encompasses more than practice and repetition of fundamental operations. No doubt most, if not all, authors who write curriculum intend that students will exit learning experiences with *understanding*. However, "textbooks are filled with facts that students are expected to memorize, and most tests assess students' abilities to remember the facts" (National Research Council, 2000, p. 9). All too often, the classroom agenda is about making sure students can recall the information the teacher has shared with them and demonstrate the baseline skills of literacy and numeracy. The common emphasis on high-stakes testing thus tends to narrow both the scope and depth of curriculum, reducing it to little more than a tool for raising test scores (Weiss, 2013). It is important, then, that curriculum specify not only what is essential for students to know and be able to do, but also what understandings they should come to as a result of learning, and that the curriculum itself is a plan for guiding students in both developing and applying the understandings that are at the core of the disciplines they study, using critical knowledge and skills in service of that goal.

Understanding connotes something considerably broader in scope than accumulating and repeating information or demonstrating basic skills. It encompasses grasping the meaning of the line in a poem, the significance of a historical event, the suggestive power of a pattern in a math problem. It means the ability to see one thing in its relationship to other things, to fully comprehend how a system functions, what consequences follow from its operation, what causes it, and what uses it can be put to.

Wiggins and McTighe (2005) present *understanding* as both a noun and a verb. *An understanding* (noun) refers to an inference, insight, or grasp of an idea that is not obvious on the surface. *Understanding* (verb) means using or applying knowledge and skill wisely and effectively—to understand is to apply an understanding (an insight or inference). The understanding teachers must pursue with students, according to Wiggins and McTighe, incorporates both the noun and verb forms—inferring beyond the facts and using what we know in unrehearsed contexts. Both are considerably more complex than recalling information and repeating skills. Both give students considerably more agency to make their way through the world. Certainly, life's challenges require more than plugging in what we have memorized; in order to meet the unpredictable, each of us must be prepared to modify, adapt, synthesize ideas and skills, and even create something new with what we initially learned.

The ability to make the leap from applying understanding in a familiar class-room context to unfamiliar new contexts is called "transfer." If a learner can solve a problem or address an issue simply by recalling information or repeating a process he or she has seen others use, that does not qualify as transfer. As Wiggins and McTighe (2005) put it, "Transfer involves figuring out which knowledge and skills apply [in a new context] and often adapting what we know to address the challenge at hand" (p. 41).

Of course, no one who is knowledgeable about principles of learning from either cognitive psychology or neuroscience would argue that fundamental knowledge and skill are unimportant. They are, in fact, *fundamental!* It's impossible to have insights about science, or to do science, if you don't know a good bit of science. Jules-Henri Poincaré, a mathematician, theoretical physicist, engineer, and philosopher born in the 19th century, knew a bit about science and about knowledge in general. He is credited with observing, "Science is built of facts, as a house is built of stones; but an accumulation of facts is no more science than a heap of stones is a house."

If the primary goal of learner-centered instruction is to help students create meaningful, productive, and satisfying lives in an increasingly uncertain world, we will need to help them "build houses" rather than just "gather stones." Knowledge and skills are necessary for the architecture of sound lives but not sufficient. Further, students do not have to "master the basics" before they can do meaningful work in a content area (Fullan et al., 2018). For many students, the basics become both clearer and more valuable when they are doing compelling work that calls on them to *use* fundamental skills, vocabulary, and information rather than simply to store them.

For all these reasons, curriculum documents should specify what students should *know, understand,* and *be able to do* in order to learn deeply. Curriculum is (or should be) a means for ensuring that learners can not only thoughtfully and actively use essential knowledge, understandings, and skills in concert with one another and with affective and social awareness but also self-assess, justify, and critique their work for the purpose of learning better (Wiggins & McTighe, 2005). David Perkins, an early advocate for classrooms that engage the minds of learners, emphasized that the verb form of *understand* should be the focus of learning: "Understanding is more a matter of what people can *do* than something they *have.* Understanding involves action more than possession" (1991, p. 6).

Figure 6.1 represents the interaction of knowledge, understanding, and skill in the form of a mobile—the kind that might hang over a baby's crib or in a modern art gallery. As the elements on the mobile turn together to generate the learning opportunities described in the curriculum, students come to see how knowledge (concrete information), understanding (abstract or big ideas), and skill (tools and processes) work together to reveal meaning and power in the content they are learning.

Figure 6.1: The balanced interaction of knowledge, understanding, and skill in learning experiences

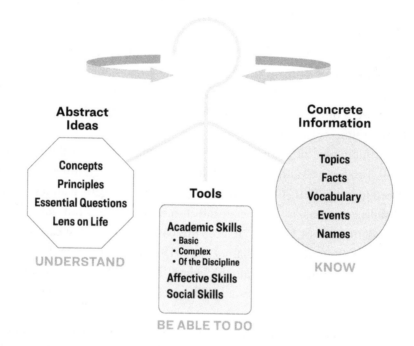

Toward the ends of engagement and understanding (both insight and transfer), curriculum should do the following:

• Guide students in mastering key knowledge, understanding, and skills of the disciplines;

• Help students uncover, recognize, understand, and apply the significant concepts essential in a discipline that explain the structure and workings of the discipline, human behavior, and the physical world;

• Provide opportunity for students to draw on and expand their interests in the context of the content;

• Help students grapple with complex and ambiguous issues and problems that characterize a discipline and link the discipline with the broader world;

• Guide students in progressing from novice toward expert levels of performance in the various content areas and in understanding their progress in that direction;

• Provide opportunities for practical, creative, and original work in the disciplines;

• Help students encounter, accept, and embrace challenge;

• Enable students to develop a sense of themselves and their possibilities as actors in the world; and

• Be compelling and satisfying enough to encourage students to persist despite frustration and drive home the importance of informed effort and collaboration (Tomlinson, Kaplan et al., 2009).

Long ago, John Dewey declared that curriculum should be "a tool to help students assert and accentuate their present and future power, capabilities, attitudes, and experiences" (in Gay, 2018, p. 142). More recently, the authors of the landmark book *How People Learn* (National Research Council, 2000) stressed that the ultimate goal of schooling is to prepare students to transfer what they have learned to the world around them—home, community, workplace. Those two assertions align well with the goals of learner-centeredness, including maximizing student potential and ensuring robust development of student cognitive/intellectual, affective, and social facility in order to construct and live productive and satisfying lives. Achieving those goals requires that students work with curriculum that motivates them to invest themselves in work that will help them make meaning of the world and drives home that what they learn in school is useful far beyond classroom walls.

Some Pathways to Engagement and Understanding

So how do we create curriculum that engages learners and that focuses both teaching and learning on knowledge, understanding, and skills that can translate into engagement and the two prongs of understanding—insight and transfer? There is no single right answer to that question, just as there is no single right curriculum. But there are some trustworthy design guidelines that lead to robust, meaning-rich curriculum. We'll look at three sources for generating such curriculum: (1) focusing on growing student expertise, with particular emphasis on organized knowledge and pattern finding; (2) using "big ideas" to support meaning making; and (3) drawing from the nature of the disciplines. The three sources, as you'll see, are intertwined and work in concert.

Growing Student Expertise

There is no expectation, of course, to create true content experts in kindergarten or even high school. But it's possible and beneficial to guide students along pathways *toward* expertise in ways that are developmentally suited to age groups and individuals. That's because the attributes of expertise are important in understanding the world and moving it forward—neither of which is an age-restricted activity. They serve young people well as students, as members of a peer group, and at home—and will continue to serve them well no matter their adult roles. Drawing from Earl (2013), the National Research Council (2000), and Tomlinson and colleagues (2009), we can say that experts do the following:

- Have a great deal of knowledge in the field of their expertise. They know a lot, but more important, they know the essentials of the field—the powerful, governing ideas, insights, and skills that drive the work in the field of their expertise—so not all knowledge, not random knowledge, but critical knowledge.
- See meaningful patterns in knowledge within and across content areas.
- Retrieve knowledge readily when there is a need. Their organization of knowledge provides them with a mental filing system that includes labels on the files and on the folders within the files signaling hierarchies, relationships, and functions.
- Transfer knowledge and skills across content areas and contexts.
- Pose insightful questions.
- Develop systems and habits of effective, efficient learning.
- Become increasingly self-aware, able to determine what knowledge is needed; able to retrieve relevant knowledge, insights, and skills; and able to monitor their own progress, adapting their course as warranted. They reflect on the adequacy of their own thinking processes.

Using "Big Ideas" to Support Meaning Making

Wiggins and McTighe (2005) talk about "big ideas" as worthy intellectual priorities in a vast sea of knowledge; as linchpins that hold knowledge together in coherent segments; as conceptual Velcro that makes facts stick together because the facts make sense together, thus enabling us to recall and retrieve information; and as umbrella ideas.

Big ideas help us see meaning in what we are learning, and in that way, they are catalysts for both engagement and understanding. They are engaging not just because they are central to a content area or pursuit but because they are often highly relevant to individuals' lives and experiences. They are catalysts for understanding because they are quite literally "*a-ha* producers." Wiggins and McTighe (2005) emphasize that big ideas can take several forms:

- **Concepts**—such as adaptation, equity, fairness, force, symmetry, balance, mitosis, oppression
- **Principles**—such as "form follows function" and that a scientific theory in one branch of science must hold true in all other branches
- **Themes**—such as good over evil, man's inhumanity to man
- **Points of view**—such as nature versus nurture, conservative versus liberal
- **Paradoxes**—such as freedom requiring limits, imaginary numbers, that people both seek and resist change
- **Theories**—such as natural selection, the big bang, historic recurrence
- **Recurring questions**—such as *What is truth? Is there life on other planets?*

Big ideas are broad, abstract, and universal such that they are applicable within and across subject areas, times, experiences, and places. They bring together different examples that share common attributes, give us a conceptual lens for studying a content area or disciplines, and point to ideas that are at the core of expert understanding of content areas or disciplines. In this way, they help us organize knowledge and give us power of transfer (Erickson et al., 2017; Wiggins & McTighe, 2005).

Concepts and principles are particularly powerful in helping people engage with and understand (have insights about and transfer) what they are learning—first, because they are the building blocks of every discipline, and second, because using them to frame knowledge helps us organize knowledge meaningfully and usefully, moving us in the direction of expert thinking. Concepts are most often represented by one word (e.g., *energy, scarcity, justice*) or two or three words in a set that make a unit of meaning (e.g., *supply and demand* or *cause and effect*). Principles are "truths" that help us unpack a concept to see how and why it works as it does. It's by applying principles, for example, that we see how concepts can be "universal" or "generic" (applicable across disciplines or content areas) or "content specific" (have special meaning and importance in a particular discipline). Figure 6.2 provides a few examples of universal concepts and leaves space for you to add some that you use or might use in your teaching. Figure 6.3 gives some examples of concepts and principles specific to disciplines or content areas.

Figure 6.2: Some examples of universal concepts

Patterns	Communication	Perspective
Systems	Influence	Diversity
Balance	Cause and Effect	Organization
Interaction	Time	Cycles
Relationships	Revolution	Exploration
Renewal	Change	Power/Powerlessness
Representation	Order	Culture
Conflict	Interdependence	Equilibrium
What else would you add?		

Determining which concepts and principles or other forms of big ideas make sense for you, your students, and the content you teach is not as straightforward as it might seem. Like interpreting a poem or a work of art, or understanding a scientific breakthrough or a historical event, "unearthing" or "crafting" concepts and principles takes patience and practice. There are books (such as those cited in this chapter) that are quite helpful in thinking about concept-based teaching. Other good sources are the websites of discipline-related organizations for educators, such as the National Council of Teachers of Mathematics (nctm.org), National Council of Teachers of English (ncte.org), National Art Education Association (arteducators.org), National Council for the Social Studies (social-studies.org), National Association for Music Education (nafme.org), and Society of Health and Physical Educators (shapeamerica.org). Judicious internet searches for other trustworthy sources of discipline-related concepts can be useful. Trust

Figure 6.3: Some examples of subject-specific concepts and principles

Content Area/ Discipline	Subject-Specific Concepts		Subject-Specific Principles
History/ Social Studies	Justice/Injustice Revolution Primary Documents	Power Supply/Demand Scarcity	• People migrate to meet basic needs. • Geography provides and restricts opportunity. • Conflicting ideologies make it difficult to achieve social ideals.
Science	Habitat Structure/Function Adaptation	Energy/Matter Stability/Change Action/Reaction	• Patterns in nature help us classify and organize information. • Models can help us understand the behavior of systems. • The shape or structure of an object determines many of its functions.
Literature/ Language Arts	Perspective Voice Communication	Style Figure of Speech Theme	• Poetry connects people with ideas, beliefs, and feelings. • Myths help give a sense of order to an uncertain world. • Writing is a series of choices.
Math	Number Sense Representations Sets	Exponents Equals Part/Whole	• Patterns in math can be represented in multiple ways. • Numbers can be represented by objects, words, and symbols. • Any division calculation can be solved with multiplication.
Art	Line Color Perspective	Contrast Unity Proportion	• Artwork elicits a personal response. • Artwork reflects the culture and history of a given time and place. • Artists use the elements of art and principles of design to organize visual communication.
Music	Melody Harmony Dynamics	Beat Rhythm Dissonance	• Rhythm organizes the time and energy of sound and silence. • Making music is a way of joining the human quest for mastery, meaning, and connection. • Notes and clefs are a way of organizing the sound world.

yourself as well. Brainstorm possibilities of big ideas. See which ones seem to have the greatest likelihood of capturing what you think matters most in a unit or series of units you are teaching. Try them out. Ask your students to help you think of other big ideas. The quest is worth the effort and time it takes; you'll expand not only your thinking but also your students' engagement and understanding. Here's an example of what that can look like.

Mr. Taylor, a high school history teacher, worked steadily to help his students see history's power to illuminate the lives of human beings, including their own. One year, he organized his classes around the concept or big idea of "transmutation," which he defined initially with his students as "the state or action of changing from one form into another." Sometimes he and his students used terms like *transformation, evolution, revolution,* or *devolution* as substitutes for *transmutation.* Figure 6.4 shows a concept map he introduced to students in segments as the year progressed. If you read the concept map from top to bottom, like a series of statements, it would result in something like this: "Transmutation is a way to think about history as revealing a continual ebb and flow of stability and change seeking a balance. That results in historical cycles with roots in the past and ripples into the future. These cycles are also evident in major aspects of life, such as the arts, science, economics, and philosophy—and in our own personal development." Framing the study of history with this concept and flow of ideas made it thought-provoking, easily transferrable to current events, engaging because of its relevance to student interests, and particularly powerful in its connections to their lives. (I don't think I've ever seen a better definition of *adolescence* than "the ebb and flow of stability and change seeking a balance with roots in the past and ripples into the future"!)

Over time, students modified the diagram based on their growing understandings. Later in this chapter, you'll find a longer description of the work Mr. Taylor and his students did centering around the concept map as well as their movement toward expertise and drawing on the nature of the disciplines. That illustration and one other in that section illustrate how curriculum designed to support student engagement and understanding using big ideas derived from the nature of a discipline can make learning dynamic, memorable, durable, and applicable for learners of varied ages.

Figure 6.4: A concept map showing history as the study of patterns changing over time with parallels to students' lives

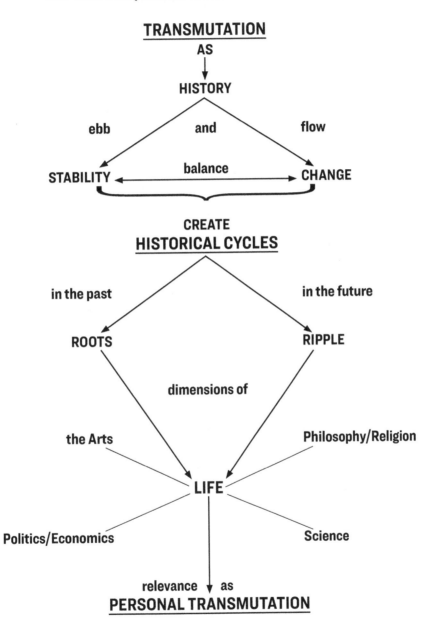

Source: Original graphic by Wes Taylor.

Drawing from the Nature of the Disciplines

When I was about 15 years into my life as a middle school teacher (and simultaneously working on a doctorate), I had one of those electric experiences of running headlong into an idea that seems to stop the world on its axis. It can happen through a song, a movie, a conversation, an interaction with nature. This one came from reading a very dense book I had been assigned in one of my graduate courses—Philip Henry Phenix's *Realms of Meaning: A Philosophy of the Curriculum for General Education* (1964). Well into the book, the author made a point that was intriguing to me. He talked about the academic disciplines "being born" as early man learned to control his environment enough to have a small amount of leisure time. Already feeling a need to make sense of life and to pass along whatever sense they could make of it to their offspring, Phenix explains, these early humans organized life according to what we would now call the academic disciplines—math, art, history, science, music, literature. I had never considered where the disciplines originated. Perhaps, even that far into my life, I thought they were generated by textbook publishers.

It was the idea that came next in the book, however, that remade my world as a teacher and as a human being. Phenix posited that by organizing and sharing their understandings in this way, these early people were asking a question that all human beings ask, from first consciousness until death: *What is life, and who am I in it?*

Reading this, it struck me that, although I had spent most of my time on this planet studying the disciplines, I had almost never asked that question, let alone found an answer to it. In that moment, I realized that the discipline of history is not, as a history teacher colleague of mine once said, "the study of dead people." The discipline of art is not about trying to create something—a painting, a drawing, a clay pot—that will not be embarrassing to display. Nor is math about computation, or science about carrying out predigested labs. Buried in all those content areas, previously hidden from my view, were answers to that eternal question: *What is life, and who am I in it?*

My next revelation was more troubling still. I was teaching English, content that I loved for its beauty and depth and wisdom, to students whom I loved because of their courage and humor and fears and doubts and confidence. Yet I was teaching English as a way to talk about plot, protagonist, figures of speech, grammatical construction, and so on. Even the concept of theme I was somehow reducing to a mechanical thing.

I don't recall whether I finished Phenix's book. I do recall that I didn't sleep that night. And that the next day, when I went into the classroom that I shared with my middle schoolers, I was a different teacher. That's not to say that I knew what to do to move from mechanics to meaning, but I was on a mission to get there, and I am still on it!

Along the way, I keep discovering all there is to gain when we teach the disciplines in a way that respects both their intrigue and wisdom as well as the capacities and interests of young people who are hungry to explore their world. Here are just a few of those positives.

Grounding curriculum in a discipline gives students systems of big ideas that function like Lego bricks. With guidance, they can learn to use these ideas to construct knowledge that helps them understand the "architecture" of the world around and beyond themselves. Over time, they become increasingly able to answer fundamental questions* about new knowledge they encounter, such as these:

- What does this information mean?
- Why does this information matter?
- How is this information organized to help people use it effectively?
- Why do these ideas make sense?
- How do these ideas and skills work?
- How can I use these ideas and skills productively?

This approach also helps students see the interconnectedness of all knowledge and the significance of that interconnectedness. They learn to ask questions like these:

- How do ideas and skills learned in one context connect to other contexts?
- How do different contexts affect my earlier understandings?
- How might I need to adjust my way of thinking and working in a new context?
- How do I know if the adjustments are effective?
- How does looking at one thing help me understand another?
- Why do different people have different perspectives on the same issue?

---

*All questions in this section are adapted from Tomlinson, Kaplan et al., 2009.

- How are perspectives shaped by time, place, culture, and circumstances?
- What are the benefits of examining varied perspectives?
- How do I assess the relative merits of varied perspectives on problems, events, and issues?
- What connections do I see between what I am learning and my own life and times?

This pathway empowers students to work increasingly like practitioners and experts within the discipline. They address issues, solve problems, and generate new ideas to make a positive impact on the world by exploring questions like these:

- What theories govern this field of knowledge and practice?
- How do practitioners organize their knowledge and skill in this field?
- How do the concepts and principles that form the framework of this discipline get translated into action by those who work in this field?
- What kinds of problems and issues do practitioners in this field address?
- What strategies, tools, and processes do practitioners use to solve problems and generate new knowledge in this discipline?
- What are the methods that practitioners in this field use to generate new questions, create new knowledge, and solve problems?
- What drives the work of practitioners in this field?
- What are the standards by which this field measures success?
- What are the ethical issues and standards in this field?

Finally, grounding curriculum in the disciplines is a way to encourage students to reflect on their own interests, strengths, traits, and goals as they consider questions such as these:

- What kinds of thinking, creating, and work do practitioners in this field do?
- To what degree are those things familiar, surprising, or intriguing?
- What is the range of vocational and avocational possibilities in this field?
- In which ones can I see myself making a contribution?
- What difficulties do practitioners and contributors in this field encounter?
- How do they cope with those challenges?
- How do I think I would cope with them?
- How are the ethical principles that guide the work of this field like and unlike my own ethical principles?

- What wisdom has this discipline contributed to the world, and how has that affected me?
  - How might I shape the discipline over time?
  - How might it shape me?

When we teach young people so they really get to know their way around a discipline—get to understand its nature, structure, and meaning—we use their time more economically and are more likely to help them make meaning. They are more likely to transfer what they learn than when we teach by topic. Further, teaching according to the nature of the discipline provides levels of depth, complexity, and coherence that are not possible when learner-centeredness is interpreted to mean students choose all or most the content they learn. Wiliam (2011b) reminds us that substantive curriculum and student voice and relevance are not oppositional:

> The curriculum should, as far as possible, be relevant and should take into account the interests, needs, and wishes of students, but within a framework of informed choice in respect [to] pedagogy and curriculum. That is to say, from the earliest ages, students should have a say in how they learn, and as they get older, also in what they learn. The curriculum should provide opportunities for students to specialize—to pursue their interests in greater depth than would be required of all students. However, students should not be allowed to discontinue the study of particular subjects until they have experienced enough of the subject to make an informed choice about discontinuing study of that subject. This, in turn, places a burden on schools to provide rich experiences that properly introduce students to the disciplines, so that they know what they are giving up. (p. 6)

When curriculum is designed to provide the substantial knowledge, authenticity, product focus, and clear and compelling standards for quality work that are key factors in student engagement (Schlechty, 2011) and understanding (Wiggins & McTighe, 2005), we are at the threshold of the kind of dynamic learning consistent with the goals of learner-centeredness. By integrating into our planning the attributes of affiliation, affirmation, novelty, variety, and choice and working collaboratively with our students, we are far more likely to extend the capacities of those students and help them build far more compelling lives than when we teach from a textbook, set of standards, scripted curriculum, or pacing guide—or when our curriculum relies so heavily on student choice that students have little opportunity to learn their way around the world.

The wisdom of all the centuries that came before us resides in the disciplines. Understood appropriately, they are the foundations for everything worthwhile that we can contribute to the world during our time in it. They were created to answer the most enduring human question. They embody everyone's history, literature, science, art, music, and drama and provide an open door to connecting students with the past and current contributions of people in their cultures to the disciplines. And, when we teach the disciplines with the power that's inherent in them, they are highly engaging, storehouses of "big ideas," and direct conduits to understanding ourselves and the world around us.

The Curriculum–Assessment–Instruction Connection

On its must fundamental level, *curriculum* is what we teach, what we want students to learn. *Instruction* is the act or process of teaching what we want students to learn. *Assessment* is seeing how the teaching and learning are progressing—the degree to which each student is succeeding in learning what we determined to be important for his or her growth. Those three elements are—or should be—so tightly bound together that separating them is not wholly possible. For purposes of understanding the roles and possibilities of each of the three elements in learner-centered classrooms, however, we'll examine them separately in this chapter and the two that follow. Still, you will see moments of merging in all three chapters. It is not possible to fully understand any one of the three elements apart from the curriculum–assessment–instruction connection ("CAI connection"). It is also not possible to develop robust curriculum without understanding the connection. The CAI connection asks us to continually consider these questions:

1. What should my students know, understand, and be able to do as the result of any segment(s) of learning?

2. In what ways might I engage students with the essential knowledge, understanding, and skill to support their success with that knowledge, understanding, and skill?

3. How will I know when they know?

4. What will I do if they don't know?

5. What will I do if they already know?

6. Who benefitted and who didn't?

7. What can I learn from these observations that will help me be a more effective teacher in both the short and long terms?

8. What can I learn from these observations that will help me support my student in becoming better learners? (Bain, 2004; Hattie, 2012; Wiggins & McTighe, 2005)

Question 1 relates to curriculum; questions 2, 4, and 5 relate to instruction; questions 3, 6, 7, and 8 relate to assessment. Or so it would seem on the face of things. As we explore curriculum a bit more—and then assessment and instruction in the coming chapters—you will notice the melding and interdependence of the questions across the three CAI elements.

The Nature and Purpose of a Curriculum Design

Wiggins and McTighe (2005) propose that "the best curricula... are written from the point of view of the desired learning, not merely what will be covered" (p. 6). These curricula specify what the learner should have achieved upon completing a segment of learning, what the learner will need to do to achieve those results, and what the teacher needs to do to support that achievement. "In sum, this sort of curriculum specifies the desired output and means of achieving it, not just a list of content and activities" (p. 6).

The purpose of curriculum, Wiggins and McTighe say, is to clarify what is essential for students to know, understand, and be able to do as the result of their work. Those outputs should be expressed in terms of student products and performances. In other words, if students can't apply, transfer, or otherwise use their knowledge in unfamiliar contexts, they have not learned as they needed to learn. Instruction and assessment practices play a critical role in helping students and their teachers see that the learners accomplish the goals of understanding and performing in ways that make the understanding evident. The curriculum design lays out the plan for all three elements in that success. The tight linkage between curriculum, assessment, and instruction means that gaining maximum traction with any one of those elements requires effective use of all three.

A curriculum design should not be viewed as static or "set" (it will evolve as the teacher and students grow and as needs change) or as "closed" (it should allow ample opportunity for student voice, interests, and needs, as well as for a teacher's expertise and interests). Nor should a curriculum design be a mandate for standardization. That is to say, although the knowledge, understanding, and skill specified in the curriculum as learning intentions will apply to all students (except those who have unique personal learning plans), there should be room for flexibility in most other aspects of a curriculum design.

I am a fan of the three-tiered answer Steven Levy (1996) gives to the question "Who decides curriculum?" and the case he makes for why curriculum ought to be the co-creation of standards-developers, teachers, and students:

> We need to have a curriculum framework so that in the course of the children's education they will be exposed to an integrated and coherent course of study. We also need to coordinate the subjects across the grades so that the children do not learn about electricity three years in a row. We need an outline of when the children are expected to master sentence structure, fractions, scientific procedure. What I want from my system is a very broad sketch of subjects to teach and the freedom to teach them out of my own design. Define the habits of mind, heart, and work that the community decides are important for all children to develop. Then let me have room to explore the topic with the children. I don't think it is necessary that every teacher teach in the same way.... I want to teach out of the natural activity of the class. I want the children to see how learning is the natural activity of people coming together. I want to begin with the students' experience and their own questions, I want them to follow their own interests. But I need to address the content and skills prescribed in the curriculum. Herein lies the art of teaching: leading the students from their own experiences and interests to the depth and breadth of the world within the framework of the subjects I am supposed to teach. I need to find the link that leads the children from their own interests and questions to the areas of the required curriculum. (pp. 28–29)

A curriculum design plan for learner-centered classrooms can draw on any number of pedagogical approaches including (but not limited to) problem-based learning, inquiry, project-based learning, experiential learning, Socratic learning, mastery learning, or a combination of approaches. Quality direct instruction that balances teacher and student roles also has a place in student-centered classrooms. Any of these avenues to learning—effectively implemented—can support three key goals of student-centered classrooms: (1) maximizing the academic, affective, and social growth of each learner; (2) encouraging student voice and agency; and (3) learning from a robust, discipline-based curriculum that stresses understanding and the transfer of knowledge, understanding, and skills that are foundational for making sense of and contributing to a rapidly changing and uncertain world. To that end, Figure 6.5 provides a framework for planning curriculum, informed by the Understanding by Design (UbD) curriculum planning approach of Wiggins and McTighe (2005).

Figure 6.5: A basic framework for planning learning-focused curriculum

Step 1: Answer the question *"What should my students know, understand, and be able to do as a result of this unit?"*
This section should include a list of the following elements that will frame the unit and define learner success in the unit: • The essential knowledge • The essential understandings (big ideas) • The essential skills
Step 2: Answer the question *"How will I know if my students know, understand, and are able to do the goals specified in Step 1?"*
This section should include: • A description of summative assessments (emphasizing performance tasks and products, but also including evidence such as tests, work samples, and teacher observations) that will allow students to effectively demonstrate mastery of and ability to apply/transfer the knowledge, understandings, and skills listed as essential in Step 1 • Opportunities for students to self-assess their work in this step
Step 3: Answer the questions *"In what ways might I engage students with the essential knowledge, understandings, and skills to support their success?"* **and** *"How will I know when they know?"*
This section should include: • Ways in which a teacher should/could *engage* students with the learning intentions in Step 1 with an emphasis on developing student *understanding* • Suggested formative assessments that should help the teacher and students follow and understand student progress toward the learning intentions in Step 1 throughout the unit of study • Success criteria for the performance tasks and targets for other evidence • Options for scaffolding students who need additional time or support in mastering the elements in Step 1 and ways to push forward the learning of students who show early competence with those elements • Time for students to work with topics of special interest to them, to work collaboratively, and to work with specific learning needs • Ample opportunity for both teacher and student voice in mapping routes to achieving the learning intentions in Step 1

Brian Greene (2005), a professor of physics and mathematics at Columbia University, asserted in a radio feature that when teachers believe deeply in each student they teach and in the power of what they are teaching to make a positive difference in their students' lives, the learning journey they map out through curriculum will engage and stretch students' minds as it reveals the power and wonder inherent in that field. He describes the sense of the impoverishment students experience when their teachers settle for lesser alternatives:

> Just as our experience playing baseball is enormously richer if we know the rules of the game, the better we understand the universe's rules—the laws of physics—the more deeply we can appreciate our lives within it. I believe this because I've seen it. I've seen children's eyes light up when I tell them about black holes and the big bang. I've received letters from young soldiers in Iraq telling me how reading popular accounts of relativity and quantum physics has provided them hope that there is something larger, something universal that binds us together. Which is why I am distressed when I meet students who approach science and math with drudgery. I know it doesn't have to be that way.
>
> But when science is presented as a collection of facts that need to be memorized, when math is taught as a series of abstract calculations without revealing its power to unravel the mysteries of the universe, it can all seem pointless and boring. Even more troubling, I've encountered students who've been told they don't have the capacity to grasp math and science. These are lost opportunities.
>
> I believe we owe our young an education that captures the exhilarating drama of science. I believe the process of going from confusion to understanding is a precious, even emotional, experience that can be the foundation of self-confidence.

Creating curriculum that energizes learning and helps students identify as learners is an art form. It takes practice, as all art does. It's a prime mechanism through which we pass along the wisdom of the past to citizens of the present so they are solidly positioned to better the time they have on this planet... and the time beyond that as well.

Analyzing Examples of Curriculum That Stresses Engagement and Understanding

To solidify understanding of the principles discussed in this chapter, let's look at some examples of teachers working to apply them—including a deeper examination of the curriculum created by Mr. Taylor, the high school history teacher we met earlier. Use the prompts following each example to kick off your own analysis.

In a High School History Classroom

Mr. Taylor's students found his history class intriguing from the jump. The idea of studying history as transmutation—the ebb and flow of stability and change seeking a balance—was different, surprising. This was not history as usual.

By the end of the first class session, they were ready to go—already thinking and making connections and seeing familiar things in unexpected ways. Throughout the course, they examined how, in a particular historical cycle, people sought both change and stability. They looked at which people favored change, and which favored stability, and why that was the case. They compared a cycle they were currently studying to ones they had previously studied and saw that music, art, philosophy, economics, governments, leadership, houses, transportation, and many other societal elements were shaped by, and subsequently shaped, the time period. They traced how the roots of one cycle very quickly began to suggest potential ripples in another and hypothesized how that time period might influence the next cycle. They regularly used the lens of a past time period they were studying to examine the period in which they were living, focusing on social media, varied reports in the news media, lyrics to contemporary songs, and excerpts from movies and television.

As the course continued, Mr. Taylor challenged his students to give evidence for or against the premise that adolescence is the ebb and flow of stability and change seeking a balance, and that it also has roots in the past and makes ripples into the future. He prompted them to use the analogy repeatedly—to think about adolescence through the lens of history, and history through the lens of adolescence. He gave students regular opportunities to use the ideas represented in the course's concept map (see Figure 6.1, p. 116) to learn more about their personal interests. What did these areas look like in the past? What were the potential benefits and costs of their transmutation?

Mr. Taylor carefully integrated required content standards into readings, discussions, and assignments throughout the course, offering support as needed to ensure everyone utilized the knowledge and skills inferred in standards in group work, individual writing, and products. He integrated into student work the methods and kinds of thinking historians use, emphasizing those approaches in rubrics and other success criteria. Students had considerable choice in how they worked on assignments and how they would demonstrate what they were learning, and their teacher helped them understand and select modes of expression in line with the goals, standards of quality work, and types of thinking prevalent among historians. In addition, many students elected to explore how one or more of the domains of interest spotlighted on the concept map (see Figure 6.1) evolved over the time periods the class was studying. This gave them a chance to test the theory that history is the study of ebb and flow seeking stability with roots in the past and ripples into the future.

 ## Points to Consider

- Thinking back about your own experiences in history classes, which of them helped you consistently engage with the content, encouraged you to make meaning of what you were learning, and empowered you to draw on what you learned in order to form opinions, solve problems, or take action? What was it in the curriculum (and instruction, of course) that made those outcomes possible for you?

- If you recall classes where what you learned was largely forgettable, what was the difference in the way content (and instruction) were presented in those classes?

In Kindergarten Classrooms

Four teachers from a well-regarded kindergarten program in a small school in Virginia had become concerned that they were "covering" so many topics and skills that their students had no way to make meaning of what they were "learning." As a new school year began, they applied to their principal for a Teachers' Learning Grant and received funding for substitutes that would allow the four of them to meet one morning a month for six months. Their goal was to think about how to make their curriculum more coherent, connected, and useful to their students.

Gathered together in a meeting room, the teachers began by listing all of the "topics" they taught on a whiteboard and were shocked to see that they had listed nearly 50 of them. These topics ranged from learning sounds, reading stories, exploring art, problem solving, and doing science experiments to family, colors, weather, poetry, coins, the Earth, senses, and dental care. (Note that the topics were not all equivalent. Some were skills, some were processes, and some were events. The teachers didn't realize the variance until well into their work.) Surveying the full list, one teacher commented, "These little folks can't find their way to their bus without the bus number hanging around their necks. How do we think they are going to find their way through all of this?"

Immediately, the group began trying to classify the information to allow for more economic presentation. After about three hours, they had created a five-column chart on the whiteboard, with each column headed by an organizing concept: Cooperation, Communication, Culture, Change, and Exploration. Under each concept, they listed the "topics" that seemed to fit there. This organization—every piece in a logical place—provided some momentary satisfaction. But then one of the teachers said aloud what the others were thinking: "Before we did this, I felt like we had too many pairs of socks lying around. We've put the socks in drawers, so they are better organized now, but we still have too many pairs of socks!"

They devoted several hours to thinking carefully about what mattered most for their students to learn and how they could organize learning experiences to provide the most meaningful ways for students to connect to these outcomes. They finally concluded that "sharing and caring"—helping students learn to care for one another and share ideas—was core to the intent of kindergarten. (Although the teachers did not use the term *affect*, this was an affective goal—and one they valued greatly.) Communication, they decided, was at the heart of everything they did with their students, so it became the central skill they designated, along with a second affective goal of appreciation. When they looked at the content areas they felt were most essential for their students, they concluded that the concepts of Patterns and Change were "themes" across all those areas. At that point, they drew a set of concentric circles that contained the various elements they had named and wrote a statement that unified the circles. It read something like this:

> We want to work with our students in a way that helps them care for themselves, care for others, and care for nature and appreciate themselves, appreciate others, and appreciate nature. Therefore, we will explore Patterns and Change in ourselves, in others, and in nature so that we may more fully understand and appreciate ourselves, others, and nature. As we learn, we will communicate about ourselves, about others, and about nature... with ourselves, with others, and with nature.

Changing instruction from disjointed and topic-based to coherent and concept-based was bumpy for a while, but the teachers continued to talk together so that their thinking and planning would align with their new focus.

Here's one example of what resulted. In this school, it was traditional for kindergarten students to study animals every spring, with each student ultimately "adopting" an animal that interested them and making a book about "their" animal. The pages in the book included facts about the animal and accompanying student illustrations. The children shared their books with parents in what became a traditional and eagerly anticipated "authors' reception" held in the school library late in the school year.

The new concept-based approach to curriculum made the learning goals of this activity a bit more complex than just presenting animal facts. Here are the two concepts and sets of principles the teachers and their students generated during the study of animals.

Rationale: There are *patterns* and *changes* in all animals, including humans.

Concept: *Patterns*
Principles (Understandings): Scientists use patterns to classify animals.
1. A category of animals shares predictable patterns.
2. We can classify animals by patterns in their size, movement, body features, habitat, food type, etc.
3. There are patterns in the life cycles of animals.
4. There are patterns in animal "families."
5. Weather and habitat determine basic patterns in animals' bodies and lives.
6. There are patterns of interdependence in lives of humans and other animals.
7. There are patterns in how and why animals communicate.

Concept: *Change*
Principles (Understandings):
1. Animals change as they grow.
2. Metamorphosis is a complete change.
3. The ways in which animals move, see, protect themselves, etc., change among classifications of animals.
4. Some animals change their habits in order to survive.
5. Some animals change their coloration to protect themselves.
6. Animals that do not adapt to change in their environments become extinct.

While this first iteration of the principles would become "tighter" in later years, even its first use shifted instruction from a series of "activities" designed for students' enjoyment to a meaningful exploration and discussion of ideas and co-developed work that captured and extended student understanding of the ideas. This was only one example of their revitalized curriculum. Throughout the year, the students practiced, honed, and applied a variety of skills articulated in their state standards in highly meaningful work.

During the authors' reception, parents with older children who had created animal books when they were in kindergarten expressed astonishment at the increased depth of student thinking reflected in this year's books. Many of the parents had also shared with teachers throughout the year surprising questions and observations their children were making, particularly related to patterns and change, at home, on family outings, in books they read together, in their family and friends, and so on.

Perhaps the most striking testimony to the positive impact the new kindergarten curriculum was having on young learners came from the local high school, which was also well regarded. In late spring, a large group of the high school's faculty reached out to the kindergarten teachers to ask for support in understanding how to use concept-based learning within and across their courses. The genesis of this request? About a half-dozen of the teachers at the high school, seen as thought leaders among their colleagues, had children in the elementary school's kindergarten class that year and saw firsthand the effect it was having. As one of the high school teachers said, "If learning this way makes that much difference to 5-year-olds, just imagine what it could do to make school better for high schoolers."

 ## Points to Consider

• If you are a relative newcomer to the idea of teaching by concepts and principles (big ideas), what do you think would be most challenging for you in moving to this approach? What would be most rewarding? If your teaching is already organized around concepts and principles, what was most challenging to you about making that transition? What have you found most rewarding?

• Thinking about the kindergarten example, in what areas (other than those they directly explored in class) can you envision the students seeing and commenting on patterns and change? How do you imagine these kindergarten teachers ensured that the concepts of patterns and change remained in the forefront of their students' thinking as each lesson progressed?

• How do you, or how might you, go about keeping students' focus on the big ideas rather than only or largely on the information in the curriculum?

Looking Ahead

Adam, one of my university students, asserted that differentiation was just common sense. Pleased that he had drawn that conclusion, I asked him to explain his thinking. He began by pointing to his own school experiences, noting it was evident to him that an affirming and challenging learning environment was necessary for students to really invest in learning. He went on to explain that when the curriculum is flat and uninspiring, it is predictable that student learning will generally be flat and uninspiring as well. Next, he introduced formative assessment into the picture by saying that it was just logical that a teacher who cared enough about learners to create a learning environment and a curriculum that were continuously inviting for every student would want to know every day how each student's learning was unfolding. "So, of course," Adam said, "those teachers just naturally use formative assessment for that purpose." He continued, "I think I just figured this out, but through frequent formative assessment is how teachers know *when* and *how* and *for whom* they need to differentiate instruction!" His final commonsense assertion was this: "And of course you can't teach flexibly in an inflexible classroom, and you have to learn how to create a flexible classroom."

So far, we have looked at the nature of learning-focused environments and intellectually engaging curriculum. Adam was correct that it is difficult to maintain one of those conditions without the other. Those statements capsule Chapters 5 and 6 in this book. Adam's thoughts about the role of formative assessment in learner- and learning-focused classrooms lead nicely into the next chapter, which examines the often-overlooked power of formative assessment in teacher and student growth and success. Later, we'll look at the link between dynamic instruction and the other elements Adam mentioned.

◌ ◌ ◌

7

Learner-Centered Assessment

*The most important assessments that take place in any school
building are seen by no one. They take place inside the heads of
students, all day long. Students assess what they do, say, and produce,
and decide what is good enough. These internal assessments govern
how much they care, how hard they work, and how much they learn.
They govern how kind and polite they are and how respectful and
responsible. They set the standard for what is "good enough"
in class. In the end, these are the assessments that matter.*

—Leah Berger, Libby Rugen, and Ron Woodfin in *Leaders of Their Own Learning*

When I was a young teacher, my relationship with the concept of assessment was uneasy at best and adversarial most of the time. Assessments meant tests, tests meant grades, grades meant report cards. They all brought a heaviness into the classroom that seemed oppositional to the excitement and satisfaction of learning that characterized the work my students and I did on most days.

I recall with precision standing at the door to the classroom I shared with my young adolescents on a day report cards would be distributed. Some students joked nervously about being grounded as a result of poor grades in one subject or another. Some sat hunched in their desks, their faces looking absent. Some twittered about rewards they would "earn" for good grades. As I talked with the kids entering the room, I had a devastating insight. Even though it was the end of the first marking period, I realized I could go home that evening and complete report cards for the rest of the year with alarming accuracy.

Something was dangerously wrong with the test-grade-report system that had been an immutable feature of school during all of my years as a student—yet here I was, perpetuating it as a teacher because I had no reasoned alternative to offer. Had I been aware enough to follow this thought more deeply, I might have asked, "Is the test/grade/report system benefitting students? What is the purpose of assessment? What do I really want to assess? How well do grades communicate meaningfully to students and their parents? What are alternative ways to assess learning other than tests? What assessment practices are most likely to contribute to developing young people who care to learn and who have the skills and mind-sets necessary to do so?"

I was *not* aware enough to ask these questions.

The State of Assessment in Schools

In her presidential address to the American Educational Research Association (AERA) in 2000, Lorrie Shepard expressed deep concern about the negative effects of external accountability testing. She saw that the heavy emphasis on such testing, and the subsequent judgment of schools, teachers, and students, could lead to de-skilling and de-professionalizing teachers. She worried also that both teachers and students would come to believe that their effort in school should be in service of externally mandated rewards and punishments rather than in pursuit of the excitement of ideas (in Earl, 2013). As I argue in Chapter 1, these fears have become reality.

While the cost of focusing the bulk of classroom efforts on raising standardized test scores has been (and, at this point, continues to be) ruinous in its impact on teaching and learning, there is a second and related culprit at work. It's that the same mindset that almost deifies standardized testing propels assessment practices in schools and classrooms as well. Few schools have moved beyond the sense I had as a novice teacher that judgment is necessary to make sure students are learning what they should learn, that classroom tests are necessary to judge student performance, and that grades are the best way we have of conveying a student's level of performance to the students themselves and to parents, who expect and even demand that the test/grade/report system remain a centerpiece of schools and schooling. The perceived *rightness* of that process is perhaps best evidenced now in the reality that many schools require teachers to give students a specified number of grades each week and rapidly post the grades on websites for parental consumption. So pervasive is the emphasis on grades that when students beyond the primary grades receive an assignment, they ask in chorus, "Will this be graded?" If the answer is no, the assignment is too often relegated to "Why bother?" status.

Many schools still use the terms *assessment, grades,* and *report cards* as near synonyms—a reality that works as a detriment to learning. As Burke (in O'Connor, 2009) observes, "Traditional grades... have little to do with learning because they are competitive, punitive, and encourage game playing by students and teachers alike" (p. 238). They encourage grade-grubbing instead of learning and are often used by teachers as control mechanisms in spite of a lack of evidence that using grades punitively improves either behavior or achievement. Reeves (2017) lists as the first of five persistent myths about grading that grades motivate students. All in all, it appears we often use grading practices that do little to encourage student growth (Black & Wiliam, 1998).

What's more, grades are discouraging, even dehumanizing, for many students. Berger (2003) recalls that by 3rd grade, it was clear to him that there were *good students* who got *good grades* and *bad students* who got *bad grades*. Other kids considered classmates in the bad-grades group to be stupid, and the kids in the bad-grades group spoke of themselves as stupid and let everyone know in a variety of ways that they hated school. Those who routinely got Cs and Ds on their report cards thought of themselves as "C students" or "D students." Although only in 3rd grade, they had already given up trying to be something else. In these instances—and there are many of them—grades function to make the learning environment anything but invitational to students. This corrodes the trust that many teachers work hard to establish, demeans rather than dignifies young humans, and leads far too many students to believe that learning is not for them.

The test/grade/report approach to assessment also diminishes motivation to learn in another group of students—those for whom school is nearly always easy. With a high skill level and low challenge, they drift into boredom. Further, accustomed to making good grades with minimal or modest effort, they can come to believe that they should not have to work hard. After all, they make good grades, which means they are smart, and smart people don't have to work for grades, right? When presented with a challenge that is appropriate for their level of performance, these students often reject the challenge and even get angry with the teacher for "unfairly" giving them work that's "harder than everyone else's." Here, Earl (2013) captures the experiences of many advanced and struggling learners related to grades:

For some students, the certainty of praise and success in school has become a drug; they continually need more. For many other students, year upon year of "not good enough" has eroded their intellectual self-confidence and resulted in a kind of mind-numbing malaise. (p. 15)

So advanced students can easily—almost automatically—become habituated to working for grades rather than working to learn. Struggling students see no escape from the indictment of low grades and give up on learning. It is easier to fail at something you don't invest in than to continue to fail at something you invest in heavily over an extended period of time with no hopeful results. In both cases, the outcome is reduced motivation (Dweck, 2006).

In sum, "judgment-based" summative assessment commonly dominates the school assessment landscape. The quality of a student's learning is judged with an eye to passing on that judgment to parents and students in the form of test and report card grades that signal students' relative position compared to their peers. Teachers may *intend* classroom testing and grades to benefit, extend, or deepen student learning, but that's a purpose woefully unrealized.

The observation I made while standing in my classroom door more than 40 years ago still holds in many schools and classrooms. Students who make high grades early in the year will, on the whole, continue to do so. Students who earn poor grades early in the year will, on the whole, continue on that path as well. The persistent low-scoring students are grouped for "remedial" classes or groups. The persistent high scorers are placed in advanced classes or groups. The kids in between find themselves in "regular" or "standard" classes or groups. Thereafter, the kinds of assignments doled out to each group are more likely to cement teachers' perceptions of students than they are to change any individual student's academic trajectory.

As teachers, we see these unhappy consequences, yet the way we think about, frame, and enact assessment practices is so fundamental in our experiences that we believe them to be inherently right, untouchable. I remember a teacher in a school where I was making a presentation that touched briefly on the impact of grades on learning whispering this advice to me during a break: "I don't think we can mess with grades here. In this state, we have three religions: Baptist, football, and grades. It's just not smart to tamper with any of them." In truth, I suspect the same statement could be made in most U.S. states, with just a little variation in the first and second "religions." Indeed, "many of the grading practices in U.S. schools are based on tradition, not evidence" (Brookhart, Guskey, McTighe, & Wiliam, 2020, para. 5).

Envisioning a Better Way

Assessment in learner-centered classrooms has a very different goal and seeks very different outcomes than the assessment that's common in many schools and classrooms. Like all other elements in learner-centered pedagogy, it's designed not to judge but to help maximize students' intellectual, affective, and social growth. In fact, assessment in these classrooms exists to ensure that student growth escalates consistently rather than stagnates.

It is past time to move away from the test-grade-report model of assessment and to focus instead on assessment that contributes to the process of learning and the progress of the individual student (Burke in O'Connor, 2009). What would it be like to embrace the kind of assessment that is more concerned with optimizing student thinking and learning than with measuring and reporting it? Earl (in Earl & Cousins, 1995) offers this hypothesis:

> I can imagine a day…when assessment and evaluation are not viewed with foreboding and terror; not separated from teaching and learning; not used to punish or prohibit access to important learning. Instead, assessment and teaching/learning will be reciprocal, each contributing to the other in ways that enhance both. Assessment will reveal not only what students know, and understand, and can do, but will also capture how those new learnings came about and will provide a range in variety and quality of work that shows the depth, breadth, and growth of each student's thinking. This wealth of information will, in turn, be used to provoke further learning and focused instruction. (Chapter 1, Location #205)

Earl makes three other assertions that frame her vision for classroom assessment—statements that precisely mirror key goals of learner-centeredness. First, she states that the primary purpose of school is to *optimize learning* for *each student* who comes there. Next, she expands on what she means by *each student*, explaining that, in her vision, schools would educate all children as we now tend to educate students whom we believe to have the greatest academic capacity. It would no longer be acceptable for schools to sort their students and cull the ones who don't fit the school's image of a capable learner. Finally, Earl elaborates on what she means by *optimizing learning*, explaining that all students would not only learn the foundational skills of literacy and numeracy but gain competence and confidence in a broad array of subjects as well as skills in those subjects that are and will be fundamental to success in the world of school and the world beyond school (e.g., assessing, interpreting, and applying information; critical thinking and analysis; solving novel problems; making informed judgments; working independently and in groups; discerning appropriate courses of action in ambiguous situations). Further, each student would consistently practice with tools that will empower them to adapt their new knowledge in response to new information as well as with the habits of mind necessary to function wisely and with civility in a world that is fast paced, rapidly changing, and unpredictable.

You probably recognize that Earl's statements reflect a growth-mindset view of student capacity to learn important things (the focus of Chapters 3 and 4 in this book) and a view of curriculum that centers around sound knowledge of the disciplines with an emphasis on understanding and transferring learning to unfamiliar contexts (the focus of Chapter 6). In addition, the statements relate to a view of education as that which prepares students intellectually, affectively, and socially to develop productive and satisfying lives in the world they do and will inhabit (the focus of Chapter 2).

The linchpin for accomplishing the vision for more promising, equitable, and excellent approaches to teaching and learning is an understanding of assessment that shifts the focus from *judging learning* to *developing the skills of learning*. The rest of this chapter explores what that shift means, why it matters, and what it might look like in practice.

A Foundation for Understanding Assessment

Because we understand and use terms differently in different contexts, it is reasonable to begin an examination of the role of assessment in learner-centered classrooms by establishing a shared understanding of vocabulary that describes the nature and purposes of various forms of classroom assessment.

There are essentially two kinds of classroom assessment: *summative* and *formative*. The purposes of and audiences for these forms differ in significant ways.

Summative Assessment

Summative assessment is assessment *of* learning. Its purpose, noted earlier, is to judge student work—to rate and report achievement to students, parents, and others who need to know a student's status at designated intervals (e.g., guidance counselors who are key to establishing students' class schedules in middle and high school).

Although insight into how a student is faring at intervals during a school year can provide valuable information for stakeholders in that student's education, summative assessment is limited in its capacity to help students grow as learners. A metaphor offered by Wiliam (2011a) helps to illustrate why that's the case. At the end of a quarter of swimming meets, a coach would not hand a swimmer a card that says C+. That would be of no use whatsoever in helping the swimmer improve her performance. Neither would it be helpful for the coach to assign a value of 2 points to each of four areas of development—arms, legs, breathing, timing—and tell the swimmer she's a 5½. By contrast, if the coach has carefully observed practices and meets, making notes on what the swimmer is doing in each area, she can detail specific strengths in each area and explain specific ways in which the swimmer could modify her timing and breathing to improve her performance.

By definition, summative assessment is after-the-fact assessment, used when it is reasonable (although not always accurate) to assume that students have had ample time, practice, and support to become proficient in what the summative assessment measures. These end-point assessments occur (or should occur) only a few times in a unit of study or inquiry. They are most common at transition points between major topics within a unit or inquiry, at the end of a unit or inquiry, or at the end of a grading period, semester, or school year. Their purpose is to measure the student's proficiency with knowledge/understanding/skill designated as essential in the curriculum design plan.

Summative assessments generally apply a judgment in the form of a grade meant to reflect a student's degree of competence with those learning targets or learning intentions. They can take the form of a test, product, performance, or combination of these. In an ideal world, every summative assessment would reveal all students demonstrating proficiency through their answers, products, and performances because the teaching and learning in the classroom were of a caliber to support that outcome.

As noted, summative assessments are typically used at transition points. After the summative assessment is complete, teachers and students alike assume it's time to move on to the next topic or inquiry. Thus, summative assessment is rarely used as a serious learning tool through which focused feedback from the teacher, combined with careful student analysis of the work, extends both student proficiency with learning intentions and student awareness of how to extend the skills and habits of mind that lead to increasing independence as a learner.

Formative Assessment

In contrast to summative assessment, *formative assessment* occurs often throughout the learning cycle, and its goals are markedly different. We can dig into formative assessment's purpose and its practice by focusing on four key terms: *pre-assessment, ongoing assessment, assessment* for *learning*, and *assessment* as *learning*.

Pre-assessment, sometimes called *diagnostic assessment*, is a kind of formative assessment distinguished by its timing. Used prior to the start of a new unit of study or inquiry, pre-assessment is quite useful in helping a teacher begin teaching a unit with a reasonable sense of which students may already have knowledge of content that will be introduced and which students lack command of the prerequisite knowledge, understanding, and skill that the teacher might expect students to have acquired via prior learning experiences. Pre-assessments can also help teachers spot misconceptions students have about a topic—valuable insight they can use to steer students toward accurate understandings before the misconceptions become more problematic for learning. When students take a pre-assessment, there is no expectation from the teacher or the students that they should show mastery of the new content. And because most of the content reflected on a pre-assessment has not yet been taught, pre-assessments should not be graded.

Formative assessment that occurs throughout a unit or inquiry rather than at its outset is typically called *ongoing assessment*. Some experts (e.g., Earl, 2013) also call attention to two subcategories of ongoing formative assessment that reflect the purpose of the assessment: assessment for learning and assessment as learning.

Assessment *for* learning can occur at any time during a unit of study or inquiry and should be a continuing feature of instruction. Its role is to help *teachers* see how to teach more effectively (Stiggins, 2004). Many teachers who see formative assessment as central in their work use assessment *for* learning almost daily, daily, or even multiple times during a class period or learning block to glean insights about student progress that will inform their planning for upcoming lessons. In addition to providing clarity about a student's academic growth, assessment *for* learning can also shed light on a student's social or affective growth, particularly through classroom observations and conversations. In sum, teachers use assessment *for* learning to gain a clearer understanding of a student's current learning status with targeted goals or outcomes for the purpose of adjusting their instructional next steps to better support that student's learning.

Assessment *as* learning has a related but different purpose. Its mission is to help *students* develop a clearer understanding of how they are progressing toward designated learning outcomes, learning goals, or learning intentions. It is self-assessment, but the kind of self-assessment focused on helping students make personal sense of the learning targets and become better pilots of their own learning success (Earl, 2013).

Teachers who value assessment *as* learning teach students to do the following:

- Pay close attention to learning goals and success criteria as they work;
- Monitor their own work in relation to the goals and criteria for quality work;
- Connect new knowledge to things they already know as a means to making sense of the new content;
- Think analytically about their work;
- Ask productive questions when they do not understand something;
- Develop a repertoire of strategies for moving forward with their work when they are stuck;
- Be mindful of how they learn, study, and create quality products;
- Reflect on the attitudes and habits of mind they bring to their schoolwork;
- Appreciate and learn from mistakes; and
- Tolerate ambiguity in the process of learning.

In reviewing this list, you may notice (as many have pointed out) that assessment *as* learning is essentially the process of learning (Black & Wiliam, 1998; Earl, 2013, Hattie, 2012; National Research Council, 2000). Teachers who are committed to the goals of learner-centeredness make certain that students are not left to their own devices to figure out what successful thinkers and learners do. Instead, they step up to provide dependable mentoring in "learning to learn" throughout the school year; assessment *as* learning is one of their tools. Figure 7.1 contains teacher practices that support assessment *as* learning.

Whether an assessment is summative or formative has to do with the *purpose* and *timing* of its administration, not the nature of the assessment itself. In other words, the same test or other measure could be used for formative or summative purposes (Hattie, 2012). Similarly, a single assessment can serve as both an assessment *for* learning and an assessment *as* learning. In those instances, the teacher will both (1) analyze and reflect on the responses of each learner in order to plan and teach more effectively in the short term, and (2) provide time, opportunity, and support for each student to analyze his or her responses and plan for next steps in learning to promote continuing growth with the learning targets.

Figure 7.1: Strategies for effective assessment *as* learning

- Create a learning environment in which students feel safe to take chances and where support for learning is consistently available.
- Model and teach the skills of self-assessment.
- Guide students in setting goals and monitoring their progress toward the goals.
- Provide models of quality work at varied levels of complexity that reflect the learning goals and success criteria.
- Work with students to develop clear criteria of good practice in learning and to monitor use of those criteria as they work with challenging tasks.
- Provide frequent and challenging opportunities for students to practice the skills and attitudes of successful work.
- Monitor student metacognition as well as their learning and provide descriptive feedback to students on what they observe.
- Guide students in developing self-monitoring mechanisms to both affirm and question their thinking.

What else would you add?

Source: Earl, 2013.

We have talked about the ideal outcome of a summative assessment being all students demonstrating competence with the intended learning outcomes. The goal for formative assessment—whether it comes in the form of a pre-assessment or ongoing assessment *for* or *as* learning—is different. In assessing formatively, the goal is to see what a student has accomplished and what he or she has not yet accomplished (Hattie, 2012). Given this, student error is not only expected but *sought*, because it shines a light on areas for student growth. If a formative assessment resulted in a set of "perfect papers" or observations of flawless work, the most likely conclusion would be that all students in the class were being significantly underchallenged.

An important caveat regarding ongoing formative assessments is that they should rarely, if ever, be graded. They take place during the long span in an instructional cycle when students are encountering new information and developing new understandings and skills. When students who doubt their capacity receive grades too early in the cycle, the result is often a sense of resignation: "See, it's just like always. I'm no good at school." And when students who are accustomed to high grades receive grades too early in a learning cycle, anything less than excellent results can incline them to focus on what it will take to raise the grade rather than what next steps they might take toward a deeper understanding of the content.

In recent years, as schools have begun to focus professional conversations around the value of formative assessment in furthering student learning, extensive observations suggest that many teachers who give formative assessments either grade them and move on (Earl, 2013), or take a look at the assessment responses and stop there because they are not sure what should come next (Tomlinson & Moon, 2013). Experts on formative assessment who advocate its use to full effect remind us that the goal of such assessment is to inform adjustment to teaching and learning practices so that students will learn more effectively and efficiently than would have otherwise been the case. Said differently, if a formative assessment does not result in one or both of those changes in the short term, it does not qualify as a formative assessment (Black & Wiliam, 1998; Hattie, 2012).

With a shared understanding of basic terms and principles related to assessment, we'll move next to exploring in more depth why formative assessment can be so powerful for learning in a student-centered classroom.

The Potential of Formative Assessment in Learner-Centeredness

Dylan Wiliam (2011c) provides this practical argument for formative assessment:

> Assessment is a central process in education. If students learned what they were taught, we would never need to assess; we could instead just keep records of what we had taught. But as every teacher knows, many students do not learn what they are taught. Indeed, when we look at their work, we sometimes wonder if they were even present in the classroom. In fact, it is impossible to predict with any certainty what students will learn as the result of a particular sequence of classroom activities. And because we cannot teach well without finding out where our students are starting from, we have to assess. Even if all our students started out at the same point (a highly unlikely situation!), each of them will have reached different understandings of the material being studied within a very short period of time. That is why

assessment is the bridge between teaching and learning—it is only through assessment that we can find out whether what has happened in the classroom has produced the learning we intended. (para. 1)

Formative assessment is the unsung hero of student success in learner-focused classrooms. It *is* the bridge between teaching and learning—connecting teacher to student, and student to student as well. It is how teachers can know the degree to which what happens in the classroom is making a positive difference in students' development toward learning targets and, more to the point, what sort of difference, if any, it is making in the growth of each learner individually. That is the case because in learner-centered classrooms, teachers understand that young people learn "in individual and idiosyncratic ways" (Earl, 2013, p. 27); therefore, the teacher's concern is with the development and welfare of each individual, not only of "the students."

In essence, formative assessment is consistent, persistent, moment-by-moment teacher watchfulness of students—and of each student—as they learn. Which students seem clear about the purpose and nature of their work, and which do not? Where is there evidence of understanding or misunderstanding? Who might need to go backward to gain competence and confidence with precursor knowledge and skills even as they try to move forward with new content as well? Who is clearly working without sufficient challenge? What is the level of a student's engagement? Confidence? Motivation? Which students seem able to move themselves ahead in the learning process, and which ones seem lost or frozen? Which students are working collaboratively to good effect? Which ones are struggling with skills of collaboration—and which ones are unable to contribute to the success of others in their group? When there is any impediment to forward momentum in learning, the teacher asks, "What needs to change here to set learning on the right course?" The focus is, as it should always be, on what's next for a student (Wiliam, 2011c).

Hattie (2012) reports that integrating formative assessment into minute-to-minute and day-by-day classroom practice can boost students' learning efficiency a remarkable 70 percent. According to Earl (2013), in the short term, effective formative assessment can draw students' attention to the most important aspects of the content, give students opportunities to practice skills and consolidate learning, and allow teachers to plan and guide subsequent instructional or learning activities that are responsive to student learning needs. Further on, in the mid-term and long term, formative assessment can help teachers not only communicate and reinforce learning intentions and success criteria but also foster students' ability to choose and employ effective learning strategies, boosting their agency and autonomy and sense of themselves as capable learners. It can even influence student choice of subsequent courses, activities, and careers.

The Process of Assessing Formatively

Formative assessment is, or should be, more a process or a practice than a specific strategy or instrument. It's a kind of sleuthing that involves continual and purposeful hunting for clues about student progress, interpreting those clues, and acting on them in the near term to improve the match between instruction and learners' next steps in learning.

Varied Forms, One Purpose

Whether conducted as pre-assessment, ongoing assessment, *for* learning, or *as* learning, formative assessment can also be either informal or formal. *Informal* formative assessment gives a teacher a general sense of how things are going. An example might be a teacher asking students to hold up a green card if they understand the difference between weather and climate, a yellow card if they think they generally understand but still have a few questions, or a red card if they need to read and talk about weather and climate some more in order to understand. Other examples of informal formative assessment might be a teacher observing that a number of students "tuned out" when they were asked to draw a picture that shows how length times width equals area, or a teacher having a doorway exchange with a couple of students about a homework assignment. In all these instances, the teacher is able to glean a general sense about how learning is progressing. Significantly, gathering *informal* formative assessment data is about getting this big picture; it's not meant to support conclusions about the state of specific students' learning or about the learning status of all students who responded in a given way or who appeared to be having a similar reaction (Tomlinson & Moon, 2013).

By contrast, *formal* formative assessment allows teachers to link the work of specific students with specific learning targets. In that way, formal formative assessments are more useful in understanding and responding to learning needs of identifiable individuals or groups of individuals. Formal assessment requires that a teacher have clear targets for talking with students, observing them, or analyzing their work. It also requires a record-keeping system—online or on paper—for recording how a student is progressing with targeted goals at a given time. Being able to associate a need with an individual is generally more precise, and therefore more powerful, in planning for and extending student learning.

Teachers can formatively assess students' ever-changing learning status using a broad array of formats and strategies. One common format is exit tickets, which themselves can take varied forms—anything from a one-word answer to a specific question to a "write for one minute" response that synthesizes the important information and ideas related to a topic or issue. For example, at the end of a history class in which students have read about and discussed events and circumstances that led up to the Vietnam War, an exit ticket might ask two questions: (1) *What do you believe to be the most important event or circumstances that led to U.S. involvement in the war?* and (2) *Why did you select the answer you provided as opposed to other answers you might have reasonably provided? Be sure to give specific examples and reasons.* And exit tickets can be employed at all grade levels, even before students gain written fluency. In a 1st grade classroom, for example, students might complete a storyboard showing the beginning, middle, and end of a story their teacher just read to them.

Exit tickets can also take the form of 3-2-1 cards. For example, after 2nd graders have listened to a story and discussed the way the author used language to interest readers in the story, a 3-2-1 exit ticket might ask students to "write or draw and label three things in the story that made you want to keep listening, two places the author used language that got your attention, and one thing you'd like to know about what happened after the story ended." A variation on this is the 1-2-3 exit ticket, which generally begins by asking students the one most important thing (to know about fractions, or word order in German, or fusion vs. fission) and move on from there. Exit tickets of any kind can help students reflect on processes as well as content. For example, a 3-2-1 exit ticket might ask students to explain three areas in their current work that they know they could improve, two steps they will take to make those improvements, and one way the teacher could be helpful in supporting those improvements.

Formative assessment can also occur in teacher–student conferences, as teachers observe students working individually or in small groups, as students make presentations in class or online, through analysis of work students turn in, by directly asking students what is going well for them in class and what isn't working for them, and through many other channels. You'll find more examples of formative assessment formats in the classroom illustrations at the end of this chapter.

Principles That Govern Effective Formative Assessment

The "means" of formatively assessing student learning are not as important as the principles and practices that undergird effective formative assessment. They illuminate what distinguishes formative assessment from just another classroom "exercise" and speak to the qualities of formative assessment that represents a teacher's commitment to maximizing student learning. Figure 7.2 presents key principles and practices that characterize effective formative assessment, and Figure 7.3 shows the flip side: the conditions under which formative assessment will likely fall short of its potential to promote student learning.

Figure 7.2: Conditions that support effective formative assessment

- Formative assessment happens continuously, but not intrusively, throughout an instructional cycle.
- Assessments are carefully aligned with the learning intentions/goals/targets established in the curriculum design and taught in class.
- Assessments focus on the task and on learning, not on the student
- Students have clarity on learning intentions/goals and success criteria.
- Students aim for understanding, not just recall.
- Status have multiple ways to express learning.
- Students recognize formative assessment as a low-stakes or no-stakes process designed to help them learn, not to judge them.
- Students receive effective, actionable feedback.
- Teachers emphasize progress by clarifying where the student is now in a learning progression, where he or she needs to be, and what the student might do to progress in that direction.
- Teacher and students recognize the role of motivation and self-concept in learning.
- Students are comfortable admitting when they don't understand something and are encouraged to ask reflective questions.
- Students analyze their own responses and thinking and use what they discover to gain more control of their own learning success.
- Students are interested in supporting one another's learning.
- The teacher uses results to rethink and adapt instructional plans.

Sources: Berger, Rugen, & Woodfin, 2014; Earl, 2013; Fullan et al., 2018; Hattie, 2012; Stiggins, 2004; Wiliam, 2011a.

Just administering a formative assessment counts for little in terms of promoting learner progress. The power of formative assessment resides (1) in how the teacher uses the information generated to create instruction that is more responsive to students' learning needs than would have been the case without insights from the assessment and (2) in the feedback the teacher provides to students as a result of the assessment, along with guidance in how to think about and use the feedback to support further learning. Both student use of feedback and teacher use of assessment information occur after the assessment's administration. Both, however, are essential in effective formative assessment *practice* because feedback (a cornerstone of assessment *as* learning) propels students forward in learning, and applying insights from student responses to formative measures or observations (a cornerstone of assessment *for* learning) propels teachers forward in the practice of their craft. In the next two sections, look at the role of those two sources of feedback in effective formative assessment practices, why they matter, and how they relate to student-focused pedagogy.

Figure 7.3: Conditions that hinder effective formative assessment

- The teacher does not consistently enact the belief that all students can learn and succeed.
- The classroom environment feels unsafe or unsupportive to a learner.
- The learner does not have a sense of trust in the teacher and/or peers.
- The teacher assesses quantity of learning rather than quality.
- Greater emphasis is placed on grading than on feedback.
- There is an emphasis on comparing students to one another.
- Feedback is used more for managerial or social purposes than for helping students learn more effectively.
- The teacher does not understand an individual student well enough to know that student's culture, strengths, and learning needs.
- The teacher does not consistently use formative assessment information to plan instruction that is more responsive to students' needs than would have been the case without using the formative assessment information.

Sources: Berger et al., 2014; Black & Wiliam, 1998; Earl, 2013.

Teacher Feedback to Support Student Progress

Despite my long-time belief that *assessment* was a euphemism for *judgment*, the Latin root word for *assessment* means "to sit beside" or "to sit with" (Berger et al., 2014) and conjures an image of the teacher as a listener, learner, mentor, and guide. Feedback is central to assessment *as* learning and shifts the focus of assessment from making judgments about student learning to supporting the student in developing insights and strategies for knowing when and how to take important next steps in learning (Earl, 2013). Feedback is the bedrock of such learning—"lightning in a bottle" (Moss & Brookhart, 2009, p. 12). In fact, Hattie (2012) reports that formative assessment has an effect size of 0.79 on student achievement—twice the average effect size of all other schooling effects.

The term *feedback* has its origins in engineering, referring to a context in which information about the current state of a system was used to change the future state of that system (Wiliam, 2011a). In schools, the term *feedback* is often, and incorrectly, used to mean any comments a teacher makes to a student about his or her work. In that instance, comments such as "Nice job," "You need to work harder on this point," "I can see that you're making progress here," and kindred written or spoken remarks fall short of the definition of feedback and, therefore, fall short of providing the kind of support that moves learners and their learning forward.

The intended outcome for teacher feedback is for students to use it to understand how their current performance aligns with desired outcomes—where the work is off base, why it's off base, and steps they can take to get back on base and move forward toward success. More precisely, feedback should help the student acquire the skills and habits of minds that are characteristic of thoughtful learners, think metacognitively (think about their thinking and how it is or is not working to support success), and become increasingly independent as a learner (Earl, 2013). We recognize this progression as a student's movement along the path toward agency as a learner. Agency is not only a prime goal of learner-centered teaching but also a characteristic of people who have the confidence and skill to successfully tackle many of life's challenges. Understood in that light, feedback in a learner-centered classroom is a systematic, informed, and sustained process of teaching young people how to be learners, problem solvers, and architects of their own success. In Figure 7.4, you'll find a collection of strategies for making feedback useful to your students.

Here are a few top-level guidelines for delivering feedback:

• **Avoid praise or judgment.** Hattie (2012) advises that teachers should always help students feel worthy and welcome in class—a precursor for student trust in the teacher and environment as a whole—but feedback should be simply actionable information.

• **Limit your focus.** Offering feedback on too many issues can create student overload and be discouraging.

• Avoid comparing any student's work to any other student's work. Feedback should promote learning, not competition.

Figure 7.4: Strategies for making feedback useful

- Provide when the student has a specific need for it—while the student is working on a task or very soon thereafter.
- Focus it on the learning intentions and success criteria specified for the activity or assignment, and make sure the learner is aware that this is what you're doing.
- Phrase feedback so that the learner sees what you see in the work.
- Specify what in the work needs attention—where it is inaccurate, ineffective, or incorrect—and why.
- Specify what the student can do next to move closer to desired outcomes.
- Be economical and focus on guiding the student to do a few things better; what matters is not how much feedback you provide but how much a student receives and acts upon.
- Phrase feedback in a way that prompts the student to think rather than respond emotionally.

What else would you add?

The timing of feedback also merits careful consideration. Teacher feedback is most useful to a student when that student has some knowledge, understanding, and skill related to the content or task at hand but just doesn't know how to move forward—the student doesn't know what a next step might look like. In other words, a student is most likely to need feedback when a task is "appropriately challenging," which means a little too hard for that student and thus creating some uncertainty about next steps. Feedback is not useful when a student is "lost in the woods"; the next step for that student is reteaching. When a task poses little or no challenge for a student, feedback is not necessary (Hattie, 2012); at these times, the best response is to direct students to appropriately challenging work that will be slightly out of reach and, thus, will require feedback to support the reach.

And, of course, there is the content of the feedback to consider, which depends on the individual student. Those who are working to build basic knowledge and vocabulary need corrective feedback to help them solidify what is correct or incorrect. They may also need assurance that they have support to move ahead. When students have made sense of basic concepts in the content but are not yet seeing connections or extending the basic ideas, it's often beneficial to provide feedback that assures that they are on the right track and are applying the right methods or strategies. In addition, feedback should indicate how they might extend those strategies, or suggest other approaches when their use of a strategy is not productive. Students who are working at advanced levels in a content area will benefit from feedback that points out their effective application of concepts or skills and provides suggestions for continuing to work with abstractions that can lead them to broaden or deepen understanding and applications of the content (Hattie & Yates, 2014).

Peer Feedback and Student Progress

In a strong learner-centered classroom, positive peer interactions are potent contributors to every student's academic, social, and affective development. Those interactions can build trust, create lasting friendships, provide broader perspectives on events and ideas, increase motivation, and contribute to sense making with content and skills. They can assure young people that they are never alone in learning. And they can also be a valuable source of feedback, reducing uncertainty and building confidence and motivation to persevere.

Peer feedback is not automatically effective, of course. One study (Nuthall, 2007, cited in Hattie, 2012) found that 80 percent of the verbal feedback a student received in class was likely to come from peers. That study also concluded that most of that feedback information was incorrect.

One factor that leads to useful peer feedback is a learning environment characterized by positive peer relationships and a solid sense of trust. A second factor is a teacher who takes an active role in ensuring that students know the purposes of feedback, how to provide it, and how to have conversations around feedback rather than just making a statement and moving on. Students can also become better partners in their peers' learning when teachers provide prompts for feedback, such as guiding questions, sentence openers, or question stems that students can use to generate feedback that would help a peer understand how to complete a task successfully (Hattie, 2012). Sometimes a template or organizer designed around an assignment is useful—especially when there are guiding questions for each element or step.

It can also be worthwhile to give learners an example of student work from years past and ask them to provide feedback on it that they believe would help the original author revise the work to be clearer or more effective. Afterward, a teacher-led class discussion or fishbowl conversation focused on the kind of feedback the students think would be most helpful to them if they had authored that particular work can clarify or gel student thinking. Certainly, it's beneficial for a teacher and students to co-construct a list of characteristics of fruitful feedback—and to revise the list from time to time, based on students' experience in providing and receiving peer feedback. The opportunity to talk about feedback can prompt ongoing thinking about what kind of feedback is most likely to help a peer grow and how to deliver that feedback so peers can listen openly.

The relationship between peer feedback and student-centered pedagogy is multidimensional. Establishing a learning community based on trust, respect, and partnerships makes both teacher and student feedback more likely to be effective in supporting student growth. What's more, giving students multiple opportunities to learn how to be effective providers and recipients of peer feedback contributes to a sense of community. Extending student agency and voice are central goals of student-centeredness. Both of those attributes are more likely to be realized in a classroom where peer interactions, including providing feedback, are valued and nurtured. At the same time, as peers learn to provide and benefit from peer feedback, they are extending their agency and developing their voices.

Teacher Use of Formative Assessment Information

Learner-centeredness, by definition, requires instruction that is responsive to the needs of individual students as well as those of the class as a whole. Information a teacher derives from formative assessment is key to achieving that goal.

During instruction, the teacher engages with students in something of a call-and-response process. The teacher (or the teacher and student together) determines what a unit, sequence of lessons, or pathway to a product or performance will look like, taking care to craft the steps so that students will move forward in specified knowledge, understanding, and skill. Students then do the work associated with the unit, lesson, and so on. Knowing that students don't learn as a "pack," the teacher watches and listens as the lesson unfolds, often systematically taking notes on clues about how learning is progressing for individual learners and the class as a whole, and on the level of student confidence and motivation. The teacher then has frequent opportunities to observe students as they work or to look at the work students have submitted. This is when the teacher provides feedback for a student and also derives greater clarity about each student's steps forward in learning or missteps.

Next, the teacher reviews student formative assessment data and engages in a pattern-finding exercise. Which students did or did not appear to understand a key idea? Who does or does not use a targeted skill appropriately? Who seems hampered by language or vocabulary? Whose confidence or motivation is flagging? Those students who seem lost in the assignment will need reteaching. Those who have a reasonable sense of direction but still need additional practice should have opportunities to strengthen weak spots; these will not be the same across students and will therefore call for varied practice activities of varied duration and with varied scaffolding. Students whose work indicates seamless progress need "next steps" that prompt them to think more deeply and to venture into the unknown. Tomorrow's lesson—or next Monday's—as currently written will likely not be the learning opportunities indicated by the formative assessment analysis. And so that lesson needs to change. Otherwise, learning for some students, and maybe most of them, will be hampered.

In learner-centered classrooms, learning doesn't end for students or their teachers when a class or lesson reaches its conclusion. It continues as a teacher interprets evidence of the lesson's impact on varied students; provides feedback that will help students move forward in knowledge, understanding, and skill; and adapts upcoming instruction to further support that growth. It continues as one student draws on what she has learned about content and her ability to shape her learning journey to revise her goals, and another student draws upon his new learning and most recent learning journey to determine new strategies that will serve him well. In this way, the interactive and interdependent cycles of teaching and learning move ahead.

Grading Practices That Benefit Learning

A noteworthy number of schools don't issue traditional report cards with a grade for each subject. Instead, they may use student and teacher narratives, portfolios of student work, and student performances as a means of demonstrating the quality of student learning. Often there are public audiences that view these presentations and provide feedback to students on their work. In most cases, educators and students in those schools would tell us that when grading no longer occupies center stage, attention shifts to learning.

Other schools, in increasing numbers, have adopted standards-based grading, replacing letter grades with more transparent indicators of student achievement on delineated state or school-based learning standards. The aim in these schools is to replace the mystery that often surrounds grades with clarity about a student's degree of mastery on specified learning goals.

In many schools, of course, traditional grades are still a fixture. In those places, and certainly in classrooms that aspire to be learner-centered, there should be honest and even courageous conversations among educators about whether traditional grades are the best way to encourage learning, the negative impacts of traditional grading practices on individual students and groups of students, the goals of grading, and what our current best evidence suggests constitutes learning-friendly grading practices. We don't have to—should not continue to—adhere to practices that reflect habit more than reason.

Berger and colleagues contend that "nothing is more important in fostering growth in students than the degree to which they care…if students don't care, they are not going to work hard" (2014, pp. 6–7). Grades are extrinsic motivators—rewards and punishments. Using grades stems from the assumption that external motivators cause students to care about learning. Some students "learn" for tests and grades. Some shut down learning to protect themselves from additional failure and pain. Many become co-dependent with grades (Wiliam, 2011a). In fact, students who are motivated to learn because the learning itself is rewarding, and because they believe in their capacity to progress as learners, grow more academically than students who learn for the sake of rewards (Dweck, 2006).

In schools where grades will continue to prevail, there are practices that can make the test-grade-report cycle more learner- and learning-friendly. Here are a few of them*:

• Work to make curriculum and instruction compelling enough to motivate students to learn (e.g., it is connected to students' lives, attached to students' interests, focused on creating meaningful products that have a real audience, and designed to provide opportunities for student voice and choice; see Chapter 6).

• Ensure that students understand clearly what the learning targets are.

• Ensure that tests mirror those learning targets.

---

*This list of suggestions was compiled from Berger, 2003; Earl, 2013; O'Connor, 2009, 2010; Tomlinson & Moon, 2013; and Wiliam, 2011a.

- Ensure that students know what the success criteria are and understand what they will need to do to achieve those.
- Collaborate with students in developing rubrics.
- Assign grades only to summative tests and products, not to formative assessments, class practice, or homework. Don't grade students while they are still learning new content.
- When computing report card grades, weigh a student's recent work more heavily than his or her earlier work.
- Give students multiple opportunities to succeed, including reteaching and reassessment opportunities. (Ron Berger [2003] notes that in a school of his design, the only two grading options would be A and "not finished." Work would be expected to go through multiple drafts and would not be considered complete until it represents high quality for that learner.) Guskey (2019) points out that more than 50 years ago, Benjamin Bloom asserted that assigning different levels of "not-mastery" is unnecessary. Both Bloom and Carol Dweck (2006) seem to prefer a category called "not yet." In agreement with Berger, and likely Dweck as well, Bloom held the belief that "given sufficient time and appropriate types of help,…95 percent of students…can learn a subject to a high level of mastery" (in Guskey, 2019, para. 9). One part of Bloom's "appropriate conditions" is a teacher providing to a student consistent feedback that is both diagnostic (reiterating precisely what a student needed to demonstrate and ways in which the student has met those criteria) and prescriptive (pointing to what the student needs to do next to improve his or her learning).
- Emphasize student growth over comparison with others. (Hattie [2012] commends "+1 learning" in which the teacher and each student focus on progressing one step forward from where they were the day before. Wiliam [2011a] suggests three possible grades for an assignment: a minus sign, a plus sign, and an equal sign. A minus means the work is of lesser quality than previous work. An equal sign means the work is of about the same quality as previous work. A plus sign means the work shows advancement over previous work. No student can get a plus without advancing.)
- Match assessment methods with learning goals. When curriculum emphasizes understanding and application, performance tasks or products will generally be more revealing measures of learning than tests.
- As often as possible, give students options for expressing learning.
- Don't only use the mean when computing grades—use median and mode as well.

• Talk with students about grades and what you do to try to make them helpful for learning and to be sure they have a reasonable sense of how their work might translate into a grade.

• Invest heavily in assessment *as* learning to help students focus on progress, become increasingly adept at understanding how to learn effectively, and become increasingly confident as learners.

• Use narrative progress reports to students and/or parents between report cards to support shared understanding of student progress.

• Consider "3-P" reporting of grades. In this format, each student receives a grade for *performance* (solely focused on mastery of learning targets/standards), *process* (habits of mind and work), and *progress* (movement forward from a starting point). These grades should *not* be averaged but reported separately (Guskey, 1994, 2020). The three separate grades help students and parents understand the strong link between sound habits of mind/work, forward movement, and ultimately success with performance goals. They emphasize to students that multiple aspects of their work are important in their success (Guskey, 2020). The 3-P approach does much to dignify, encourage, and stretch each learner. It also communicates more clearly to parents about a child's work than does the single-amalgamated-grade approach (Guskey, 2020), which is significant since the primary goal of grading and reporting is, or should be, communicating *usable* and *understandable* information about a learner's achievement and other qualities to key stakeholders (Brookhart et al., 2020).

To argue for much broader and wiser use of assessment in schools is not to argue that all grades have to be eliminated; rather, it points to the reality that schools, students, teachers, and parents have become so fixated on grades that actual learning has become secondary. The argument here is to recognize the potential damage of *over*-grading, which is both well documented in research and clearly visible in classrooms, and to balance the scales in favor of feedback that stems from authentically implemented formative classroom assessment. This approach raises teacher quality and learner effectiveness, increases achievement for students across the spectrum of learners, and "forges learning partnerships between students and teachers that make a huge difference in what happens every day and every minute in the classroom" (Moss & Brookhart, 2019, p. 24). That's a lot of encouragement for a teacher to keep learning and moving forward.

Analyzing Examples of Formative Assessment in Learner-Focused Classrooms

Now let's look at examples of teachers in varied grades and content areas applying principles and practices of classroom formative assessment. In this chapter, you'll find the prompts for reflection at the conclusion of the fifth and final example.

In an Algebra 1 Classroom

Jennifer McCalla (in Coté, 2019) has a strong interest in classroom formative assessment and particularly in assessment *as* learning. She and colleagues developed "learning target trackers" and student self-assessment tools to help learners engage in metacognitive behavior. To prepare for chapter assessments, she created "closure stations" for each chapter to serve as a self-directed review for her math students. Each table in the classroom focused on a different learning target (typically there were six or seven targets for a given test) and had a corresponding set of practice problems, along with an answer key (see Figure 7.5).

Figure 7.5: An example of a learning target sign on a "closure station"

Station 1

Skill: I can solve a system of equations and prove that my answer is correct.

LT #8: I can solve a system of equations by substitution.

Which of the following system(s) would be easiest to solve using substitution? Why? Then solve the system(s) that you choose.

1. $y = 5x - 7$
   $-3x - 2y = -12$

2. $-3x - 8y = 20$
   $-5x + y = 19$

3. $-3x + 3y = 4$
   $-x + y = 3$

Before they started the closure stations, Ms. McCalla asked her students to prioritize the learning targets and number them from weakest to strongest in the "learning target" cells on their planning grids. They would then visit the closure stations in that order. As she observed students at work, she saw that this was a great way to differentiate student learning practice based on a student's awareness of their current strengths and weaknesses. Completing the closure stations also allowed all students the experience of becoming their own agents for improving their understanding. Ms. McCalla noted that the students did not follow their friends to the stations but rather visited in the order in which they rated themselves. Students later commented that they appreciated knowing clearly which learning targets would be the focus for the upcoming test. As the next chapter test approached, students were again asking Ms. McCalla to use closure stations, which ultimately became a staple in the classroom.

An interesting side benefit of having the students prioritize their learning targets was that, as students went to the station that was their first priority, Ms. McCalla was able to physically see which learning targets individual students believed they needed the most support to achieve. That added to her evolving understanding of each student's progress. Figure 7.6 provides an example of a student tracking guide from Ms. McCalla's Algebra 1 class.

In Middle School Math

Heather Tackett developed a strategy called "Test Correction Teams" to enable students to learn from questions they had when summative tests were returned to them. She had previously asked her students to correct errors on those tests but found that the students had so many questions that they could not make the corrections unless she could spend extended time with each of them. That solution was simply not feasible.

So the next time Ms. Tackett returned a set of student tests, she placed students in groups of four, working as a team to ensure that each student would be able to get the assistance necessary to explain and correct mistakes they had made on the test. Each team contained one member who had really struggled with the test, one or two who did reasonably well on the test, and one who had demonstrated mastery. Ms. Tackett had graded each problem on a four-point rubric, and any problem that received less than a 4 had to be corrected and submitted for additional credit. She noted that it was a rare occurrence when any student had no corrections to make. The results of her initial experiment with Test Correction Teams was so impressive that she made it a regular feature of a summative assessment cycle.

Figure 7.6: An example of a student tracking guide

Algebra 1

Name _____ Pd _____

Chapter 4 Closure Stations

Rate yourself on how well you know each learning target based on your results that you recorded on your learning tracker. Then prioritize the stations by numbering them from 1 to 6 (1 being "I need more practice with this target" and 6 being "I'm good with this target.")

Station	Learning Target	Overall, How Well Do You Know the Target?			
1	SKILL: Solving Equations	1	2	3	4
2	**LT #8:** I can solve a system of equations using substitution.	1	2	3	4
3	**LT #9:** I can solve a system of equations using elimination.	1	2	3	4
4	**LT #10:** I can solve a system of linear equations by graphing.	1	2	3	4
5	**LT #11:** I can translate a scenario into an algebraic equation or system of equations and solve it.	1	2	3	4
6	**LT #2:** I can determine if a relation (pairs of inputs and outputs) is a function.	1	2	3	4

1	2	3	4
I cannot do this by myself because I do not understand it YET.	*Sometimes I need help, but I am starting to understand.*	*I can do this by myself, but I make little mistakes.*	*I can do this without mistakes and can teach someone else this concept.*

Students tell Ms. Tackett they really enjoy and benefit from the opportunity to discuss their work with peers and fix errors in small groups. The strategy also allows her to spend focused time with each group as its members collaborate, assisting as necessary and also gaining insight into common questions across groups so that she can focus her instruction in those areas. She feels the process results in greater student engagement in learning from their errors and greater ownership of their learning. Test correction teams disperse at the end of the class period, so the groups are not fixed. In addition, students work in collaborative groups for much of their day and are accustomed to working in many kinds of groups. Test Correction Teams just seem like business as usual.

In a Kindergarten Classroom

Kindergarten teachers in an Illinois school were working with an instructional coach to strengthen their understanding and use of pre-assessments. An upcoming unit in math required students to be able to explain and understand the concept of symmetry. Talking together about pre-assessing students for that concept, the teachers agreed that none of their students would be familiar with symmetry. A pre-assessment on symmetry, they felt, would take valuable class time and yield little information that would be useful in their planning for the unit. The coach who was working with the teachers suggested that they teach and illustrate the concept of symmetry in class for a day and then use a pre-assessment. Reluctantly, the teachers agreed to that plan.

On Day 1 of the unit, the teachers led their students in an exploration and discussion of symmetry using a number of artifacts in different media. Then, over the next couple of days, the teachers conducted a one-on-one pre-assessment of each student in their class by giving a student a brown lunch bag containing several objects. Students reached into the bag, pulling out one item at a time and explaining whether they thought the item was or was not an example of symmetry and why they answered as they did. After the teachers analyzed student responses and met together to share what they learned, one of the teachers wrote this to the coach:

> We were all amazed by the results of our symmetry pre-assessment. We had all made assumptions about the kids that were not true! Vocabulary really made a difference in the "tell me why" part of the pre-assessment. Every one of us ran into more than one student about whom our before-the-unit conclusions were wrong. So often we teachers draw conclusions about kids on the fly and say, "I know my students" and then determine what "group" they should work in and how well they will learn. This pre-assessment made us face the fact that, without this early information, we really *didn't* know our students!

In a 5th Grade Classroom

Ede Marquissee felt strongly that students in her very diverse classroom would benefit from her metacognitive approach to teaching and consistent use of formative assessment to inform her teaching and help students better understand, plan for, and take control of their learning. Her metacognitive teaching called on her to talk with students about decisions she made in her planning and ask for their input. This modeling of reasoned thinking, she believed, would serve as an example of careful decision making. The student input not only kept students from feeling that school was done *to* them but also gave her excellent ideas for ways they could all learn together more effectively.

Students in Ms. Marquissee's class were accustomed to her using varied forms of formative assessment multiple times a day. They also understood how she used what she learned from studying their assessment work to know how to help each of them learn better. About four months into the school year, she said to the class, "You're used to the different ways I try to understand how you are learning so that I can help you learn as well as possible, and I'm going to keep asking you to work with me in those same ways. But last night, I had a new idea, and I want to see if you'll be willing to give it a try with me."

She continued, "I realized that I don't always need to be the one to figure out how you're doing with what we are studying. You know yourselves well enough now to know that without me. So I'm thinking we might try something we'll call a 'windshield check.' Here's how it would work."

Ms. Marquissee explained that sometimes when they had been working with a topic or skill for a while, she would stop and ask them to tell her how well they were understanding. The windshield represented how well they could "see"—understand what they had been discussing and practicing together. Each student would select one of three choices about how clearly they were "seeing" the ideas. Ms. Marquissee explained:

> If your windshield is clear, that means you are confident you understand and can use the ideas or skills. If your windshield has bugs on it, that means you can generally see where we're going—but there are a few messy or uncertain areas as well. If your windshield is muddy, that means something got in your way to keep you from being confident with the new ideas yet. Once you tell me how your windshield is looking right now, I'll ask you to come to a place in the room where there will be some practice for you that will help make sure your windshield gets clearer—that your understanding gets better.

The students had great trust in their teacher and in one another, so only rarely did a student describe their "windshield" inaccurately. When that happened, Ms. Marquissee sat down with the student to explore the reasoning behind the student's answer. Most of the time, the student self-corrected his or her choice. If not, she requested that the student try a particular task to see if it was helpful.

Later in the year, a student said in class one day that he thought he and his classmates were good enough at understanding themselves, so now they could suggest *when* a windshield check was needed rather than the teacher having to make that decision all the time. Ms. Marquissee was delighted with the suggestion, and the class added another layer of depth to their assessment practices.

Ms. Marquissee's students made remarkable strides in self-understanding and academics during the year—a new phenomenon to many of them. She was an energetic, innovative, determined teacher who wanted her students to learn and to love learning, so the days they shared were full of surprises, creative approaches, and purposeful productions. Asked which of the things she had used with her students made the most difference in their growth, she responded without hesitation, "Oh, it's the windshield checks. I have no doubt about that."

She went on to explain that this form of assessment *as* learning* had been particularly productive for two key reasons. First, the students were the decision makers and took that very seriously. They "owned" their progress. Second, there was almost no wasted time between when a student needed clarification and when he or she was able to get it. Both of those things were effective and efficient. You could almost see the students developing confidence and agency, she said.

In a World Languages Classroom

Ms. Wanamaker conducted weekly check-ins with each of her World Languages students. Sometimes she scheduled mini-conferences with them at her desk while the class worked on a variety of independent or small-group tasks. Sometimes she walked around as students worked at stations based on their needs in one of the components of language proficiency. Students had a matrix of competencies in their classroom work folders and in their online portfolios as well. These teacher–student conferences centered on two or three competencies, often with the students suggesting two and the teacher suggesting one. Competency

---

*Read more about the windshield check technique in Brimijoin, Marquissee, and Tomlinson, 2003.

areas included oral language production, listening and understanding, reading fluency, vocabulary, sentence structure and grammar, and cultural fluency. Within those areas, the teacher introduced new competencies throughout the year.

Each week, Ms. Wanamaker asked students to be ready to share with her one area where they had grown over the prior week (with examples to support their choice) and one area they were targeting for growth that week, along with examples of the learning approaches they were planning to take. Students shared examples in both competency areas from their work folders or portfolios. Sometimes Ms. Wanamaker's choice of competency area was one in which she had observed student growth and sometimes one in which she wanted to present a challenge to the student. She kept notes from the check-ins on student-specific competency matrices.

She built time into the class schedule each week for whole-class or small-group discussions of "barriers and passages," during which students shared strategies that had worked for them in strengthening their proficiency in a specific competency and barriers they were still encountering. As the end of each quarter of the school year approached, Ms. Wanamaker asked each student to create a brief analysis of their most important progress areas (passages) and one area of difficulty (barrier) that they would take on as a challenge in the next quarter. Both she and her students felt the clarity and specificity of competencies, regular check-ins with the teacher, peer debriefings, and regular student reflections had helped them grow stronger in language development and in personal development.

 ## Points to Consider

- Based on the information here, what do the teachers in these five scenarios have in common in terms of their beliefs about and uses of formative assessment in the classroom?
- What differences do the scenarios suggest?
- At some point, all of these teachers made the transition to using assessment practices that actively support learning as central in their goal of maximizing student learning. How do you imagine that transition looked and felt?
- What might have had to change in their teaching *prior to* a significant change in assessment practices?
- What might have had to change *as* or *after* their assessment practices shifted markedly?

• Moss and Brookhart (2009) comment that formative assessment "flips a switch, shining a bright light on individual teaching decisions so that teachers can see clearly (and perhaps for the first time) the difference between the *intent* and the *effect* of their actions" (p. 10). How do you interpret that statement?

Looking Ahead

At the end of Chapter 6, I referenced the conclusion of Adam, one of my university students, that differentiation (and I would extend that to say quality teaching in general) involves a hefty dose of common sense. He had recently realized that, unless formative assessment is a way of life in a classroom, a teacher has scant basis from which to differentiate instruction. Likewise, envisioning any sort of learner-centered classroom without a relatively clear and evolving understanding of the various points on which students are located along continuums of academic achievement, affective development, and social growth hobbles a teacher's intent to place students at the center of instructional decision making and action.

Another of my students, Davis, reached a similar conclusion about the necessity of formative assessment in planning for *the* student as well as the *students*. He wrote that formative assessment greases the wheel of differentiation (and I would again extend the comment to include any form of learner-centeredness). In the next chapter, we'll consider the "next logical step" after formative assessment—learner-centered instruction.

8

Learner-Centered Instruction

*In what universe does standing up in front of 30 people to "teach"
something make any sense? Are they all learning the same thing? Who
thinks that's a good idea? Are they all ready for the same content in
the same way? Is their genius going to shine through that whole-class
instruction, or is that simply the easiest way to express stuff? To "cover" it?*

—Terry Heick in *TeachThought*

Instruction is where it all comes together—or, perhaps more accurately, where
determined teachers try their very best to make it all come together. Instruction
is the arena in which philosophy, beliefs about learners and learning, ideas about
the role of the teacher, plans for building community, curriculum design, and
assessment meld into a live-action drama centered on the uniquely human capacity to learn from the past and present in order to contribute to a better future. Wiliam (2011a) captures the stakes when he writes, "The greatest impact on learning
is the daily lived experiences of students in classrooms, and that is determined
much more by *how* teachers teach than by what they teach" (p. 13).

This chapter, as others, draws on the work of experts in various education-
based domains because, as I noted in Chapter 2, my goal in the book is to synthesize our current best understanding of quality educational practices drawn from
research and classroom experience. I want to share my reason for emphasizing
one particular resource in this chapter, because it might otherwise seem like an
odd choice. The book is *What the Best College Teachers Do* by Ken Bain (2004),
a Harvard professor and researcher. It might seem a misfit to provide guidance to
K–12 educators, my primary audience, from a research study of excellent college

instructors. What I have found, and what I hope you'll see as you read on, is that truly excellent teachers, no matter the age of their students, are most often learner-centered. The instructional practices of the outstanding college teachers in Bain's study absolutely mirror those commended for K–12 educators in respected research compilations (e.g., Bloom, Hattie, National Research Council) as well as in the writing of education specialists (e.g., Black, Brookhart, Duckworth, Earl, Erickson, Gay, Guskey, Love, Wiggins & McTighe, Wiliam) and education practitioners who write for colleagues who teach in a variety of grade levels (e.g., Berger, France, Levy, Steele). So, as you'll see shortly, I have framed the majority of this chapter around questions Bain poses in *What the Best College Teachers Do*. As I hope you will also see, these questions are the ones teachers who strive to be excellent ask and seek to answer in classrooms at all levels of learning.

It has long been reassuring to me to see that we really do know what quality educational practices look like and we understand how and why they work. That's not to say we don't need to continue to grow in understanding, but as David Perkins remarked nearly 30 years ago, we already know enough about how learning works to do a much better job of educating young people than we currently do (in Earl, 2013). Our need, as I proposed at the outset of the book, is not to find the next "new thing" to add to our teaching repertoires but rather to seek to (1) better understand what we know to do, (2) apply what we have or will come to understand, and (3) invest in the application at as high a level of quality as possible.

We'll dig into that work in this chapter.

A Fundamental Framework for Learner-Centered Instruction

There is no recipe for instruction. To address all its elements in all possible contexts for the variety of students who arrive at school in all different age groups would require an encyclopedia rather than a recipe card. Instruction designed for primary students will vary in evident ways from instruction designed for high school students. It will vary when teaching is inductive versus when it is deductive. It will have a different feel in a block schedule than in a 49-minute class period. It will have a different tone if the teacher has an exuberant personality than if he or she is quiet and reserved by nature. And whatever the age group, content, or teacher proclivities, instruction in one classroom will—if we take seriously the familiar statement that every student can learn—differ from instruction in every other classroom as the teacher attends to varied learner needs. In fact, because of learner variety and the unpredictability of learning itself, instruction in a particular classroom on any Tuesday morning will (or should) be noticeably different than it will be during the same time period on Wednesday morning.

Nonetheless, there are principles and practices of quality instruction that are remarkably stable across contexts from preschool through university levels. Learner-focused teachers tend to ask themselves similar guiding questions as they plan, implement, reflect on, and continue planning instruction. There are also some common classroom practices that reveal misconceptions about teaching and learning that learner-focused teachers must reject based on considerable research over many years and the goals of student-centeredness. These questions and the rejection of certain practices and the embrace of others are informed by four philosophical assertions, which should be familiar by this point in the book:

1. The student is at the center of instruction and instructional decision making.

- You must begin with the student. You don't begin by thinking about what you know or your own ego. As Steele (2009) points out, "The moments of the class belong to the student—*not the students*, but to the very undivided student. You don't teach a class. You teach a student" (p. 96).
- Like any other human characteristics, learning is diverse and different for each learner (Earl, 2013).
- Students do not simply "store" knowledge they hear; each student learns in a particular, personal way. Each child gives personal shape to his or her understanding and to the way that he or she comes to understand things. The teacher may be teaching a class, but all learning is ultimately an individual process (van Manen, 1991).

2. The goal of instruction is to make sure that each student has the opportunity and support necessary to maximize his or her intellectual, social, and affective capacity.

- The goal is to ensure that each student learns, not just that all students were taught (Hattie, 2012).
- The ultimate goal is to help each student be able to transfer what he or she has learned into everyday settings of home, community, and workplace—to be able to adapt what they know for changing circumstances (National Research Council, 2000).

3. Effective learner-centered instruction is necessarily also

- **Knowledge-centered,** with an emphasis on making sense, making meaning, thinking and problem solving, and transferring/applying knowledge to new contexts that connect with students interests and concerns;
- **Assessment-centered,** in that it's used to support more effective learning and more effective teaching; and
- **Community-centered,** with an emphasis on connecting students with one another (to support academic, affective, and social development) and connecting students and student learning with the broader community (National Research Council, 2000).

4. Effective learner-centered instruction rests on teachers who are

- Invested in the welfare and development of each learner in their care;
- Committed to contributing to equity and excellence;
- Passionate about teaching;
- Eager to learn and grow toward expertise in the disciplines in which they teach and in instructional approaches that support students' academic, intellectual, affective, and social growth; and
- Boundary-breaking change agents (Bain, 2014; Gay, 2018; Hattie, 2012; Levy, 1996; National Research Council, 2000; Steele, 2009).

Decisions regarding learner-centered instruction hinge on these assertions. In various schools and classrooms, there will be many variables in cultures, community norms, student needs, available resources, curriculum, allocation of time, and so on. Nonetheless, claiming learner-centered instruction in any context should indicate eagerness to place the student at the center of educational policy and practice and determination to live inside the four assertions.

Dwyer (1995) identifies parallel practices that educators will need to leave behind and embrace in order to better prepare each learner for a promising life in both the near and long range. Here are seven key adjustments necessary for achieving quality learner-centered instruction:

- Shifting **classroom activity** from largely teacher-centered or didactic to largely *learner-centered and interactive;*
- Shifting the **teacher's role** from fact dispenser or expert to *orchestrator, collaborator, and fellow learner;*
- Shifting the **students' role** from listeners and learners of information to *collaborators, sense makers, and sometimes-experts;*

- Shifting the **conception of knowledge** from facts that are accumulated and replicated to *understanding that can be applied and transferred;*
- Shifting the **measure of success** from quantity mastered to *quality of mastery;*
- Shifting the **focus of assessment** from test scores to *wide-ranging student performance;* and
- Shifting the **focus of instruction** from listening and seat work to *communication and collaboration.*

Twelve Questions That Guide Learner-Centered Instruction Across Contexts

I referred earlier to the guiding questions that learner-centered teachers ask as they plan, carry out, and reflect on their instructional practices. Now I want to provide a closer look at the kinds of questions I mean and the practices that emerge from them.

The questions I've chosen draw from those posed in *What the Best College Teachers Do* (Bain, 2004), obviously focused on excellence in university teachers. I have adapted the questions—adding, deleting, combining, and factoring in perspectives from *The Inspired Teacher* (Steele, 2009), written about excellence in K–12 teachers, and the work of others to make them more familiar to K–12 instruction—but their core remains as reported in Bain's book. To avoid repetition, I will not cite Bain (2004) and Steele (2009) further in regard to specific questions, but I will cite all authors (those two included) as I incorporate their ideas in the principles and practices that relate to each question. As always, because classroom elements are so closely bound to one another, principles and practices provided below one question could often be classified under others as well.

Just one more note: the questions Bain captured were most commonly asked by "the best college teachers," regardless of content area, location, or level of students. It is interesting that very few of these college teachers had any formal training in pedagogy. What they did have was common sense and clarity about what they wanted for their students. They also learned though experience, trial and error, and dogged reflection what was fruitful in accomplishing their vision. In the end, the pivotal element they share is learner-centeredness. All this is encouraging because it suggests that most of us who are teachers can make our way to excellence by following that same path.

1. Who are these students? How will I get to know them well enough to guide them productively?

- Remember that the more we learn about a student—what's happening in their lives at home and in the classroom, for what reasons, and what the contributing factors are—the more we see every action in its context, allowing us to react more appropriately (Steele, 2009).
- Be diligent in getting to know each student. Make that an early and continuing goal for your work (Bain, 2004).
- Use morning meetings, class forums, or 5-minute check-ins, transition times, and class breaks as opportunities for students to talk with one another and with you about things in their lives that matter to them (Fullan et al., 2018).
- Actively pay attention to students' backgrounds and cultural values as well as to their particular strengths so that you can build on what they bring to the classroom. Unless the connections are made explicit, they often remain inert and do not support learning (Wiliam, 2011a).
- Resist thinking of students as winners or losers, able or not able. Look for and draw on the individual value of each student and the unique contribution each student can make to the class and the work of the class (Bain, 2004).
- Early in the school year or course, begin to compile a list of each student's special interests. If you find after a few weeks that you're lacking information for some students, find ways to elicit it (Bain, 2004). Options might include doorway conversations, surveys, listening for the interests students express in class discussions, and providing students with choices to study a topic more deeply or broadly and noting their choices.

2. What big questions will the course or units I teach help my students answer? What skills and abilities and qualities will I need to help them develop to pursue answers to those questions? How will I build the class around those questions?

- Work to have a good understanding of the content you teach. The more deeply you understand a subject, the more ways you'll be able to relate it to students' lives (Levy, 1996).
- Plan backwards. Begin with the most essential and insightful "big ideas," concepts, or principles that will shape teaching and learning in a course or unit of study. Then decide on the knowledge and skill students must acquire in order to make sense of, apply, and transfer these big ideas (Bain, 2004; Wiggins & McTighe, 2005).

• Be deliberate in considering various possibilities for essential questions. Ask what lies behind each possible question you generate. Consider which will ultimately help students see the power and importance of the learning before them and want to achieve understanding (Bain, 2004).

• Pull out, and draw students' attention to, what Levy (1996) calls "the genius" of every topic: "What is essential about the American Revolution? What is unique about the world of plants, what distinguishes them from all other forms of life? What is the genius of grammar? Finding the genius guides me in sorting through the pile of available information. It gives meaning and purpose to even the most mundane skills" (p. 30).

• Teach in alignment with the organizational system of the content area you are teaching and ensure that students are building new information and skills using that framework (Steele, 2009).

• Relate new knowledge to a student's existing knowledge or experiences (Bain, 2004; Love, 2020; Noddings, 2005).

• Ask students questions designed to draw out their experiences and questions that will help them project content and principles they are studying into the world. Levy (1996) offers this illustration: "[The question] 'If you were to disappear today, how might I find out something about your life?' prompts the children to think of the kind of records and artifacts that are evidence of their existence. Then I might ask, 'How do we know anything today about Paul Revere?' Having reflected on their own artifacts helps them understand the methods of the historian in interpreting the past" (p. 31).

• Draw on concepts, principles, and big ideas that are relevant to experiences and concerns across ethnic groups, geographies, and times, such as identity, culture, courage, power/powerlessness, and justice/injustice (Gay, 2018; Love, 2020).

• Help students discover how the essential questions and essential understandings they are learning about in a discipline are evident in other disciplines and in aspects of life beyond the classroom (Bain, 2004). Teach students to read concept maps that represent what they are studying and to create and use concept maps themselves.

• Be engaged in and passionate about the content you teach and its value for the world. Think of your class preparation as great meals you are preparing to nourish the development of your students; invite students to come sit at the table, enjoy what is before them, challenge it, and interact with others and with you about what they are experiencing and have experienced related to the ideas "on the table" (Bain, 2004).

• Design—or guide students in the design of—authentic summative applications of what they are learning so that it's clear to them that the work they do has purpose and so that they have practice applying and transferring what they learn (Bain, 2004).

3. What mental models or misconceptions will students bring with them to class that I will want to challenge? What information and skills will they need in order to revise their thinking?

• Knowledge is constructed from existing knowledge; it's not something that can just be imparted or received. Therefore, it is critical to draw out and pay attention to the incomplete understandings, false beliefs, or naïve explanations of concepts that learners bring to class with them. If we ignore their initial ideas and beliefs, the understandings they develop may be quite different than ones we intend (National Research Council, 2000).

• Think about the most common misconceptions or misunderstandings students might have about a topic they will study soon and create a pre-assessment that asks students to share what they know about these "facts," ideas, or theories. This provides an early window into thinking that may be a barrier to student learning and will suggest areas in which you will need to help students reconstruct their thinking. Be alert to other misconceptions that may arise later in the unit or study (Wiggins & McTighe, 2005).

• Include items on most if not all assessments that call on students to explain concepts, theories, processes, or big ideas. When reviewing their responses, look for gaps they may have between an accurate understanding and a misunderstanding or misconception (Wiggins & McTighe, 2005).

• Use a variety of models and strategies to help students integrate new knowledge with their current knowledge and to understand and form principles that represent the content and discipline(s) in which they are working (Steele, 2009). This means developing a repertoire of models and strategies (e.g., inquiry-based learning, reflective writing, synectics, Socratic circles, community-based learning, case-based learning, problem-based learning, concept attainment, concept development, producing hypotheses, supporting a hypothesis with evidence, making inferences) and using these strategies to respond to both the nature of the content and the nature of the students you teach.

• Give students plenty of opportunity to talk with you and one another about lesson content; this is how they develop and refine their understanding. As France (2020) notes, "It is through discourse and discussion that children are able to wrestle with idea, recognize their own misconceptions, and channel background knowledge to communicate distinct ideas with clarity and precision" (p. 39).

4. How will I help students who have difficulty understanding and using reason and evidence to answer the big questions? How will I help those who lack background knowledge and skills? How will I extend the learning of all students?

• Pay close attention to individual students' starting points and their progress—both on learning tasks (Gay, 2018; Wiliam, 2001a) and on goals related to autonomy, agency, and collaboration.

• Have faith in each student's ability to achieve and express this faith in varied ways to individuals and the class as a whole. Ensure challenging expectations for all students and provide the support and encouragement necessary for success (Bain, 2004).

• Connect new information to prior learning or experiences. You might use analogies or comparisons to familiar objects, movies, life at school, the student's community, and so on (Bain, 2004). Levy's advice is to ask, "What experiences have the children had that are miniature examples of the principle or concept I want them to understand?" (1996, p. 31). When they have not had any such experiences, look for ways to provide one before going forward with the instruction via demonstrations, real or virtual field trips, and so on.

• Distill or simplify major principles and complex ideas to the point where they are clear enough for students to get a foothold. Help students grapple with ideas and information in order to construct a more complete understanding (Bain, 2004).

• Provide flexibility in assignments and assessments in ways that broadly draw on students' individual strengths, experiences, and goals (National Academies of Science, Engineering, and Medicine, 2018).

• Present projects and performances as opportunities rather than commands. Guide students to see how their work is important and can make a difference for the world and for their own growth. Early on, walk students through components of the work, making certain that they understand what it requires and how to accomplish its challenges. Then gradually shift power to the students so that they have increasing ownership of their work (Bain, 2004).

- Understand the extra burden placed on some students by geography, physical or emotional challenges, financial status, and injustices related to race, culture, religion, gender, and sexual orientation. Work to counter those extra weights (Bain, 2004; Love, 2000).

- Teach through multiple modes. Incorporate videos, music, pictures, art, student movement, stories, demonstrations, concept maps, modeling, and so on (Love, 2020; Steele, 2009).

- Understand that students from some cultures best express learning in ways that can combine movement, rhythm, music, art, high levels of energy and sensory stimulation, storytelling, emphasis on emotion and feeling, and social connectedness rather than in more traditional, mechanistic modes. Providing opportunity to learn in those modes opens the way to affective engagement for far more learners (Gay, 2018; Love, 2020).

- Based on observation and other formative assessment information, adapt instruction to include opportunities for students to gain necessary background knowledge and skill and opportunities for students who already show mastery to encounter a new challenge that will further their learning (Steele, 2009). Make sure that added "challenge" brings intellectual stimulation and is not just additional work or hard labor.

- Provide social scaffolding to complement learning interventions. This might include training in thinking critically, talking analytically about learning problems, and explicitly teaching social knowledge and skills that support effective interaction in school and society (Gay, 2018).

- Many students who do well in school do not develop good understandings or the capacity to think and think about their own thinking because they have become "performance learners" who work to please teachers or to make top grades rather than to become deep thinkers and questioners who pursue understanding. We need to move them from mere performance learning to those levels of deeper and more meaningful learning through example, mentoring, and the assignments we propose for them in order to help them understand more deeply and recognize the nature of the learning that is open to them. To that end, teachers need also to understand the emotional conflicts that prevent highly capable students from engaging in this more meaningful kind of learning (Bain, 2004).

- When students have difficulty in class, look first at potential problems in your lesson design rather than assume students' preparation or intelligence is the main factor (Bain, 2004).

5. How will I help students stretch their thinking? How can I help them deal with multiple perspectives on questions or issues?

• Help students become metacognitive—more aware of their thinking—by expecting them to make sense of new information and ideas and ask for clarification when something does not seem to make sense to them (National Research Council, 2000).

• In class discussions, ask questions that require analytical thinking, synthesis, critique, and consideration of multiple sides of an issue. Create assignments and products that call on students to look at an issue, problem, or topic through varied lenses and, when appropriate, require them to use analysis with evidence, synthesis, or evaluation to sift through and draw conclusions about the varied vantage points they have explored.

• Pose complex questions but provide ample time for students to think, jot notes, or share ideas with others before seeking student responses. Ask them to reflect aloud on their thinking as they respond (Black & Wiliam, 1998) and prompt them to build on one another's responses.

• When presenting a problem or complex issue, give students a choice between different possible answers or responses and ask them to vote on their choice. Collect the responses and read a few to the class, encouraging students to expand on their responses (Black & Wiliam, 1998). Have students meet in triads or quads to debate the choices. Then take the vote again.

• Minimize the practice of calling on students with raised hands, which gives students a choice to opt out and affords only a few students the opportunity to increase their academic prospects (Wiliam, 2011a).

6. How will I find out what students' hopes and expectations are for the course and what their interests are? How will I address those hopes, expectations, and interests to support learning?

• Remember that all students want to learn; the challenge is to figure out *what* they want to learn and find some common ground. While you likely have a better grasp of what learning a discipline would entail, your students will prioritize learning based on what they view as important and useful to them. Start with the experience and interests of students and patiently forge connections to the content in your curriculum (Noddings, 2005).

• Survey students early in each semester to get a sense of their interests. You might also distribute a list of critical questions you plan to address in upcoming units ask them to indicate their level of interest in these inquiries. Encourage students to dig more deeply into topics or connections to topics that are intriguing to them (Bain, 2004; Levy, 1996).

- Root student investigations, products, and performances in the key concepts, skills, and knowledge of the disciplines in which they are working, then give students the opportunity to decide as many details of the work as is feasible to encourage motivation, competence, autonomy, and collaboration (Fullan et al., 2018).

7. How will I help students learn to learn, to examine and assess their own learning, and to read more thoughtfully, analytically, and actively?

- Teach, model, assess for, and commend the attitudes, skills, and habits of mind that undergird learning and success. These include self-awareness, open-mindedness, active listening, empathy, appreciation of diversity, flexible thinking, metacognition, striving for accuracy and quality, appreciation, questioning, ethical responsibility, clarity of communication, decision-making, learning to learn, collaboration/teamwork, self-regulation, sense making, seeking multiple perspectives, responsible risk taking, thinking creatively, and thinking logically (CASEL, 2019; Costa & Kallick, 2008; France, 2020; Gall, Gall, Jacobsen, & Bullock, 1990; Rimm-Kaufman, 2020). Significant gaps in these areas can be barriers to academic, intellectual, affective, and social success. Remember that learners' development in regard to these attitudes, skills, and habits of mind will vary widely at any age, and it is unwise to assume important building blocks are in place.

- Embrace the responsibility to help students become better, more self-conscious learners who use the procedures and standards of the discipline in their work (Bain, 2004).

- Be certain all students have a clear picture of the learning targets. Students are generally good at assessing themselves and one another, but only when they know what they are meant to attain. Emphasize the overarching rationale of the work to counter students' tendency to see schoolwork as a set of arbitrary exercises (Black & Wiliam, 1998).

- Call students' attention to what is unique and distinctive about the reading material associated with a lesson or class. Break reading into identifiable strategies, being sure to use strategies suited to the discipline. (For example, in science, it is often useful to look for classification, process, problem solving, and experimentation patterns in the text in order to better understand how it is organized and what sorts of questions it will present, explore, or answer. In history, students may find it helpful to look for the story the text is telling, causes and effects that drive the story, and methods the writer uses that lead you to find the story reliable or cause you to be uncertain of its accuracy.) Model reading and analytical thinking regularly in class and give students opportunities to grapple collaboratively with complex text (Bain, 2004).

• Focus less on *your* "classroom performance" and more on getting students actively involved (Bain, 2004).

• Teach students how to clarify the goals they are working toward; think about, give, and use feedback in individual and group contexts; transfer knowledge from one form or context to another; connect big ideas with their own experiences; reflect critically on their beliefs, thoughts, and actions; think analytically and creatively; and think about themselves as change agents in the world around them. They need to know when something makes sense or doesn't, realize when they need more information, consider the strategies they might use to understand someone else's meaning, identify the kind of evidence they need to accept particular claims, and be capable of building and testing their own theories (Berger et al., 2014; Gay, 2018; National Research Council, 2000).

• Use classroom activities that focus on sense making, self-assessment, and reflection—skills that they will need to assume more responsibility for the learning process (National Research Council, 2000).

• Structure the class in a way that encourages students to learn and benefit from their own mistakes (Bain, 2004).

• Ask students to keep a work diary that describes what they are learning, steps they are following to achieve goals, indicators of their progress, their level of confidence in their work, and their perceptions about the quality of a final product or performance (Hattie, 2012).

8. *How will I find out how students are learning before summatively assessing them, and how will I provide feedback before and separate from any summative assessment?*

• Build in opportunities for students to express their understanding during instruction through class discussions, homework, projects, performances, and teacher–student conversations (Black & Wiliam, 1998).

• Use formative assessment to refine instructional plans so that they more effectively reduce the gap between where a student currently is relative to learning goals/intentions and where the student needs to be (Heritage, 2010).

• Watch students carefully as they work independently, interact with peers in small groups, and participate in class discussions. Look for patterns in what you see and adjust what comes next in response to those patterns (Bain, 2004).

• Regularly engage students in understanding their own growth toward learning goals and developing the skills and attitudes necessary to support their own learning success (Heritage, 2010).

• Ask students to think aloud during lesson activities, and maintain a non-threatening atmosphere in which they feel safe to do so. Give them opportunities to struggle with their thoughts without threat of assessment or judgment and to come up short, receive feedback on their efforts, and try again before facing any grading (Bain, 2004).

9. *How will I find out what my students already know as we begin to work together? How can my students and I best understand the nature, progress, and quality of their learning throughout our time together? What are effective ways to determine how they are developing intellectually? Whether they are reasoning well? Whether they have and can use essential knowledge and skill?*

• Create assignments and performances that ask students to use essential knowledge and essential skill to act on an essential understanding. This might include asking them to support the understanding with evidence, take a different position on the meaning of the understanding than one reflected in current content, relate the understanding to their own life, compare how the understanding applies in another time or setting or problem, create an analogy for the understanding with a non-school-related pursuit, or illustrate the understanding in different content areas or different segments of the same content area (Tomlinson, Kaplan et al., 2009; Wiggins & McTighe, 2005).

• Develop in-class assignments that call on students to use the aimed-for knowledge, skills, and understandings and examine possible misconceptions. Observe student thinking and conversation as they work (Earl, 2013).

• Demonstrate to students through words and actions that you are as interested in how they are growing as thinkers as you are in how well they do on assignments (Bain, 2004).

• Provide stories, illustrations, case studies, or scenarios related to target content and ask students to respond or propose solutions in ways that apply essential knowledge, skills, and understanding. Be sure the directions for the work include indicators of quality.

• Help students design ways to think about and extend their own learning. For example, you might guide their creation of protocols, reflection stems, checklists, interior monologues, interviews, and so on (Bain, 2004).

10. How can I interact with my students in a way that fuels their interest, curiosity, motivation, and thinking? How can I ensure that they interact with one another in ways that support understanding?

• Let students see your passion for a topic and its ideas—ensure that they see your joy in learning about it. Help them identify and develop their passions as well.

• Look for "stories" within the content you teach and try presenting it that way, with progression from beginning to middle to end, and with dramatic tension between a protagonist and antagonist. "What's the story of a plant?" Levy (1996) asks by way of example. As he points out, "[Young people] pay attention to a story… a story keeps all the children involved and motivated. It facilitates memory and increases understanding" (pp. 31–32).

• Set appropriately challenging goals and structure groupings, discussions, and assignments to support students in achieving the goals (Hattie, 2012). The goals must be challenging enough to maintain student engagement but not so difficult that they lead to discouragement (Wiliam, 2011a).

• Plan opportunities within each class session for students to grapple with ideas and issues or problems in small groups and to propose, present, and defend solutions to the problems.

• Teach the skills of collaboration (e.g., respect, empathy, self-awareness, appreciation of diversity, careful listening, communicating clearly, asking fruitful questions, building consensus, seeking multiple perspectives, recognizing the contributions of others, resilience, apologizing when called for). Observe students as they work to understand which of those skills they are using effectively and which they are not yet applying. Continue to engage individual groups and the class as a whole in figuring out how to make their collaborative work support and extend their learning (Gay, 2018).

• Use discussion protocols for collaborative work when students would benefit from guidance and structure in this area (Berger et al., 2014).

• Use voice, body language, pauses, careful listening, appropriate humor, storytelling, and questioning to stress the importance of what students are learning and their involvement in learning it. Make sure you are consistently reflecting your enthusiasm for both the content you teach and the students you teach (Bain, 2004; Steele, 2009).

• Create activities that allow for a wide range of participation inclusive of various developmental and content-mastery stages.

• Learn about students' cultures and first languages and design activities to honor and build on both. While teaching English is a goal of classrooms in the United States, all students can expand their language awareness and ability to communicate by learning about the varied patterns and perspectives that are consistent across languages. Remember, to indicate in any way that any learner's language is "less than" is to make the learner feel "less than" as well, curtailing both communication and enthusiasm for learning (Gay, 2018; Love, 2020).

• Use questions that reflect the question-asking patterns of varied cultures. Examples might include questions designed to seek a "right" answer, questions that invite expressive input, and questions that encourage storytelling or sharing experiences (National Research Council, 2000).

• Build student trust in you as you listen and respond to their ideas, and build trust among students as you help them learn to work together successfully.

11. How can I make clear the standards for quality work we will use in class and help students understand why those standards are significant and learn to assess their own work using those standards? How can I support each of my students in reaching for excellence?

• Support students in learning how to judge the quality of their own work fairly, accurately, and productively (Bain, 2004).

• Guide students in observing and understanding the goals and standards of the discipline so they can do work that mirrors that of practitioners, producers, creators, or problem solvers in the field. This might mean working from theories that are important in the discipline, posing questions that reflect the structure and concerns in the field, learning to use tools and processes that enable independent learning or research in the discipline, sharing learning in ways that practitioners share their findings, pursuing standards of quality work in the discipline, and so on (Tomlinson, Kaplan et al., 2009).

• Ensure that most student work, class discussions, teacher–student conversations, and feedback focus on understanding and development, and call students' attention to this practice. For example, ask them to consider and answer questions like these: "What evidence of your development can you offer?" "What is valuable in this piece of work?" "In what ways does your work exhibit deep thinking?" and "What meaningful contributions are you making to the group?" (Bain, 2004).

- Provide models that illustrate what quality work looks like. As Berger (2015) observes, "Showing students… models of beautiful, sophisticated work, created in their school or schools like their own, creates a ripple effect among those students about what is possible" (para. 11).

- Provide students with stakes-free practice analyzing the quality of work by sharing work samples from past years' students (with no identifiers attached) along with those assignments' learning targets and criteria for success. Ask them to discuss which elements in the various pieces are strong or weak and why (Earl, 2013).

- Remember that not all learning can be pre-scripted. Give students opportunities to suggest alternate learning intentions (learning goals/outcomes) and success criteria—as long as they are related to the mission of the lesson, unit, or product at hand (Hattie, 2012).

12. How can I create assignments that students will find fascinating—authentic tasks that will arouse curiosity and challenge their thinking? How will I create a safe learning environment in which students can tackle these assignments with optimism and be willing to try, fail, receive feedback, and try again?

- Explore the possibilities of play. Students tend to progress through an important stage of playfulness with ideas before they are ready for serious, deep work in the subject and before they actually seek corrective feedback in order to grow in the discipline (Bloom, 1985). Teach to evoke curiosity, joy, and passion in students. Premature seriousness kills the joy that is nearly always a precursor to passion. Perseverance is important, and all students can learn it, but passion comes first (Duckworth, 2020).

- Provide for open-ended exploration. Dedicate a significant portion of class time and homework time to meaning-rich challenges that will not have readily evident solutions, that will call on students to do both divergent and convergent thinking, and that will engage students with both curiosity and the uncertainty that nearly always accompanies invention (Fullan et al., 2018).

- Normalize failure. Students learn through making errors, receiving feedback on errors, and examining the errors. If each student is appropriately challenged, all of them will make errors, and analysis of error can become a class norm. Everyone should be bewildered at various points in a learning cycle. Failure is the gateway to learning for every student (Fullan et al., 2018; Hattie, 2012).

• Balance assignments so that students have opportunities to build on strengths and develop competence in areas that are difficult for them (Steele, 2009).

• Emphasize growth over speed and ease. Let students know that you see complex learning as a path that is often uneven and uncertain. Your goal is for them to learn from the difficulties they encounter; to make sure that happens, you'll be coaching, mentoring, and providing feedback for them along the way. Stress to students that you are more interested in where they end up than you are in how rapidly they work. Then be sure to enact that perspective when issuing grades (Bain, 2004; O'Connor, 2010).

• Connect students with the mentors they need. As students dig deeper into areas of personal interest, they may need mentoring beyond what you can offer. Explore opportunities to link these students with practitioners in the field who can extend their capacity and help them become creative producers (Bloom, 1985).

• Allow retakes. Settings in which students can retake tests, or take different versions of a test, reinforce to students that the work they are doing is challenging, but with practice and support, they can meet the challenge (Duckworth in McKibben, 2018).

• Conduct systematic reality checks on your instructional practices. Are your expectations for student work clear? Are students experiencing any major problems in accomplishing these expectations? How are student groups functioning? What are students connecting with in the content, what are they pleased with in their work, and why? What are their plans for the work's next steps? Use these check-ins to affirm your faith in their ability to accomplish high-quality work and your ability to assist them (Gay, 2018).

• Seek student input. Ask students, individually and as a group, what makes the class a good fit for them and what changes they would suggest to make it a better fit. When you incorporate their suggestions, point that out to the class (Gay, 2018).

In student-focused classrooms, and certainly during instruction (which claims the principal part of the school day), "every act centers around and ultimately springs from a concern for student learning" (Bain, 2004, p. 163). The goal is the fullest possible development of each learner intellectually, affectively, and socially. The principles and practices we've reviewed reflect that goal as seen through the lens of both research and real-life application.

For teachers who set their professional compass in this direction, every instructional moment is "another opportunity for pulling more from students and giving back more. Every hour is a chance to find out what works best. The job of improving instruction never ends" (Steele, 2009, p. 49). But engaged and inspired teachers would not want it any other way. They grow as their students do. They "use instructional insights and skills the way great painters use oils" (p. 50). To an observer, the practice of inspired teachers may look easy, natural, and obvious, but it is the fruit of years of growth and mastery and the reflection of deep commitment. Like the fictional version of artist Georges Seurat in the musical *Sunday in the Park with George*, these teachers apply themselves faithfully to the ongoing challenge of "bring[ing] order to the whole… through design, composition, balance, light, and harmony" (Sondheim & Lapine, 2000, pp. 575–576).

Analyzing Examples of Instruction in Learner-Focused Classrooms

Now, let's go through five different scenarios—all examples of instruction in learner-centered classrooms. These examples reflect different grade levels and subject areas, but the various teachers' instruction uses the questions, principles, and practices we've looked at in this chapter. You'll find prompts for analysis at the very end.

In a 2nd Grade Classroom

Ms. Jurey wanted to introduce her young students to several ideas about the concept of thinking—specifically that (1) people can think in different ways, (2) people can be aware of and think about their thinking, (3) different kinds of thinking can help us do better work and make better choices, and (4) we can learn to choose a kind of thinking that will help us in a particular situation.

Initially, she and her students studied the brain and learned that people can make their brains stronger just like they can make their bodies stronger—by working hard and making smart choices about how to work. Then, as the year progressed, Ms. Jurey and her students had many conversations about ways we can help our brains help us learn better. They talked about organizing learning into categories, connecting ideas to experiences, and focusing on goals during work. They devoted time to figuring out how math works and how to use feedback from the teacher and classmates to create improved drafts of important work.

Throughout the year, students learned language related to thinking as it applied to current work they were doing. At one point, for example, they learned about and applied the terms *convergent* and *divergent* to work they were doing in math and writing. They ultimately concluded as a class that getting the right answer to a math problem called for a convergent solution, but that they might arrive at the correct solution more often if they tried divergent routes to solving the problem when they got stuck along the way. They also decided that while informational writing calls for convergence more often than writing fiction, both kinds of writing can be more effective if the writer understands when and how to use both convergent and divergent thinking.

As Ms. Jurey's students shared products and performances with their classmates, it was common for them to introduce their work with comments like "You'll see me *working with comprehension* when I explain the main idea of my project. You'll see me *applying what I learned* when I propose a solution to the problem my work addressed. You'll see me *evaluating my work* when I explain to you where it meets the criteria for success in our rubric."

The 2nd graders began to use terms and practices related to thinking in both their classroom and out-of-school lives. They also pointed to evolving evidence that using their brains in smart ways made them both work smarter and feel smarter.

In Middle School Math

Tracy Frank and her colleagues saw homework as a critical tool for furthering their students' mathematical thinking and understanding. They set out to clarify the various purposes homework assignments might serve, including reinforcing a lesson's concepts, translating previously learned concepts into more complex contexts or to deeper levels, previewing upcoming lessons, teaching simple concepts not covered in a lesson, and providing opportunities for enrichment or extension.

To help themselves mindfully attend to these various purposes—and to encourage their math learners to push ahead with challenging problems—Ms. Frank and her colleagues labeled every problem in their homework sets as "green light," "yellow light," or "red light." Green light problems were required review exercises accessible to all students. Yellow light problems were generally extensions of a day's lesson or a preview on an upcoming lesson and were optional for all students. In some cases, students could exchange green light problems for yellow light problems if they felt confident they knew the green light material well. Red light problems, generally extension or enrichment problems, were also optional for all students.

Ms. Frank and her colleagues found that using this Traffic Lights strategy, which gave students voice and choice in modifying both the content and length of a homework assignment, both was empowering to students and resulted in increased student engagement in the review and preview process.

In High School U.S. History

Most of Mr. Locado's students had never left the small mountain town where their school is located. As they began their course in U.S. history, several of them explained to their teacher that they felt both separated *and* separate from the rest of the country, which they largely knew only through television, movies, and popular music.

Mr. Locado's instructional approach was to use the familiar to help his students think about and connect to the unfamiliar. He felt that if he and his students reflected first on what it meant to live in their time and place, they would be better prepared to ask the same questions about other times and places in the United States—and better prepared to recognize similarities and differences between their life in a rural, mountainous, coal-mining region in 2018 and life in other places and times in the country.

So he challenged the students to answer this question: "What does it mean to live in coal-mining country in your time?"

Drawing on an approach called Entry Points that stems from the work of Howard Gardner, Mr. Locado introduced five "windows into a world." He wanted the students to dig deeply into the meanings of their time and place by using one of five "lenses" to probe that meaning. Students could select from these options:

• A narrational approach to learning about and sharing what they learned through words and stories;

• A quantitative, number-oriented investigation through data and records;

• A foundational or philosophical investigation of background history, roots, beliefs, and rationales;

• An aesthetic approach to understanding grounded in art, music, dance, and drama; or

• An experiential investigation through personal experiences and the experiences of others.

Each student chose an entry point of interest to them individually. Then, during the 10-day period students spent looking for information and examples through their lens of choice, Mr. Locado played interviews from the American Folklife Center and shared data sets that revealed trends in health, population shifts, occupations, income ranges, and contributors to local economies from areas outside their own. He guided paired, small-group, and class discussions of both the content and perspectives offered by the various examples students found. Mr. Locado provided the class with a rubric that indicated criteria for quality work in the areas of planning, research, expression, and interpretation, and he conducted one-on-one conversations with each student throughout the research period to keep them on track.

In the end, each student presented three examples (interviews, stories, songs, data sets, news reports, personal reflections, photographs, family histories, artifacts, etc.) that they considered meaningful representatives of their research, explained why they selected these examples to share with the group, and explained each example's significance for answering the question of what it means to live in coal-mining country in their time. Mr. Locado could see his students were clearly interested and often moved by what their classmates shared and the commentaries that probed the meaning of the examples. This activity marked an important beginning for the students in realizing that the time and place in which they lived, as well as the history of that place, gave them a way to connect with and understand other times and places in a country that was, in fact, *theirs* too.

As the year progressed, students often specialized in different lenses to think more deeply about the various time periods and people they were studying. They continued to collect examples from their own culture to help them explore similarities and differences between their local world and the broader world of the United States. Mr. Locado also worked with the students to expand and refine the research and presentation processes and success criteria for their ongoing investigations. The time he and his students spent early in the year preparing for this first investigation set the stage for many more.

In High School Biology

Ms. Patel used "synthesis groups" throughout the year to focus her biology students on making meaning. At key points in every unit of study, she asked the groups to convene and bring together their growing knowledge on the topic at hand to push forward their own learning and that of their classmates.

The specific challenge for the group varied with each meeting, but students learned to be prepared to share their thinking clearly, to listen to one another carefully, to distill the group's best ideas and share them effectively, and to respond in an informed and appropriate way to questions and challenges from other groups. Students found the challenges of synthesis groups motivating and took pride in generating and sharing ideas that enlisted the thinking of classmates. They also said that the challenges caused them to think more deeply throughout the unit and left them better prepared for end-of-unit performance assessments.

One day, about three-quarters of the way through a unit on the human circulatory system, Ms. Patel issued the following synthesis group challenge:

> During today's class, I'd like you to work with your synthesis group to do the following:
>   1. Review and agree on the key understanding or principle that best reveals the meaning of, or helps you make sense of, or could be said to be "the punchline" for our study of the circulatory system.
>   2. Find at least two ways of expressing that key understanding or principle in relation to the contents of the unit—for example, an analogy, a concept map, a model, a meme, a Gary Larson–type cartoon, and so on.
>   3. Be sure each mode of expression
>   —Makes clear what the key understanding or principle is,
>   —Illustrates how it helps to make sense of what we have been studying, and
>   —Accurately shows how key knowledge and skills come together to form an understanding.
>   4. Be ready to present your group's work in four minutes or less.
>   5. Be sure everyone in your group can interpret both modes effectively and can address questions and challenges from your classmates.

In a Middle School, Across Content Areas

Teachers in a North Carolina middle school wanted to help their students begin to think deeply about doing quality work instead of just checking off requirements and collecting "points" for product completion. Teachers in several content areas worked together over the course of a semester to create a rubric that could guide classroom conversations about the habits that support quality work and focus student attention on quality as they completed major assignments.

First, the teachers debated categories they might include in the rubric that would speak to indicators of quality across disciplines. Ultimately, they concluded that "Quality of Thought," "Quality of Research," "Quality of Expression," and "Habits of Mind" were foundational in all their disciplines. Then they brainstormed long lists of attributes for each category—without comment, judgment, or revision. Once the group felt a brainstormed list for a category was complete, the teachers worked together to select items from the initial collection that seemed particularly relevant to the developmental stages of their students and to the content they taught. Finally, they debated how to "distribute" the indicators across a continuum of development. Repeating that process three more times, they found themselves occasionally moving an indicator from one category (row) to another, or from one column (level of quality) to another.

Early in their work, the teachers made three decisions that they felt would be important in student motivation and learning. First, they decided they would *not* equate a column with points or a point spread. Their goal was to keep the focus on quality of work. Second, they decided not to include a column that represented less than acceptable work. Third, they decided not to label the columns with familiar labels like good, progressing, apprentice, and so forth. They chose instead to stress growth and personal best goals. The teachers worked with each student or team of students to set goals in any column that their most recent work suggested would be steps forward for them. Teachers then spotlighted one or two of those goals as current personal best targets for the student or team and supported them in focusing on these targets throughout the work. Individual students and teams also had the option of adding one or two additional success criteria that were important to them.

Teachers adapted the rubric as necessary for a particular piece of work or student. Generally, however, the majority of the rubric indicators remained relatively constant within and across classes. Teachers and students worked throughout the year to examine, discuss, apply, get and give feedback on, and revise work based on the categories and criteria represented on the rubric. Both students and teachers agreed that the students' work was of higher quality than it was with earlier guides and supports.

Figure 8.1 shows the rubric categories and indicators in the categories. This format served as a common foundation from which teachers in all core subjects could craft a rubric that more precisely reflected specific content and related performance assessments. All teachers used it to ensure they emphasized the same

Figure 8.1: A generic cross–content area rubric to help students focus on quality work

Quality of Research	• Uses appropriate range of resources • Gives credit appropriately • Accurately captures key ideas and issues • Makes ideas his/her own, doesn't "copy and paste" • Carefully logs research process and sources	• Screens resources for the most valid or valuable options • Effectively blends ideas from several sources • Identifies patterns and themes in research • Synthesizes sources effectively	• Weighs evidence for positions from varied views and sources • Makes and supports generalizations that show depth of understanding • Raises questions that point to the next level of research
Quality of Thinking	• Poses and seeks answers for important questions • Uses logical progression of thought • Supports ideas with evidence	• Balances the big picture with detail • Elaborates thoughts effectively • Draws valid and supported conclusions from evidence • Makes connections • Shows evidence of self-aware thought	• Looks at ideas from varied viewpoints • Makes unexpected and important connections • Shows insight • Seeks creative approaches • Shows self-regulation of thought based on purpose
Quality of Expression	• Develops a flow of ideas that's easy to follow • Structures piece with a clear beginning, developed middle, and sound conclusion • Uses appropriate vocabulary • Shows work with mechanics	• Varies sentence structure effectively • Uses effective transitions to guide the reader • Structures the piece so the beginning catches audience attention, the middle is well-elaborated and supported, and the end captures the essence of the piece and "punches" key point(s) • Makes powerful word choices • Shows care and general accuracy with mechanics	• Shows development of own voice • Seems genuinely to care about ideas and issues • Uses effective imagery and figures of speech • Uses sophisticated, professional-like language • Uses strong mechanics throughout
Habits of Mind	• Thinks and plans before acting • Asks questions to ensure understanding • Evaluates own work according to established criteria • Listens to ideas and input of others • Shows periodic persistence • Attends to directions and goals	• Asks probing questions • Is aware of and reflects on own thinking processes • Applies knowledge to new situations • Persists with tasks despite difficulty • Proposes criteria to improve own work • Seeks and uses feedback for improvement	• Regularly seeks meaning and deeper understanding • Shows appreciation, pleasure, or wonder with learning • Adjusts thinking and work appropriately for task/situation • Respects perspectives different from own • Seeks quality more than comfort or ease • Is highly invested and engaged in work

valuable skills and habits of mind but did so in ways that enabled students to see how those skills and habits of mind were useful in varied contexts.

Figures 8.2 and 8.3 share one example of the rubric's use—with students in a U.S. history class during a unit on the American Revolution. The teacher, Mr. Lambert, framed the class's exploration of history around four key beliefs:

1. History tells the story of people in a given time and place.
2. History is best learned as a story, not as dates, names, and facts.
3. The stories of history help us understand ourselves and our world.
4. Students should learn to work as a historian does.

In the class's unit on the American Revolution, these four beliefs were evident in the work students were asked to do. Figure 8.2 provides an overview of a team product assignment. Figure 8.3 shows the rubric Mr. Lambert created for the unit by modestly modifying the generic rubric he and his colleagues developed.

Figure 8.2: Assignment highlights for a team research product

Name _____ Class Period _____

Here Comes the Revolution: Part 1
Assignment Highlights

KUDs for Part 1 of the Unit (leading up to the Revolution)

Know:

Terms (meaning & significance): colonies, colonists, American Revolution, King George, England, Britain, taxation, quartering soldiers, Townshend Acts, Stamp Acts, closing the western territories, restricted trade, repression, representation, revolution, evolution, 1776.

Key Fact: The American Revolution happened after the colonists had had a taste of freedom in the colonies for more than 10 years while England continued to try to control the colonies and colonists.

Understand:

About History & the Work of Historians

- History is a story about a people.
- There is almost always more than one way to interpret an event or series of events.
- Historians tell the stories of history based on the best information available related to the events, feelings, and people in the story.
- History should help us understand the multiple perspectives that surround events.
- Historians make a case by providing research evidence for what they believe is the most accurate and complete telling of the story possible.
- The themes of history often repeat across times and places.

About the Beginning of the American Revolution

- As people experience more freedoms and a better life, they often become unwilling to give up those things.
- Revolutions are often first evolutions.

Be Able to Do:

- Tell the story, with evidence, of how events and experiences in the colonies made the colonists increasingly unwilling to lose their new freedoms and expectations, ultimately leading to the American Revolution. (Part 1 of your Team Assignment)
- Make connections with countries in other parts of the world whose citizens are struggling against oppression for their freedom. (Part 2 of your Team Assignment—later in the semester)

The goal of Part 1 of your team's work is to (1) select five key events that took place before the American Revolution actually began, (2) research those events in trustworthy sources, (3) understand the cause and effect relationship between each event and the American Revolution, (4) select or propose a format for presenting, illustrating, and narrating cause and effect patterns of five key events or experiences in which British actions angered many colonists, ultimately contributing to the start of the Revolution. Your work should reflect your understanding and application of the unit's learning goals (KUDs).

Possible visual formats for your work include an animation, a video, an infographic, a dramatic monologue or dialogue, a children's book, a series of storyboards, or another format your group proposes to the teacher.

Whatever format you decide will best present your ideas, you will also need to (1) create a written explanation of the visual presentation, including details of the events and interpretations of those events that you gathered through research, and (2) a narrative that explains the research process you used and how you decided which information was accurate and representative of the varied perspectives of colonists about the five events and the idea of a revolt against England.

The rubric attached here should guide your work and help you evaluate the quality of the process your group follows, the worthiness of the story you tell, and the degree to which the story represents the variety of experiences and opinion of colonists who experienced the events that make up the story you tell. The teacher will give you feedback based on the rubric as you plan, as you work in class, when you turn in drafts, and after you present your work.

Your team will have time to work in class over the next month, but you will also need to complete and contribute individual work to support the success of your team's product.

Throughout the next month, we will explore and discuss the time period that your team's story will reflect. There will also be two check-in dates on which you will need to turn in drafts of your work so the teacher can give you feedback. You will also have opportunities to talk with the teacher about your ideas as you are working together in class.

Your team members are:

1)   3)

2)   4)

Your team's check-in dates are:

1)

2)

Figure 8.3: A rubric created by a middle school history teacher

Team Rubric for "Here Comes the Revolution"

Quality of Thought	• The question we are trying to answer in our work is clearly stated and explained. • The question is important for the goals of the assignment. • The order in which we present and explain our ideas is logical and clear to our audience.	• We use evidence that helps us tell "the story" of key events as well as providing details that support "the story." • We make useful connections across events and resources. • We explain our thinking so our audience understands clearly why we drew the conclusions we did and why we presented them as we did.	• We look at opinions of varied groups about a topic or event rather than assuming all colonists had the same beliefs and reactions. • Our connections are important and/or insightful. • Our approach to answering our question is original, appropriate, and surprising. • The method(s) we use to share our findings are original, appropriate, and surprising.
Quality of Research	• We use multiple resources to seek evidence that leads to the answer(s) we provide for our question. • We provide enough evidence to support our answers to the question. • The sources we use as evidence are reliable and trustworthy. • We use paraphrasing and direct quotations correctly.	• We screen sources to be sure they were valid. • We discover and explain themes or patterns that occurred across sources. • We effectively blend ideas and information from multiple sources into meaningful units rather than generally using ideas from one source at a time.	• We explain how we decided to use particular evidence or sources when the information in those sources was contradictory. • We make or support generalizations that show depth or breadth in our thinking. • We raise questions that point to the need for additional study, thinking and/or research.
Quality of Expression	• Our explanations are easy to read and understand. • We use vocabulary that shows our understanding of the events we explain. • We use cause and effect to tell an unfolding story with a beginning, middle, and end. • Our presentation shows attention to punctuation, spelling, and grammar.	• The beginning of our presentation sets up our question and the early events related to the question. The middle elaborates and supports details that happened over time. The end captures the outcomes and importance of the events. • We consistently use accurate punctuation, spelling, and grammar. • We vary sentence structure in narration effectively.	• Our presentation shows that we have developed "voice" as a researcher and/or as the characters or individuals we portray. • Our expression suggests that we genuinely care about the ideas, issues, and characters/individuals we introduce. • We use effective imagery and/or figures of speech. • We use language and mechanics like a professional would.

| Habits of Mind | • Our work reflects the intent of the assignment.
• We show evidence of evaluating the quality of our work based on the criteria for success.
• We ask for assistance to be sure we are working in a productive direction.
• We considered several options at key points in our work before moving ahead with next steps. | • We ask questions of one another, the teacher, and texts that demonstrate a desire to understand ideas with accuracy and depth.
• We use feedback to improve our work.
• We persist with the work when it is difficult or uncertain.
• We proposed criteria to improve our work. | • Our work indicates that we thought deeply with ideas we were considering.
• We work with our team in ways that enable us to adjust our thinking, decisions, and expression as needed.
• Our work indicates that we worked for quality rather than simply for completion of the assignment.
• Our group works effectively as a team. |

Success Indicator(s) Set by Your Team	How Success with the Indicator(s) Will Look

Figure note: This rubric is a customized version of the generic rubric in shown in Figure 8.1.

In Elementary Science

Ms. Brighton was a relatively new teacher. She wanted to help her students search for understanding in their science class, and she had a good sense of what it meant to organize and teach units based on concepts and corresponding principles. She could always derive one or two principles from a unit that she felt confident "got at" the core intent of the topic. However, Ms. Brighton was not confident in her ability to always find *all* the important concepts embedded in the content, or that the ones she did select were ones that would be most enlightening to her students. More to the point, she wanted her students to think about the unit content and discover meaning for themselves.

She talked with her students often about understanding versus remembering, pointing out that while it's important to remember and use important information, without understanding how a topic works, it's hard to apply what you remember in useful ways. They talked as a whole class about "concepts" (and how concepts help us organize and categorize information) and about "principles" (and how principles help us explain or elaborate on a concept). In most lessons, students were asked to relate a concept, a principle, or both to the content of the lesson, which helped them become more comfortable with the relationships among concepts, principles, and information.

The science room Ms. Brighton shared with her students had a wall-sized whiteboard on one side of the room. As each unit began, she would display a chart with 4 columns and about 10 rows. In column 1, she would write one or two principles that she felt were central to understanding and working with the lesson's concepts and tell the students that she was reasonably confident that these principles would help them understand the chapter or topic they were about to begin studying. Then she would issue the invitation for them to look for other principles that could help the class explain how the chapter or topic made sense—and perhaps help her polish the wording of the principles she had proposed. Students' contributions were added to column 1.

As the unit continued, Ms. Brighton would ask the students to focus on a specific principle (including those she had proposed) and work with thinking partners to show how it did or did not help explain what they were learning about. After these small-group exchanges and a larger class discussion, she would update the chart by placing an X in column 2 of the chart ("principle tested and accepted"), column 3 ("principle tested and rejected"), or column 4 ("principle's utility uncertain at this time"). The review and modification process continued throughout the unit, with students looking eagerly for principles they might offer to the class for testing. In this way, they become accustomed to making sense of content through the application of concepts and principles. Over time, the students transferred that process beyond science units to other content areas and to examples from their own lives.

Points to Consider

- Choose two or three of the scenarios here to reflect on as they relate to the ideas in this chapter and to your work. After you read through the scenarios you've selected a couple of times, refer back to the 12 questions that learner-centered teachers typically ask as they plan (or co-plan with their students), deliver, and review their instruction, beginning on page 176. Each scenario included in this section represents more than one of the questions and certainly more than one of the practices associated with the questions. Using highlighters, sticky notes, or notes, link the questions and practices in this chapter to specific events or practices within your selected scenarios.

• In each scenario you chose, first note which of the 12 questions you believe teachers were considering as they planned instruction for their students (or co-planned it with them). Then, reflect on how each of the practices reflects the teacher's beliefs about learners, learning, the role of the teacher in learner-centered classrooms, building community, curriculum design, and/or assessment.

Looking Ahead

Freeman Hrabowski, president of the University of Maryland, Baltimore County (UMBC), is firmly rooted in my pantheon of educators to emulate. Since beginning his role at UMBC in 1992, he has worked with his colleagues to re-imagine a school that was once a largely unheralded commuter college. Under his leadership, UMBC has become an innovative and successful university. One of its often-celebrated accomplishments is its record of supporting African Americans and other students of color in earning degrees in math and science. Many of those students now play cutting-edge roles in groundbreaking math and science research and applications throughout the United States. Hrabowski has been named one of America's best leaders, one of America's top 10 university presidents, and one of the most influential leaders in the world, among scores of other honors. He chaired President Obama's Advisory Committee on Education Excellence for African Americans and received an honorary doctorate from Harvard.

It is not his impressive list of honors that makes his work remarkable, of course; his remarkable work has led to the recognitions. The reason I have chosen to write about him here is because what Hrabowski and his colleagues do directly aligns with the beliefs and practices that this book advocates, explains, and illustrates.

In a *60 Minutes* feature (Schneider, 2011) examining the philosophy that drives UMBC faculty and their president, Hrabowski talks about his own work as a professor of higher mathematics. With an animated smile and a visible passion for teaching, he explains that when he and his students do math, they get goosebumps. When his astonished interviewer responds by saying, "Goosebumps? From doing math?" Hrabowski simply nods, smiles more broadly, and affirms, "We get goosebumps from doing math!"

The goosebumps don't come from checking off a list of completed problems, of course; they come from discoveries of principles and connections, from the insights that are characteristic outcomes of a kind of teaching that convinces each student that he or she is capable of mastering, applying, and even extending important ideas. They come from an environment in which respect is an inviolable norm, in which students see *one another* as teachers. The goosebumps happen because students in these places work to solve real problems in a very real and challenging world. They happen because of teachers' deep and abiding interest in each student and recognition that their role is to care *for* their students rather than simply care *about* them. Goosebumps happen in places where teachers' careful and detailed planning increases the likelihood that students will be able to make discoveries that fuel not only their next steps in learning but also their fulfillment through learning.

I see many of the characteristics of UMBC classrooms in the 12 questions that form the spine of this chapter. They are the kinds of questions that guide instructional planning in life-shaping classrooms from preschool through university doctoral studies. They are essential questions that excellent teachers learn, over time, to ask and to answer.

I hope you will have an opportunity to watch the *60 Minutes* visit to UMBC and to think about what you see in relation both to this book and to your own work. I also hope that you will see in Chapter 9 many of the principles and practices commended throughout the book, as that chapter explores several concepts that unify and provide grounding for those principles and practices.

 C3 C3 C3

9

Concepts That Unify the Elements of Learner-Centeredness

*We need people who are drawn to the profession not
because it is easy, but because it is hard—a job that is so
difficult that one's daily experience is of failure, but one where
each day, to quote, Samuel Beckett, one can "fail better."*

—Dylan Wiliam in "Teacher Quality: Why It Matters and How to Get More of It"

This chapter is devoted to three clusters of concepts that are foundational to learner-centered instruction: (1) equity and excellence; (2) expectations, challenge, and "teaching up"; and (3) flexibility and differentiation. All these concepts present challenges for teachers and the "systems" in which they teach. All are concepts that educators need to reexamine, see anew, and recommit to in order to become fully learner-centered. Although all of them have appeared in various forms and locations in this book, directly addressing them here is necessary, I believe, to highlight their centrality in achieving the goals of student-centeredness. They are the mortar that binds together everything we've examined to this point.

Teaching for Equity and Excellence

While equity and excellence are sometimes presented as competing variables, they are, or should be, conjoined aspirations in schools in a society that envisions education as a common pathway to opportunity for all. Indeed, the complex demands of the 21st century seem to mandate that every young person have equity of access to excellent learning opportunities in order to thrive in and contribute to the time in which they live. Both equity and excellence are variable commodities across contemporary schools, with full access to truly excellent learning opportunities likely far scarcer than many of us would like to admit.

Equity

Three quarters of a century ago, Mahatma Gandhi asserted, "My notion of democracy is that under it the weakest shall have the same opportunities as the strongest." The World Bank (2005) describes equity as equal access to the opportunities that allow people to pursue a life of their own choosing and that enable them to avoid extreme deprivations in outcomes. The struggle to actualize these definitions of equity in the United States (and many other parts of the world) has been protracted and significantly unrealized. Some may continue to debate about whether people who live in poverty are somehow responsible for their own plight or whether it is the result of societal structures that systematically impede opportunity for groups and individuals. It seems to me that we have, and have had, more compelling evidence for the latter, given the numerous inequities consciously and unconsciously embedded in institutions and policies that continue to act as barriers to opportunity that would otherwise be open to all members of a democratic society. In the 19th century, Charles Darwin declared, "If the misery of the poor be caused not by the laws of nature, but by our institutions, great is our sin."

In fact, policies at federal, state, and local levels confer preference by race, economic status, and geography, creating inequities in access to jobs, health care, housing, and quality education. Working in concert, those inequities perpetuate economic outcomes that now define low-income communities of color. Further, the inequities create societal divisions, undermine community, discourage civic participations, and lead to distrust in institutions that should equitably represent to all citizens the ideals of democracy.

Teachers cannot *directly* address disparities in housing, health care, wages, and so on, but many educators, and I am one of them, believe that high-quality learning opportunities can empower students to develop tools for addressing these inequities. In other words, teachers can prepare students to seize for themselves opportunities the status quo would deny them (Love, 2020). To echo Darwin, if we do not teach with that aim firmly in our sights, great is our sin.

The vision of learner-centered classrooms detailed in this book proposes that quality teaching places the student at the center of thinking, planning, teaching, and reflecting in order to guide each student in realizing and extending his or her intellectual, affective, and social capacities to the greatest extent possible. Realizing that goal requires us to provide

- A learning environment that summons the best efforts of each student;
- Curriculum rooted in the wisdom of the disciplines, designed to be relevant to student experiences and to focus on understanding, build students' thinking skills, and position them to use important skills and ideas in meaningful contexts;
- Assessment practices that enable the teacher to closely follow student growth and adjust learning experiences in ways that move each student forward and that enable each student to develop agency in their own learning; and
- Instruction that guides students in exploring their own strengths and interests, in understanding the significance of the critical knowledge and insights uncovered through time by human beings, and in developing the skills and habits of mind that undergird success as learners and citizens of the world.

An education premised on these principles and practices should be the right of every student—the eager, frightened, marginalized, impoverished, challenging, and challenged. Every one of them. That's a tall order, but no other purpose appropriately serves the young people we teach, the society in which we live, or our profession.

Excellence

The term *excellence* can be defined through both "exclusive" and "inclusive" lenses. Seen through an exclusive lens, *excellence* refers to "pinnacle performance"—the three-time Super Bowl champs, the Nobel or Pulitzer recipient, the inventor whose work changes the course of a generation. Excellent schools should, and do, contribute to pinnacle outcomes.

But that contribution shouldn't come at the cost of a more inclusive definition of excellence, which is about setting and achieving a high standard, doing work of distinction, doing work that's valuable. Aristotle suggested that excellence is not an act but a habit. Looked at in that way, excellence means aspiring, believing in one's capacity to grow, working toward goals or criteria that are personally challenging, studying quality work, developing the skills of success, working with commitment, and being willing to do the unglamorous work necessary to create a high-quality product.

Ron Berger, author of *An Ethic of Excellence* (2003) and chief program offi-cer of Expeditionary Learning schools, agrees that what we might think of as A-level work reflects achievement that is exceptional and of high quality. How-ever, he argues that this designation is not intended to be impossible to achieve or even rare. It is intended to recognize when a student's work on a particular assignment, or in the class overall, reflects a high degree of sophistication and craftsmanship achieved through stringent revision, persistent preparation, and careful execution—the outcome of applying the *habits* of excellence. Berger explains that teachers who seek to "open up" excellence for a range of learners are careful to craft long-term targets in such a way that each student knows what it means to meet these targets and achieve exemplary status. Those teachers also fully support students throughout the process of creating quality work. In this view, "excellence" is not a status accorded lightly. It applies only to products that give clear evidence of meeting or exceeding high standards. Berger contends that teachers can mentor excellence in many students and that many students can learn and apply the habits of excellence (Berger et al., 2014).

The aims, principles, and practices of learner-centered instruction focus squarely on helping young people pursue quality in intellectual/cognitive, affec-tive, and social domains. A learner-centered teacher does not envision excellence in these three domains as the purview of a narrow band of students; it's to be attainable by all, through guidance and instruction the teacher provides. Equity, then, is not the enemy of excellence, as policymakers seem to have assumed (Wiliam, 2011a). Our schools can and should aspire to achieve both simultane-ously and for the full spectrum of learners.

Similarly, empathy and rigor are not antithetical. Learner-centeredness leads to classrooms in which students develop empathy and respect for their peers and learn to work as teams to enable each learner (equity) to succeed to such a degree that they consistently and successfully push against what they have perceived to be the limits of their capacity (excellence). Learner-centeredness is *not* a guaran-tee of "A work" or a promise of excellence for everyone, but it *is* an invitation for each student to aspire to accomplish things that "lift them up."

Marva Collins (1992), an educator known as a champion of equity and excel-lence for students living in poverty, says she discouraged her students from being average, adding that she believed each of her students could learn significantly so long as she did not teach them that they could not. She explains, "I will teach them to think for themselves... to have the fortitude to build their own bridges... to face unflinchingly the problems of life as a challenge of living... never to rest on their past laurels… to know that excellence is a never-ending process and that they will never arrive in the land of the done." As a result, Collins expected her students to "light the world with excellence, with self-determination, with pride" (p. 262).

This is an inclusive definition of excellence, not a diluted one. The "equity hypothesis" (Fullan et al., 2018, p. 24) proposes tackling inequity through universal pursuit of excellence, arguing that "deep learning" (becoming productive learners, thinking like global citizens, working collaboratively, functioning creatively, and thinking critically) is necessary for all students but that it may be even more advantageous for students who have been previously alienated and underserved in school. Teaching for excellence is, therefore, the most likely path to equity in schools.

Expectations, Challenge, and "Teaching Up"

At a point during my high school years when it was a stretch for me to see myself as even marginally competent in any aspect of school, my German teacher asked me to help her plan a statewide language conference for high school students. Another teacher asked me if I would like to conduct a research study on the relationship between student grades and access to a car in high school. I was sure they were asking the wrong person but too timid to say so. I knew I would be a failure and embarrass myself and my teachers. I hoped they would realize they had made a serious error in presenting those options to *me*, but in light of my total lack of ability to speak up, I started down both paths in a state of terror.

As it turned out, these undertakings were life changing. In both instances, the teachers seemed unwavering in their conviction that the work I was doing would meet the professional-level standards they had established. Both treated me as though I could reason and fill in the gaps that stood between where I began and a successful conclusion. Both talked with me and coached me as though I were more colleague than student. By the end of that year, I could barely reconcile who I had become with who I was when I entered their classes. It took me a couple of decades to understand what had provoked the transformation.

Expectations

Many students—I'd argue most—are astute observers of the expectations that teachers hold for them and tend to live up (or down) to those expectations.

One of the most compelling moments I can recall from the Olympic Games had nothing to do with a medal ceremony or the competition that led up to a medal. It occurred in a first-round qualifying heat in swimming, when a young man representing his small African nation walked onto the pool deck with terror in his eyes. He was a runner who had been recruited by his country to represent it in the Olympic swimming competition so that their slot would not go unfilled. As I recall, he had trained for only a few months prior to the competition and never in an Olympic-sized pool.

It was clear from the first moment he began to propel himself forward that he was in trouble. He flailed, gasped for air, and flailed some more. Observers in the stands stood with hands over their mouths. They followed his progress up and down the pool as he got further and further behind his competitors and more and more depleted of oxygen. In time, the spectators began shouting encouragement to him and clapping. Long after all the other swimmers in his heat had completed the required laps, he struggled on, meter by painful meter.

As an armchair observer, I was alternatively terrified for the swimmer and angry that no one on the sidelines jumped in to help him. When he finally finished the race, too exhausted and breathless to stand, a reporter approached him. "You appeared to be struggling," she said, stating the obvious. He nodded. "Was it as hard for you to swim as it seemed?" His response indicated he thought he might drown. "If you were that frightened," the reporter asked, "why didn't you just get out of the pool?" The answer he gave spoke to my deepest experiences as a young learner and my deepest conviction about teaching. Still fighting for air, he pointed to the stands and said, "All those people were cheering for me. I couldn't let them down."

In a classroom where the teacher both literally and figuratively cheers on each student and supports each student along the uncertain road to producing high-quality work, equity and excellence come together on behalf of all students—including those who would typically be on the school's sidelines. Wiliam (2011a) asserts, with research backing him up, that "education *can* compensate for the failures of society, provided that education is of high quality." In the study Wiliam cites, in the classrooms of teachers whose students made the most progress, students from disadvantaged backgrounds made just as much progress as those from advantaged backgrounds, and students with behavioral disorders made just as much progress as those with no such diagnoses. Those teachers expected great things from each of their students and engineered the classroom to turn those expectations into realities.

Measure this approach against our long-standing proclivities to label students and then to "track," "stream," or "group" them accordingly. From a very early age, children are fully aware of which classrooms or groups within a classroom are viewed as deficient. The struggles of children deemed "lesser than" are magnified by the practice of sorting based on perceived limitations, and their sense of efficacy continues its downward spiral. Hattie (2012) observes that educators love labels. While acknowledging that the issues to which we attach labels are real, he objects to the way we medicalize the labels and then use them to classify young people and to explain why a student can't learn.

The intent behind what we think of incorrectly as "ability grouping" may be well meaning, but the results are nonetheless generally destructive. Students move from low groups to tracked classes as they transition from elementary school to middle and high school. In low-track, low-status classes, students of color or from low-income backgrounds occupy most of the seats. Often in these classes, as Gay (2018) observes, "instruction is emotionally flat and intellectually dull.... Approaches emphasize teacher dominance, didactic and large-group teaching, a narrow range of learning activities, workbook assignments, and very little interactive dialogue" (p. 63). Hattie (2009, 2012) isn't a fan of ability grouping either, ranking it a lowly #131 out of 150 influences on student academic growth and at one point referring to it as a disaster.

There's further support for the "disaster" verdict in a recent study that found 40 percent of all racial segregation occurred as a result of tracking *within schools* rather than differences between schools with imbalanced resources. Tracking leaves Black and Hispanic students isolated in low-track classes at higher rates than their White and Asian American peers. They have less access to advanced courses, further education, and ultimately occupations that provide health care and support a tenable life for themselves and their families (Sparks, 2020). As we expect less of students, they expect less of themselves, and these low expectations are fulfilled. For all these reasons, there is no place for low expectations at the classroom, school, district, or national level—no place in policy or in practice.

Challenge

"If you would hit the mark, you must aim a little above it. Every arrow that flies feels the attraction of the earth." Those words, penned by Henry Wadsworth Longfellow in 1882, have stood the test of time. It is still the case that the gravitational pull of "good enough" is strong and that humans must extend their reach to escape that undertow. This is the case in the classroom as in most other arenas.

Challenging oneself and being challenged by others is key to extending one's reach.

The concept of challenge is a personal one, both in and out of the classroom. In the classroom, it is relative to a student's current performance with and understanding of particular learning intentions and success criteria (Hattie, 2012). It is not about ability but readiness—not a prediction of future ceilings of accomplishment but an indicator of the next steps in a particular segment of learning (see Sousa & Tomlinson, 2018; Tomlinson, 2017).

Much has been written about the importance of providing the right level of challenge for individuals (versus the right level of challenge for "the class"), and the consensus is that the challenge for a learner should not be so difficult that the student sees it as unattainable based on his or her prior achievement, self-efficacy, or confidence. Rather, both the student and the teacher should be able to see a pathway by which the student can meet the challenging goal. The pathway can involve teacher support, including strategies for reaching the goal, steps to follow, and a commitment on both the teacher's and student's parts to reach it (Hattie, 2012).

The appropriate level of challenge has been described in a variety of ways, including zone of proximal development, moderate challenge, desirable difficulty, just manageable difficulties, realistic challenge, and optimal challenge. In each instance, the term refers to work that stretches the student, makes the outcome seem a little uncertain but not hopeless, and calls on the student to leverage current competencies and strengths to reach a higher level of competency and strength. Appropriate challenge persistently asks a student to take his or her next step in growth—a step that, in the beginning, feels a bit too long. Especially for young people who do not see themselves as learners, the route that leads to excellence demands many next steps to next levels. Those steps involve acquiring the knowledge, understanding, skills, and habits of mind and work that are precursors to excellence. Each step taken, each new level of competency and strength attained, proves to students who doubt themselves that they can do better today than yesterday, better next week than this one, and better this year than they have ever done before. In that way, the steps elicit the motivation to persist.

These interim steps, of course, should escalate in difficulty as the learner grows. "Personal best" goals have a strong relationship to educational aspiration, enjoyment of school, class participation, and persistence with the work at hand (Martin in Hattie, 2012). Early on, personal best goals may need to be suggested by the teacher, but the student needs to participate in establishing those goals and ultimately take charge of that process as quickly as is feasible.

"Teaching Up"

The articulated rationale for placing students in groups or tracks based on a perception of ability is that it allows the teacher to teach those students "where they are." The fallacy, of course, is that teaching them where they are while other students work at more advanced levels is likely to result in the low-track/low-group students falling increasingly behind. There are absolutely times when a student needs to work with a problematic math skill or a reading competency in order to move forward, but those times should not characterize or dominate or dilute the student's academic experience. They should not trigger the creation of identifiable peer groups in which everyone is, or is perceived to be, a low performer. (We'll look further at this point in the next section of the chapter.)

"Teaching up" calls on teachers to build a baseline of rich, meaningful, "deep" learning experiences for all students. Teachers who teach up help all students form a conceptual understanding of the disciplines. They connect what students learn to the students' lives and ensure that all students address significant issues using essential knowledge and skills, regularly collaborate with peers whose entry points and interests are both similar and dissimilar to their own, examine varied perspectives, and create authentic products for meaningful audiences. These teachers ensure classrooms are literacy-rich and incorporate a wide range of resources that relate to student interests and support student learning. They teach using a wide range of strategies and approaches. They work to ensure that each student develops the skills of independence, self-direction, collaboration, and production that are necessary for success. They commend excellence as a way of life and demonstrate to learners the satisfaction that comes from accepting a challenge and investing one's best effort in achieving it. They know that when tasks help students make sense of important ideas, are highly relevant to students' life experiences, and are scaffolded so that they are moderately challenging for students with varied levels of achievement and experience, their students will be motivated to do the hard work that is the hallmark of excellence (Tomlinson & Javius, 2012).

Teaching up advocates that the teacher first develop instructional plans that would provide invigorating, meaning-making learning experiences that would engage the curiosity and interest of advanced students, then incorporate supports or scaffolding that would make it possible for students whose foundational knowledge and skills are currently less developed to access and successfully participate in those learning experiences. The supports can take a great many forms, depending on the needs of the learner and the nature of the task. In classrooms where teaching up is a way of life, high ceilings and tall ladders are hallmarks. Figure 9.1 provides varied examples of scaffolding.

There are two points to remember. First, when work is appropriately challenging for each learner in a classroom, everyone in that classroom will need scaffolding at some points. Second, scaffolding is temporary, designed to support a student until he or she learns a process or skill. As in building construction, there should be a timeline and plan for taking the scaffolding down.

Flexibility and Differentiation

I observed a 3rd grade teacher once in a school where differentiation had been an emphasis for a couple of years. My goal was to get a sense of each teacher's strengths and needs in creating a classroom that could work well for each student. As the class began, this teacher said in a voice that would have impressed an Army battalion, "I want *these* students [she called their names] to come sit where I'm standing now. I want *this next group of students* [more names] to go stand near the wall by the door." The orders continued until she had formed four groups. No one talked. No one made eye contact with the teacher. Continuing in the same tone, she gave each group a task to do, reminded them to work silently, and stood in the front of the room watching. In one group, students were supposed to collaborate to figure out how to build a specified structure. No student in that group ever spoke. In about 5-minute intervals, she told the students to stand and walk clockwise to the next place their classmates had been working, to sit down quietly and do the work at that place. At the end of an excruciating 40 minutes, the teacher directed the students to "go back where they belonged when class started" and to do that silently. When everyone was in place, she barked at the group in her drill-sergeant voice, "We just did differentiation! Wasn't that fun?" Every student in the class obediently nodded in affirmation—except one small boy in the back of the room who crossed his eyes, stuck out his tongue, and shook his head back and forth. I wanted to hug that little guy.

Figure 9.1: Strategies for scaffolding student learning

- Use peer collaboration on work that draws on multiple abilities and perspectives and (whenever possible) allows student choice for mode of expression.
- Ensure that learning targets and criteria for success are clear to students and that students know how to use them as guides for quality work.
- Streamline directions to focus students on the core essentials of the work.
- Ensure student access to content sources at varied levels of complexity, in varied media, and in varied languages.
- Lead class discussions about the work at regular intervals during an assignment.
- Help students connect the work to their own experiences and interests.
- Write directions in streamlined language, and/or with more white space, and/or using bullets.
- Provide models of quality work just above a student's comfort level.
- Use graphic organizers, charts, or pictures that guide students in various aspects of reading, research, product design, etc.
- Provide video explanations of assignments that any student can access for review throughout the duration of the work.
- Offer mini-workshops or mini-lessons to teach skills, develop ideas, refine work, or address student-suggested aspects of the work during the duration of the assignment.
- Use word walls, concept maps, glossaries, advance organizers, and other tools that support student understanding and thinking.
- Break assignments into chunks so that the work feels more manageable.
- Use multiple media and modes when teaching content and sharing directions for student work.
- Make time for learning specialists to consult with students on their work.
- Review draft work in one-on-one conversations or peer groups at regular check-in dates.
- Encourage early submission of drafts for teacher feedback with time for students to revise prior to handing in the final product.
- Lead small-group discussions on skills, processes, and topics related to student work.
- Support positive student use of peer consultation in online environments (e.g., Google Hangouts, Zoom chat rooms).
- Allow students to do the work in their first language before translating it into English.
- Include student-developed goals for both skills and "personal best" work in assignments.
- Use flexible timelines.
- Use targeted skills-practice sessions (exit ramps).
- Use modeling strategies like think-alouds and fishbowls.
- Check regularly for student understanding relative to the meaning and organization of the content and processes that will lead to task success.
- Use "hint cards" in the room that remind students how to do things they have learned earlier but may have forgotten or didn't quite learn.
- Monitor student work during classwork sessions and online to provide clear in-process feedback.

What else would you add?

Flexibility

Flexibility can be defined as the ability to cope with change and think about tasks in novel and creative ways—especially when unexpected events or stressors occur. That characterizes how I have come to think about flexibility in the class-room. It does not suggest that flexibility and chaos are kin, as some people fear. Rather, to me, it suggests beginning the day, class period, and school year with your best plan to address the needs of the people you teach in relation to the content you teach. It also suggests to me that no matter how carefully a teacher crafts a lesson or learning experience to be responsive to the varied and contin-ually shifting needs of his or her students, there is likely to be a time (assuming the teacher is observant and willing to act on observation) when something in the plan is not working for someone in the room—or for several someones. The question then is fairly clear-cut: *Do we remain faithful to the original plan, or do we adapt to the unexpected?* Often the better response is to opt for spontaneous flexibility within planned flexibility.

Without a doubt, there are times when rigidity is the way to go. There's no room for compromise when teaching a child to look right and left twice before crossing a street. School safety drills call for universal adherence to guidelines. A soldier's day is highly likely to take a wrong turn if he or she disregards or tries to debate the wisdom of the commander's order. Generally, however, when work-ing with people (including young people), there is wisdom in flexibility—both planned and spontaneous.

When a student (or two or three or a dozen) gets fidgety or chatty in the middle of an assignment in class, that's a signal that something in the plan is not working. Ignoring the signal is unlikely to benefit the student, teacher, or class. Everyone will be better served if the teacher does something to cope with the unexpected moment and think in novel and creative ways about what will work to move the student or the class ahead. When a troubling event happens at school or in the news, the choice presents itself again: plow ahead as planned, or seize a teachable moment unrelated to the day's content? Now imagine you have a student with a history of being "disconnected" in class who has now been work-ing with enthusiastic commitment on a project that is due in two days. It's clear that he won't finish the work by the deadline, despite his best efforts. Do you stick with that due date anyway, or work out an alternative plan for the student?

Circumstances differ, as do students' needs and bell schedules and class moods and magical moments. There's no answer key that can tell us whether Plan A or Plan B is the correct choice in all times and contexts. Nonetheless, making room for humanness in classrooms will often point toward flexibility rather than rigidity in unanticipated moments. Those are examples of *unplanned* flexibility governed by a teacher's internal compass or informed common sense.

Teachers who place students at the center of teaching and learning also incorporate *planned* flexibility, noting things like the following:

• Here's a spot when I want to give students a choice of how to demonstrate what they have learned.

• Here's a time when it makes sense to ask students to select a homework assignment option that's likely to help them solidify their current learning.

• I want to ask the students to change working partners three times in today's lesson, but I understand that introducing the assignment so that students are prepared to do it well might take longer than I anticipate. So . . .

　— *If we have less than 10 minutes left* when we approach the third change, I'll stop with two partner rotations and ask students to write their best headline for the meaning of the work they've done.

　— *If we have 10–15 minutes left*, I'll ask students to form "human graphs" by lining up to share their opinions on key controversies connected to the lesson.

　— *If we have 15 or more minutes left*, we're good to go for the third partner rotation.

Teachers who work toward the goals and values of learner-centered instruction come to understand that giving students voice, helping them make meaning of content (vs. covering it), and guiding them to develop agency as learners is not a by-the-clock proposition. They do the very best planning they can in order to honor both the content they teach and the humans they ask to learn it. They build flexibility into those plans because they understand the unpredictability of growing up and of learning. And they tune their instincts to respond humanely and productively to moments when unplanned flexibility may well be the most constructive option. *Flexibility* is almost—but not quite—a synonym for *differentiation*.

Differentiation

Over the years, I have defined or described differentiation in a variety of ways to help my university students and groups of teachers with whom I have been privileged to work extend their thinking about what differentiation means. Figure 9.2 shares some of those descriptions.

Figure 9.2: Some definitions of differentiation

Responsive teaching versus one-size-fits-all teaching	Shaking up what goes on in the classroom, so learners have voice and options for learning, making sense of what they learn, and sharing what they learn.
A way of thinking about the classroom aimed at honoring each student's learning needs and maximizing each student's capacity while developing a dependable community of learners	Planning for the unpredictability of the classroom
Proactively planning varied pathways to what students need to learn, how they might learn it, and how they might show what they have learned as fully as possible	Looking eyeball to eyeball at the reality that kids differ and that the best teachers do whatever it takes to hook the whole range of kids on learning
Respectful teaching	Teaching so that all kinds of kids can effectively learn together—not just occupy the same space, but actually learn and grow well together

What else would you add?

I've also metaphorically presented differentiation as a "learning journey" that requires both "highways" and "exit ramps" to ensure that students have both shared learning experiences and learning experiences that are specific to their needs and interests. On the highway, everyone explores the big ideas of the discipline or topic they are studying together. The highway also provides shared time to discuss ideas, ask questions, make suggestions to one another for successful work, and share products, performances, or applications of their learning.

Highways include time to develop a shared understanding of what it means to create a learning place designed to work for every student, to get to know one another more fully throughout the year, to laugh together and sometimes mourn together, to celebrate when celebrations are in order, and to reflect together on how we are growing and who we are becoming. The highway also includes opportunities for student collaboration when all of the collaborative groups are working with the same essential knowledge, understandings, or skills—even though the collaborative teams may approach goals in different ways. The highways are also critical to teaching up, because it is here that every student accesses the most important ideas and skills, discusses and debates them, and shares their applications. It is here that everyone learns what it means to reason—to use evidence to support ideas or opinions. It is here that "an ethic of excellence" is acted out with the full expectation that every student is part of the quest for engaged learning and quality work.

Exit ramps provide time for "patching holes" in an individual's learning, for exploring and extending interests, for pushing beyond the expectations of the curriculum design plan, for assessing one's progress both individually and with the teacher. Much effective differentiation can and should happen on the highway as, for example, a teacher presents information in varied modes, takes care with language so that students who are new to the language can understand and participate, uses examples that relate to student interests, calls on students in ways that build both knowledge and trust, checks for understanding, and adjusts accordingly. However, the exit ramps provide the most consistent opportunities to address an individual's learning needs, interests, and talents. Here, a teacher may support the success of an English language learner by front-loading vocabulary or previewing an upcoming article or text chapter, help a student with a learning disability work through or around the problem areas, and spend important time helping a student who is an advanced achiever discover and chart learning frontiers that are well beyond the perimeters of the curriculum. Exit ramps include times when students may be developing particular skills that are necessary for their own forward movement in an inquiry or an upcoming performance task. On exit ramps, a teacher will regularly meet with small groups of students and individual students to help them get back on track after an extended absence from school or to address a misconception that's evident in their work or contributions to class discussion.

Differentiation requires flexibility to address both group and individual needs. Highways and exit ramps provide that flexibility and opportunity. More to the point, highways and exit ramps, flexibility, and differentiation are all ways to proactively plan for the confluence of equity and excellence for each learner in the classroom. They are the architecture of teaching up, enabling each learner to participate in learning challenging content as well as to work on precursor knowledge and skills that are necessary for forward momentum. Figure 9.3 depicts and briefly summarizes the metaphor of highways and exit ramps.

In somewhat more academic contexts, I have described differentiation as a teacher's proactive response to learner needs, shaped by a growth mindset and guided by five general principles of differentiation:

1. An environment that encourages and supports learning;
2. Quality curriculum;
3. Assessment that informs teaching and learning;
4. Instruction that responds to learner variance; and
5. Leading students and managing classroom routines.

Teachers can differentiate through content, process, product, and affect/learning environment in response to student readiness, interests, and learning preferences through a variety of instructional strategies (see Sousa & Tomlinson, 2018; Tomlinson, 2014).

Figure 9.3: Some examples of highway and exit ramp use in learner-centered classrooms

THE HIGHWAY

In a learner-centered classroom, all students are on the highway with the teacher when

- It's time for students to get to know one another, share ideas, or celebrate.
- It's time for class meetings or discussions.
- It's time to introduce a unit or topic.
- There's information all students need to encounter, try out, or discuss in order to move forward in the unit, topic, or inquiry.
- It's time to introduce and extend concepts, principles, or big ideas.
- There's a need to share successes or concerns.
- There's a need for the teacher and students to work together on plans for curriculum and instruction, to share resources, or to create products.

EXIT RAMPS

In a learner-centered classroom, students use exit ramps for

- Small-group or individual instruction.
- Individual or small-group inquiry or problem-based work.
- Student specialty or expert-group work.
- Student-specific practice.
- Planning independent inquiries, products, performances.
- Student–teacher conferences.
- Giving and receiving peer feedback.

You will likely notice in these definitions key themes and vocabulary that permeate this book. The naturalist John Muir reflected that when we try to pick out anything in the universe by itself, we find it hitched to everything else in the universe. The major classroom elements of differentiation (environment, curriculum, assessment, instruction, classroom organization) *are* the elements all teachers use every day, whether we name them or not. They also help organize much research, teaching, and discourse about education. They belong in all discussions of quality practice, including but certainly not limited to differentiation and student-centeredness.

Likewise, equity and excellence are bound to one another and require persistent attention to both universal high standards and to individual development. In that way, the pair is interwoven with learner-centeredness and differentiation. Learner-centeredness, by definition, requires attention to individual needs and strengths in order to maximize individual growth; thus, learner-centeredness also requires differentiation. Differentiation is a non-negotiable for achieving equity as it is for achieving excellence. When we think carefully, each thread, or theme, in the book is inextricably linked to the others.

In writing about differentiation, for example, Paul France (2020) explicitly and implicitly writes about equity, excellence, honoring the individual, challenge, high expectations, empathy, learning environment, curriculum, and teaching up. Consider these observations:

• "Equity is not about giving all children the same experience or tool; it's not about providing each child a unique playlist of activities. We promote equity when we differentiate the supports given to each child, supports based on individual needs that remove barriers and help them gain access to the same high-quality education as their peers" (p. 4).

• "By building a curriculum and a classroom environment that allows for varied entry points into the same learning experiences, we allow all learners to get what they need without anyone being excluded" (p. 34).

• "Differentiation...entails engineering equitable learning environments that meet the needs of all learners, allowing for points of convergence and divergence within a multi-ability curriculum and removing barriers for vulnerable populations rather than inadvertently creating more. We can promote equity by humanizing our pedagogy and creating classrooms where diversity is expected, and inclusion is intentional" (p. 34).

There is no way to make learner-centeredness a reality without recognizing the cognitive/intellectual, affective, and social differences among learners—related to strengths and needs—and attending to them vigorously and consistently. Learner-centeredness and differentiation are inseparable. I like Lisa Westman's conclusion that "differentiation is what happens when teachers focus on student growth" (2018, p. 15) and would add that differentiation will happen on multiple levels when teachers focus on student academic, social, and affective growth.

Looking Ahead

I hope that by shining this spotlight on the concepts of equity, excellence, high expectations, teaching up, flexibility, and differentiation I have helped you see them as boldface considerations of a learner-centered teacher. These three clusters of concepts are at once foundational to everything else you have read about learner-centeredness and manifestations of its philosophy, principles, and practices.

The next chapter, the final one in this book, presents three scenarios of learner-centered teachers at work in their classrooms. The examples differ from those in earlier chapters in at least two significant ways. First, they are longer and more detailed than the earlier illustrations because they bring together the various elements of learner-centeredness that provide the architecture for this book. You'll get a sense of the teacher that is a bit more multifaceted than was possible in the shorter examples, a little bit of a wider lens on how curriculum turns into instruction, and a little deeper understanding of various ways teachers use formative assessment to benefit teaching and learning. You'll be better able to see how the elements of learner-centeredness work together to support the success of *the* student and the *students*.

The three illustrations are also different from earlier ones in that the teachers whose classrooms we will "visit" provided the information from which I built the scenarios. In every instance, I interviewed the teacher at length—and often several times. The teachers provided resources such as videos, the opportunity to interview students, samples of student work, curriculum documents, links to sources students drew on in their work, and so on. Each of the teachers reviewed their scenario—again, often several times—making suggestions for edits so the end result would accurately portray their work as they see it. As a result of these measures, you'll get a much clearer sense of the teacher's voice, beliefs, and reflections than in the earlier and briefer examples that are dependent on my memory of a teacher's work. I hope the illustrations help you better envision learner-centeredness in action in classrooms at different grade levels, with a variety of student populations, and with different approaches to curriculum and instruction. The examples, then, serve as a reminder that *quality learner-centered practices* provide a reliable compass to guide the work of teachers. They offer a broad array of approaches to and models for teaching, from direct instruction to inquiry from academic teams to product-based learning, from workshop-based to community-based learning. The success of any approach to teaching rests on the teacher's will and skill in applying our best knowledge of what constitutes quality practice *within* that approach.

CŞ CŞ CŞ

10

Inside Some
Learner-Centered Classrooms

Teaching is both an art and a science. Excellent teaching requires both as surely as humans require both breathing in and breathing out. A teacher who sets out to create an excellent practice will, along the way, become a student and a practitioner of both the art and science of teaching.

The first nine chapters in this book begin with quotes from educators whose insights have inspired and guided my own practice. This final chapter, which is largely constructed around the experiences of learner-centered educators and conveyed in their own voices, begins with words of my own, which I used as a catalyst for discussion in a university class I taught.

Most of the chapters in this book capsule our current understanding of quality educational practice in one aspect or element of teaching, describe links between that element and learner-centeredness, and finally illustrate how that element might look when translated into classroom practice. This chapter also provides images of learner-centered classrooms. The examples that follow, however, differ from earlier ones in that they provide "big picture" looks into classrooms where the teachers plan and implement those plans with *the* student and the *students* firmly in the center of all they do. They show us how the various parts of learner-centeredness become the whole.

The contexts in which these three teachers work with their students are markedly different from one another in many ways. One is an elementary school, one is a middle school, and one is a high school. Students are working with biology in one example, with history in another, and with reading and science in the third. Students in one of the schools come almost exclusively from homes in which there is often too little money to feed the family well or provide the kind of "extras" that families just a few blocks away take for granted. One of the schools accepts students by lottery without regard to income, race, or neighborhood boundaries. One of the schools is more cross-sectional, serving students who come from a defined but large geographic area and represent a broad range of backgrounds and experiences. In one of the schools, teachers work together almost daily to create and modify interdisciplinary curriculum designed to engage students at multiple grade levels. In another school, teachers use an instructional model developed by a research group to help students learn discipline-based content in conjunction with literacy skills while they develop agency as learners. The third site would probably qualify as a more "traditional" school. There, too, teacher creativity is evident in the way teachers work continually to know each student beyond the surface, to know content beyond just the facts, and to craft learning experiences that dignify both the students and the content.

On the other hand, there are some noteworthy similarities across the schools. All three administer the state-mandated standardized test late in the school year, but none of them ask or require their teachers to follow scripted curriculum or pacing guides. All three teachers you'll meet shortly would tell you that their work focuses on finding dynamic ways to help young people learn content that can make a difference in their lives—not on preparing students for a test. In all three schools, teachers are treated as professionals accountable to the expectation that they will use their content knowledge, familiarity with the standards derived from that content, and understanding of their students to craft learning experiences that directly address the strengths and needs of individuals and the class as a whole. All three of the teachers who share examples of their work in this chapter focus on cognitive, affective, and social development of their students and teach with a design to foster development of each student in all three of those areas.

As in past chapters, this one provides prompts for reflection. While reading the examples, I also urge you to look back at notes you may have taken throughout the book, passages you have underlined, or the table of contents as a reminder of the topics you have read about. Refer to figures you found useful. And keep these questions in mind:

- In what ways do the teachers in these scenarios reflect key ideas in the chapter on learner-centered teachers?

- How do the curricula they use exemplify quality curriculum? In what ways does the understanding of students and of instruction these teachers come to mirror the objectives of formative assessment as it's described in this book?

- Where do you see explicit or implicit connections with equity, excellence, flexibility, high expectations, ethics, and values? Review the questions that frame Chapter 8 and consider how these teachers seem to answer those questions in their practice.

While each of the examples here is longer than those in preceding chapters, the examples are still, necessarily, capsules of student and teacher experiences. My hope is that they will inspire you to ask and pursue answers to questions about your own life as a professional and about your own practice. In the end, I think, it's asking ourselves these probing questions and pursuing answers that matters most. There is no one right answer, after all, and when you do think you've found an answer, I believe (and hope) you'll find that the answer will continue to change as you continue to grow.

Helping Students Own Their Learning

Shelby Bellamy teaches 2nd graders at William D. Moseley Elementary School in Putnam County, Florida. In 2017, Moseley was the fifth-lowest-performing traditional public school in the entire state. As part of turning the school around, Mrs. Bellamy and other Moseley teachers began to use a new instructional process called student-led academic teaming*, which was developed by Learning Sciences International's (LSI's) Applied Research Center. In just two years, Moseley rose from a low-F letter grade in Florida's accountability system to a C. School leaders and faculty aspire to become an "A" school and believe they are on the way. In addition to the gains in academic achievement, Moseley saw improvement in social-emotional learning, academic rigor, and students taking true ownership of their own learning. Shelby Bellamy and Taylor Barahona from LSI collaborated on the account that follows.

---

*For more information on academic teaming, see Toth & Sousa (2019) or https://www.learningsciences.com/.

It's mid-morning, and Mrs. Bellamy has just delivered a mini-lesson to acquaint her students with science vocabulary she knows will be useful to them in today's assignment. She takes care not to "over-teach" the words, knowing how it is important for her 2nd graders to unlock the *significance* of the terms themselves, working as scientists do to draw on current knowledge in order to discover new knowledge.

Mini-lessons are a trusted part of Mrs. Bellamy's instructional toolkit. On other days, and with other subject areas, she might model for the students how to look for context clues if they encounter an unfamiliar word in a text or share a think-aloud about how to use a chart or photograph as a tool for understanding text. She has seen how giving students regular opportunities to watch their teacher puzzle out a word or try different approaches to unlock meaning gives them confidence that they can do so as well.

The question Mrs. Bellamy's students will explore in their academic teams today is *How are flowers and pine cones alike?* It's a question based on a science standard related to the life cycles of plants, and they'll be approaching it after having already learned about different types of plant life cycles in a prior lesson. The "big idea" of life cycles helps student focus on what's essential in the content and connect the various investigations they conduct.

Notably, when sharing the day's questions Mrs. Bellamy does not specifically ask the students to compare the life cycles of plants and pine cones. She knows that her students need to realize for themselves that focusing on the concept of life cycles (and not exclusively on sets of facts or details about plants and pine cones) rather than solely on a set of facts or details, they have found the key to what makes flowers and pine cones alike.

Students Own Every Lesson

As they usually do, the 2nd graders are working in their academic teams—typically groups of four students who work together toward a common academic goal. Once these heterogeneous academic teams are established, membership remains consistent over a period of about nine weeks so that members can learn to share the same vision and values, work together almost seamlessly, trust one another, and support one another's growth. Two key student roles on academic teams are the facilitator, who leads the team and ensures that all students participate equally, and the learning monitor, who continually tracks the group's progress toward meeting those criteria. Sometimes Mrs. Bellamy asks students to fill other roles as well.

The learning target for today's science lesson is actually derived from a reading standard: *I can describe the connection between a series of historical events, scientific ideas or concepts, or steps in technical procedures in a text.* The success criteria are (1) *I can identify the most important events, ideas, or steps in a text,* and (2) *I can explain how the events, ideas, or steps are connected.* As Mrs. Bellamy and her colleagues plan lessons together, they regularly connect reading targets to a variety of content-area texts so that their students become accustomed to applying reading skills in whatever they read.

Each Monday, Mrs. Bellamy gives every student a chart that lists the week's learning targets, success criteria, the mini-lessons she will lead, their academic teaming tasks, and exit ticket questions. Although they are only 2nd graders, each student knows how to use the chart to see what each lesson requires of them and what success in that lesson will look like.

Once in their academic teams, students discuss the lesson's learning target and success criteria. Mrs. Bellamy monitors these discussions closely, pausing at each table to listen attentively to each team's conversation. If students accurately explain the learning target and what it will mean to achieve the success criteria, she knows the team is ready to move ahead. If the early discussion suggests their grasp of the lesson isn't clear, then she poses a "small" prompting question to the team, designed to help students rethink their current understanding. In cases where the group's interpretation is just a little off course, she asks the clarifying question and moves on without waiting for an answer. If the team's explanation indicates significant misunderstanding, she waits to hear the group response to her question. If necessary, she prompts again. Her goal is not to redirect the students herself, but rather to enable them to redirect themselves. Complete student ownership of the work is a key aim of student academic teams.

Next, each team establishes a plan for its work. Today, Step 1 calls for students to read a text segment related to the question for the activity. Sometimes the students "whisper read" to themselves so Mrs. Bellamy can hear them if she leans in and listens closely. Sometimes they decide to read in pairs or to have one student read the text aloud to the group. Teams often make this latter choice when one or more team members struggle with reading. They take seriously their responsibility to support one another's success.

Today, after the reading is complete, students work independently to summarize their thinking about the lesson's question, informed by both their prior knowledge and the content in the reading. To make their thinking public, they write their summaries on a corner of a "learning mat" that rests in the center of their table. The team members then share their summaries, discuss each student's ideas, debate various options for answering the day's question, come to a consensus on a team answer, and write the consensus answer in the center of the learning mat. To help students work efficiently and with focus, Mrs. Bellamy breaks the process into steps or stages, using a timer to let students know when they should be completing a segment of work. As students develop greater agency. individually and as a group, they will be able to manage their own time more effectively.

Students Support One Another's Success

As the teams move through the stages of their work, it's common to hear the 8-year-olds ask one another questions such as "What strategy did you use to figure that out?" and "Where in the text is your evidence for that idea?" Challenging one another's thinking is a way of ensuring both group and individual understanding.

If any team member has a question or encounters a problem, that student knows to first consult teammates for help. If the team cannot help unravel the problem, the student would turn next to another team. Everyone knows they can also go to Mrs. Bellamy for help, but they know too that working first with peers to address a dilemma or gap in understanding helps them all become more autonomous learners.

As in all classes, there are times when a student struggles, feels lost, wants to give up, or is just out of sorts. Today, Emma, an English learner, is having a hard time understanding a word in the text and is getting frustrated. Her teammate, Lily, realizing that Emma is bogged down, turns to help her, but she knows better than to just give Emma the answer, because that would not help her learn. Lily asks Emma a sequence of probing questions, waiting quietly for Emma's response after each one. Other team members add helpful comments as well, including a reminder to use context clues to try to make sense of words. Mrs. Bellamy watches the exchange from a distance, pleased to see that Emma's productive struggle, in the end, deepens her learning. Emma not only figures out the meaning of that particular frustrating word but also gets the satisfaction of succeeding with a challenge that seemed out of reach just a few minutes before.

As she watches the group, Mrs. Bellamy reflects on how academic teaming supports students' social growth as well as their academic growth. Emma has taken her work seriously since coming to Moseley Elementary, but before entering Mrs. Bellamy's class and participating in academic teaming, she didn't talk with other students or play with them on the playground. In fact, Emma was so quiet that it took teachers a very long time to realize she had a significant language impairment beyond the challenge of learning a new language. Now, as a result of the bonding that happens among students on their teams and the opportunity teams provide for safe dialogue and contributions, Emma's social skills and confidence have soared. She not only interacts with her teammates consistently as they work together but plays with them as well. The combination of "push and support" on the teams gives her much-needed oral language practice and academic vocabulary acquisition and also helps her feel like a contributing part of a team—accepted, cared about, and supporting the success of every other member.

Mrs. Bellamy has been struck by how teaming allows students to shine in ways they don't or can't in a more traditional teacher-centered classroom. "Working alone most of the time, many students aren't going to be able to meet expectations; in the teams, they speak each other's language, they say things in a way that an adult might not say them, and they have a level of comfort they will never have with adults," she says. "It's just different when they learn from peers and when they learn how to work together successfully. And they develop a level of agency in the teams that I just didn't see in our students before we began using academic teams."

She refers to another student who came into her class having already attended four other schools. It was quickly evident that he couldn't read, and he only rarely spoke. The idea of being on a team was frightening to him, and he was embarrassed by his lack of literacy. But his team didn't judge him, and with their help, he began demonstrating both academic growth and social growth on an almost daily basis. While he couldn't read text at first, he could comprehend well when it was read to him, so while his teammates helped him with learning to read, he helped them understand what they had read. Now, when a student on his team is frustrated like he used to be, he will say to the student, "You don't need to be frustrated. We can figure this out. Let's work through this together!" If you ask Mrs. Bellamy, academic teams changed this boy's life. He went from rarely having anyone in his corner to having a whole team—a whole class, a whole learning community—he can count on.

Ongoing Assessment Is Key to Teacher and Student Success

As the pine cone lesson comes to an end, Mrs. Bellamy asks the teams to share their team summaries with the class and leads them in discussing and synthesizing what they learned in the lesson. Her pleasure in the students' thinking is evident.

After the discussion, each student completes the exit ticket for the lesson—a slip of paper posing a question that is related, but not identical, to the question for the lesson and calls on students to understand what they were exploring and transfer it to a slightly different context in order to answer. Also on each exit ticket is space for students to assess their own individual progress toward the learning target. The information Mrs. Bellamy gleans from exit ticket responses and exit ticket self-assessments, from team reports, and from class discussion, combined with her careful observation and systematic recording of responses during student teaming, keeps her well aware of individual, team, and class growth and learning needs. Based on what she learns, she regularly provides feedback to students and also conducts "micro interventions" with teams and individuals, as well as "full interventions" with small groups of students pulled from their groups for a short time to work directly with targeted needs.

In addition to her own persistent tracking of student progress, Mrs. Bellamy involves her students in understanding their own progress as well as the progress of their team and of the class as a whole. She notes, "My students know which targets they have and have not met before they begin a new team task. They have to be able to explain the targets so that if someone in their group hasn't yet met one of them, they are ready to help that learner move forward."

After a few more lessons, each academic team will create a comic strip that demonstrates their understanding of what life cycles are and how they work. The main character will be a plant of the team's choice, which they must both depict and describe. Mrs. Bellamy points out that the stepwise format of a comic strip is well suited to depicting the stepwise sequence of a life cycle, and the students eagerly accept the challenge of generating work that not only is accurate but also communicates clearly and demonstrates their creativity. Mrs. Bellamy smiles as she recalls the energy and creativity that last year's students displayed as they worked, including one group that named their plant "Laura-Phil" as a play on the word *chlorophyll*.

The classroom in which Mrs. Bellamy and her students work is now a place that nurtures and extends each student and their teacher. Academic teaming has proven to be a learner-centered catalyst for the academic, emotional, and social development of each student and for all-around growth of their learning community.

Helping Students Grow into a Community of Active Learners

Community Middle School in Charlottesville, Virginia, is a lab school that is part of Albemarle County Public Schools. Students from anywhere in the Albemarle district can apply for admission and are admitted by lottery. The school's charge is to establish a middle school that exemplifies the principles and practices of quality learner-centeredness, and it serves as a model and conduit for taking those principles and practices to scale in additional schools in the district. Classes are heterogeneous, with learners of all readiness levels and students from all three middle grades (6–8) working together. The daily school schedule is very flexible and changes according to the requirements of students' current projects. Recently, Community added a high school cohort that operates as an integral part of the school, using the same instructional principles and practices as their middle school colleagues. Chad Ratliff, the principal of Community Middle School, and Stephanie Passman, its head teacher, collaborated on the account that follows.

There is an evident buzz at Community Middle School each morning as students arrive, talking eagerly with their peers about a current project that's taking shape or looking for a teacher to "test-drive" an idea. The energy inside the building is high too, even for a middle school. And the enthusiasm is evident among the teachers, who are just leaving their daily collaborative planning time as the students begin to arrive. When the two groups merge, a new day of discovery begins, even though the first bell hasn't yet rung.

To backtrack a little, the teachers' school day launches about an hour before the students' does. They meet at a round table in a room that bears vestiges of whatever students are studying at the moment—a variety of materials, supplies, costumes, and resources. "These teachers have deep content knowledge," explains Head Teacher Stephanie Passman, who coordinates curricular and instructional planning in the school in addition to her own classroom duties. "That depth of knowledge is critical in creating the kinds of learning opportunities we want our students to have. These teachers don't 'own' a subject; rather, their content expertise enables them to see how multiple content areas are authentically connected."

Although each day at Community begins with homeroom time, the classes that follow are fluid, with the schedule varying with a unit of study or the particular time a unit requires. Classes contain students from all of the school's grade levels and are heterogeneous by readiness level as well. Math is the only subject that is taught at a "fixed" time in the day, but even then, it's common to see a student move from one classroom to another as he or she pursues additional practice or the next step in learning. Ms. Passman explains that the math classes are a bit like the one-room schools of the past; different kinds of learning are going in the room most of the time.

As part of the Albemarle County Public Schools, Community Middle School develops student learning experiences based on Virginia's statewide content standards, but it doesn't take long to realize that, in this school, teachers do not "cover" standards. "That term, 'covering standards,' is so teacher-centered," Ms. Passman reflects. "It almost never means the students have actually learned all those things, or that they come to see the big picture of what we ask them to learn. Here, our goal is for students to be so excited about learning that they will remember the experiences. We want them to see how readily the disciplines connect with one another. We want them to love what they are learning so that they just naturally want to master it."

Continually Evolving Curriculum

The Community Middle School teachers don't begin their planning by asking, "What do we need to cover this month or in this unit?" To avoid the kind of content overload that is common in many schools and classrooms, they begin with "anchor standards" firmly in mind. These are standards that delineate major competencies students need to master in order to be prepared to flourish in life after the K–12 years, no matter the path they elect to follow. These "big picture" standards indicate, for example, that a student needs to be proficient in presenting information, findings, and supporting evidence so that a listener can follow the student's organization and line of reasoning; or that a student can find central themes in text; or that a student can successfully analyze why individuals, events, and ideas interact in a given context or over a specific period of time. Reflective of the curriculum at Community Middle, these anchor standards move across and among content areas.

Sometimes an idea for a unit of study emerges as teachers consider how a topic (the U.S. Civil War, for example) or anchor standards (such as evaluating arguments and claims in a variety of media) might engage student curiosity and imagination. From there, they "think forward" to an authentic culminating product that would require both multidisciplinary content knowledge and application of anchor standards. At other times, the teachers begin a curriculum planning conversation by sharing a real-world problem, need, invitation, or contest that seems well suited to the interests and needs of their students. In those instances, the teachers "work backwards" to consider ways in which important knowledge, understanding, and skills from the content areas (e.g., language arts, social studies, art, science) are—or could be—embedded in a unit that would prepare the way for students to successfully address the ready-made opportunity. Both approaches to curriculum design result in learning experiences that are concept-based, engaging, and focused on student understanding of content and require transfer of knowledge and skill. In both, anchor standards are foundational to student success with the work they do. Always, the designs provide multiple pathways to student mastery and success, ensuring ongoing opportunity for student voice and choice. In that way, curriculum is co-constructed by teachers and students.

"I trust the teachers," says Principal Chad Ratliff. "I want them to have the power their pedagogical and content expertise implies." That trust has been validated in myriad ways in the years since Community Middle School first opened its doors. Certainly, consistent student enthusiasm for the school, family satisfaction with students' experiences, and teachers' excitement about their work with students are affirmations. It is also validating that from the school's early days through the most recent data, Community Middle School students have outperformed (often markedly) district and state comparison groups on mandated standardized tests. That pattern has been replicated for the cohort of high school students that has recently been added to the school.

Designing a Framework for the Morven Project

Morven Farm is a historic site on the outskirts of Charlottesville, Virginia, that dates from the mid-1700s and consists of slightly more than 2,900 acres and numerous buildings that host educational, charitable, and corporate events. It was donated to the University of Virginia in 2001. In addition to its variety of buildings, the site includes formal gardens and a Japanese garden; many works of noted sculptors; and an exhibit of African American, Native American, and English artifacts from an archeological site near Richmond, roughly an hour away. The University of Virginia Foundation invited the student body at Community to respond with proposals to the following question: *What else can we do, or what can we do better, with Morven to benefit the local community?*

As their work on the Morven Project began, students received the following charge:

You are about to make a real, lasting impact on your community.

Your task over the next two weeks:

• Learn as much as you can about the history and ecology of Morven Farm and, with a group or on your own, come up with a way to bring in members of the public for an educational or recreational experience (maybe both!). This idea will be entirely your own and will be considered by the staff at Morven.

• You will be given a reflective journal to write down your thoughts, ideas, and revelations throughout this project. There will be specific guidelines to follow for your entries to help keep you on track.

• At the end of a two-week immersion at Morven Farm, we will be hosting a "Potluck and Pitch Night" at Morven's Meeting Barn. This event will welcome members of the community including your family, University of Virginia faculty, and interested members from the Charlottesville/Albemarle area. You will present your idea on a poster or tri-fold board and guests will have the chance to read about it. *Use your time wisely and make sure you are creating the highest-quality work.*

In short, the students' job was to make informed proposals for use of a Morven Farm space that aligned with the organization's mission of bringing together people from the university, local, and global communities. Their teachers encouraged them to connect something they cared deeply about with the Morven space so that their investigation would be a catalyst for growth in themselves and in Morven. Faculty from UVa with expertise in a variety of relevant fields were available to the students for consultation throughout the two-week project.

In the beginning, students used a range of resources to learn about the history of Morven, including a visit to the farm and its gardens and structures. They needed also to understand the ecology, architecture, mission, and layout of the farm area in order to generate additional possibilities for its outreach work. Teachers guided background knowledge development; it was they who orchestrated the visit to the farm, for example, and they arranged for the expert presentations. Once students established a sense of direction with their work, they decided whether to join forces with peers who had settled on similar interests or work alone. Later, the teachers would help each student or group of students reconnect with experts whose specialty aligned with their interest-driven idea for expanding Morven's reach.

Learning Targets for the Morven Project

As is typically the case at Community, students had considerable choice in the unit surrounding Morven. Ms. Passman explains, "When a student wants to go in a different direction than what their teachers might have envisioned for any product, they know they will be heard and that we will do our best to support them in making their idea happen." Still, she notes, "Whatever a student decides to do as a culminating experience, their work must demonstrate application of the KUDs—the knowledge, understanding, and skills that frame a particular learning experience." These KUDs, then, function as a kind of constraint that helps balance the *direction* necessary to ensure that student learning mirrors the nature of the discipline(s) in which they are working with the *freedom* necessary to extend their strengths and interests. Here are the KUDs set for the Morven Project, along with a few "values," or reflection points, for students' consideration as they work and consider the benefits of their work.

Essential Questions
- What gives a space purpose?
- How can we improve our community through use of a space?
- What can the natural world teach us?

Know
- How indigenous cultures lived and worked on the land that is now Morven
- Current use of certain spaces on Morven
- How and why Native Americans gathered in the space that is now Morven
- Abiotic (non-living) and biotic (living) features of Morven (for example, rock formations, sources of water, plant species)

Understand
- The environment can tell stories that teach us more about the world we live in.
- Spaces can tell the stories of history.
- Spaces can provide people with a sense of purpose.

Do
- Develop and present a specific plan that provides a new purpose for some aspect of Morven.
- Find out and explain how your proposal can positively influence members of the community.
- Incorporate some of the natural beauty of Morven into your concept.

Value
- Your reflections on your own ideas regarding a purpose for Morven
- The opportunity to learn, from the perspective of others in your community and from history, ways in which you might make a positive impact on the lives of others
- The art of putting together elements of the natural world to find an even greater sense of your place within that environment

As students visited Morven, did background research, prepared and polished their proposals, created display boards to support their pitch, and developed their oral presentations, teacher guidance ensured that the students kept to these KUDs and focused on relevant anchor standards in several areas, including science, history, communications, and math. As always, curriculum and instruction were used to balance student freedom and choice with the teacher direction necessary to develop authentic, discipline-based products.

Potluck and Pitch Night

Over the days leading up to Potluck and Pitch Night, the energy and buzz at Community Middle School were at peak levels. Students were really invested in the ideas they would propose. They understood that their audience would include not only their parents and the parents of their friends but professors and Morven leaders as well. Some of the ideas might become part of the history of Morven, and in any case, they had worked diligently and learned a great deal in two intense weeks. They wanted their presentations to be of the highest possible caliber. So, as is often the case, students moved among teachers and spaces in the school, consulting additional resources, getting final critiques on their work, making sure their display boards looked professional, and practicing their pitches alone or in front of willing peers.

Then, on the night itself, with an adult audience gathered before them, individuals and groups presented 20-plus ideas that could extend Morven's mission of community outreach, including trails for hiking and biking, a team-building course for local businesses and companies, a corn maze with geocaches in various spots, a continental conservatory with flowers and food from every continent (except Antarctica), a zen garden, a glass-bottom fishing dock, local music in the gardens, upgrading the stables for boarding horses, horseback riding and opportunities for young people to learn to take care of horses, and adding sheep to the farm (leading to a seasonal petting zoo, sheep-herding competitions, visual aesthetics, and "living lawn mowers").

Ms. Passman notes that the school doesn't use a traditional grading system. "We list relevant anchor standards and students earn one of three indicators—*not mastered, approaching mastery,* or *mastered*." A student's work, she says, leaves a trail that makes their degree of mastery visible. "People ask us why our students work so hard if they don't get 'real' grades. When you watch them at work and as they share their products, it's clear: They do the work because the work itself is compelling for them."

Helping Students Discover Science and Themselves

George Murphy teaches biology and marine science at Fauquier High School in Warrenton, Virginia. The school serves students in grades 9–12 who live in both rural communities and outer-ring "bedroom communities" of the Washington, D.C., metro area. Fauquier High students represent a wide spectrum of experiences, economic backgrounds, cultures, and races. The school offers a broad range of both academic and vocational classes. It does not follow any designated instructional model, allowing departments and individual teachers to develop approaches that are best suited to the content they teach and to their students' needs. George Murphy and a former student, Addison Bowman, collaborated on the account that follows.

"A challenge I enjoy is inspiring students, developing in them a love of learning in general and biology in particular," Mr. Murphy says. Listening to his students talk, it seems a sure bet that he meets this challenge daily.

Mr. Murphy remembers himself as a poor student in high school biology, but his teacher, Mr. Watson, was having none of that: "Mr. Watson talked to me, and to all of us, about his fascination with observing microscopic life for hours at a time, describing life forms that he had never seen before and describing the intricate forms of life in detail. His passion was contagious. We couldn't wait to use the microscope."

While Mr. Murphy was bitten by the science bug in Mr. Watson's class, his early days as a teacher were memorable for all the wrong reasons.. "I was in a survival mode during my first year," he admits. "I had no idea what I was doing. I struggled with discipline. I had never heard of differentiation. Ultimately, I decided that if I kept students busy with labs, they were less likely to disassemble another lab table—plus, I would have to lecture less. I had not yet discovered how to lead an interesting discussion."

The Teacher Finds His Groove

Several years into his teaching career, someone gave Mr. Murphy a text called *Biological Science: An Inquiry into Life.* It used an investigative rather than a descriptive approach to teaching biology, in that students would acquire knowledge in biology through experiments involving multiple layers of inquiry. "I was hooked," he says. And he still is. His students are as well.

Today, Mr. Murphy's classroom is a sort of combination professional laboratory, museum, and library. Says one of his students, "There are always animals all over the place—chinchillas, ferrets, hamsters, birds, turtles, fish in fish tanks. It's OK if you want to go get a gecko and put it on your shoulder while you work." The room is also filled with all sorts of books. There are books on biology and on science more broadly, including Mr. Murphy's college lab manuals, but there are also many books on topics that he just thinks are interesting to learn about. He notes, "Students use the books all the time to figure out problems, deepen their knowledge on a current classroom topic, or just because the books *are*, in fact, *interesting*." Mr. Murphy says he wants students to follow their own curiosity and supports them in doing that. "I'm happy if their curiosity leads them to learn about things that are in no way connected to the content we are studying."

Students say that Mr. Murphy's room is always open for them to come in and ask him questions, read, or work on a lab or project. On the day I met with Mr. Murphy to discuss this section of the chapter—a day on which there were no scheduled classes—three students came in to work on their "yeast communication lab." As they worked, they talked with him about their experiences in and memories from class. Jason recalled the tedious and exacting process of trying to extract and purify DNA from samples of fish he and his classmates brought to class for a genetics unit. He was always the one who had to hold the digital pipette while someone else held the solution tube. "No one else had hands that were steady enough to do what Jason was doing, so he played that role for every lab group in the class," Mr. Murphy remembers.

There's Always Something Compelling to Do

"One year," recalls Maura, a former student in several of Mr. Murphy's classes, "he asked us to select an animal in the room and then form groups around our choice. We had to read broadly, figure out what questions were important to ask about the animal, and then do our own experiment designed around what we learned and the question we posed from that learning." Maura and her lab group looked into food sources for ferrets in their natural habitats and ultimately conducted an experiment to determine whether the ferret had food preferences among five available foods. (It did.) Each student was responsible for a section of their group lab report which they had to blend into one, well-composed piece to turn in together.

Maura recalls that another group chose a Green Amazon Parrot. Learning about the incredible capacity of that species to remember and reproduce sounds, they conducted an experiment to see if the bird could learn a popular song if the group played it for the bird several hours a day. Students in the class were fascinated with the experiment, although they came to strongly dislike the song they'd chosen before the experiment ended. (The bird learned and reproduced some early notes in the song but seemed to lose interest in mastering more of it. Mr. Murphy's recollection is that the bird had the capacity to learn the song but just chose not to.) "We were all aware of the labs and projects of groups other than our own, and we often worked across groups to help one another," says Maura.

As Mr. Murphy's students work together, he moves continually around the room, observing what they are saying, asking, and doing. This not only helps him get to know the students individually but also serves as ongoing formative assessment. He explains, "I see good out-of-the-box thinking even when students aren't there yet. When I see a gap in knowledge or understanding, I ask questions to lead the student or group to think more deeply; they nearly always recalibrate their thinking." He pauses and adds, "The students have ongoing dialogues too, and they consistently help one another evaluate their ideas and processes."

"His class is always engaging," a student reflects. "It makes us all mentally curious. Our labs often cause us to raise more questions than we answer. We just want to know *more* and more about the subject. His class feels to all of us like a break from what normal classes are like."

Students point out that Mr. Murphy intends them to see that it's perfectly fine not to know an answer. Says Maura, "He tells us over and over there's no such thing as a dumb question in this class. He says he's never heard one."

"When I don't know the answer to what they're asking," Mr. Murphy echoes, "I tell them that I don't know, and we work together to find the missing information. Labs often don't work out. It's like that for scientists." Persistence is imperative for good science. For example, he and his students have been trying for 25 years to breed sea urchins as a part of their study of embryology. "These creatures are at the bottom of the food chain, incredibly vulnerable. We can begin with 2,000 embryos and in less than a month, we're down to 10." He and his students have read widely about the complexity of breeding sea urchins and have consulted multiple times with experts at Stanford University who are "the preeminent breeders of this species." The Stanford scientists breed sea urchins to learn about the impact of climate change on them. "We got really close one year," Mr. Murphy recalls, "but just as it looked like we would succeed, there was a snowstorm and no one could get to the school, so the room got too chilly for the embryos and we missed our goal again." He adds, "There is always room for a teacher to grow as well as for students."

"Students learn to work together like a good family," Maura remembers. "We laughed a lot, but we were always focused on doing whatever we could to make a lab a success. We helped one another and encouraged one another every step of the way." Another student concurs, "A member of our lab group will sometimes stop and say, 'Wait! Should we do this, or should we do this?'" They puzzle through the work together.

A Favorite Lab Among Many Favorites

In recent years, thanks to "incredible leaps in genetic engineering and forensics technology," Mr. Murphy wanted to introduce his students to electrophoresis—a lab technique used to separate pieces of DNA based on their size and electrical charge. DNA is cut up into little pieces by molecular scissors called restriction enzymes and then placed in a gel in an electrophoresis chamber, where an electric current moves the pieces through the gel at different rates, depending on the fragment size. After staining the gel, you get what looks like a barcode—a DNA fingerprint. Each species, each organism, has a different DNA fingerprint. Using those fingerprints, we can tell whether two people are related or whether a hair sample left at a crime scene matches the DNA of a suspect.

It's now possible to run electrophoresis with only a very small piece of DNA, but that requires a thermal cycler, which costs far more than a high school science department can afford. So, Mr. Murphy and his students tried thermal cycling by hand. It didn't work, but as always, the students were captivated by the process and learned a great deal. Then, a career-switching teacher at Fauquier High, who once worked for the National Institutes of Health, called on some earlier connections in the field who were able to get two thermal cyclers donated to the school. The Forensics Lab is now a favorite of Mr. Murphy's students.

Maura recalls the excitement she and her classmates felt as they tested DNA of three suspects from a fictional crime scene. The process is arduous and exacting, requiring students to make "the buffer that will be used in the gel that is used to run the DNA through as well as covering the chamber where the experiment is run. This needs to be done ahead of time, so it is ready for the lab. We made it the day before or the morning before our afternoon lab." That is Step 1 of about 15 or 20, each more complex than the previous one—each planned and completed by the students with much coordination among lab groups. "When we saw the DNA fingerprints begin to emerge, we were in awe. We were ready to keep making buffer for the rest of our lives. We never wanted to stop."

"Can we do the Forensics Lab again even though we won't be in Biology anymore?" Mr. Murphy's students regularly ask. The answer is yes. In another class, students bring in samples of fish of varied kinds, both fresh and canned, and test the DNA to see if what they were told they were purchasing was actually what was purchased. In yet again another class, they test their own DNA. Learning this, a prospective student eagerly suggests, "A DNA database! Let's make a DNA database for students in the class!"

Maura thinks back on a trip Mr. Murphy and his Marine Biology students took to Andros Island. Students had to develop their own research group, design an experiment they would conduct at the field station where they stayed, figure out and pack everything they would need for the experiment, decide how to run the experiment, and be responsible for their procedures and results. In addition, they went on excursions to varied marine sites on the island, worked with scientists at the field station, and attended lectures every evening. The students had just enough spare time to snorkel and swim a bit in the blue waters. Mr. Murphy, she says, "gave us so many opportunities to learn and grow inside and outside the classroom—and to make memories that will last a lifetime."

Amid all this unconventional work, Mr. Murphy still does plenty that teachers traditionally do. He gives students tests, for example; they are legendary for the mental gymnastics they ask of students in applying and transferring what they learn. He grades lab reports, which require careful, accurate, and precise work. "But what I really care about," Mr. Murphy says, "is that students grow—that their content and processes develop over time. So, I use something like a portfolio of their work samples, and I factor growth over time into their grades. Because growth is what matters most." As a side note, he mentions that as standardized tests began to dominate teaching and learning, he didn't change a thing about his practice. The reason was simple: "I don't teach to raise test scores. I teach to help create a hunger to learn, a fascination with the world." Perhaps it's not a surprise to learn that Mr. Murphy's students do well on the mandated tests anyhow.

Maura, completing her sophomore year in college as this chapter was written, says she was totally well-prepared for her science major in college. "I had solid content knowledge, a sound understanding of lab procedures, the skills necessary to work in a lab group, and comfort with using the many resources that are important in science. I know the difference between taking good notes in class and taking appropriate notes in a lab. I know how to stay on top of content and my goals all the time. My professors are amazed when I tell them what I did in my high school science classes." Maura pauses then admits, "I just wish we had the kind of labs at the university that we had in Mr. Murphy's class."

Points to Consider

- In many ways, the three teachers and classrooms in the examples differ significantly. Still, all three reflect the goals and attributes of learner centeredness. What would you say are the most important commonalities across the three scenarios that bind them together as representatives of quality learner-centered pedagogy?

- Take a look back at Figure 3.4 (p. 44) and use this model for thinking about and addressing the needs of students in learner-centered classrooms to reflect on each of the three examples. Which elements do you see in all three classrooms? Which do you see in one or two of the classrooms but not all three? Can you point to elements common to all three classrooms that these teachers achieved in *different* ways? Before you answer, review Figure 5.3 (p. 87) and its strategies for building community.

- Figures 3.1 (p. 38) and 3.2 (p. 39) compare "power relationships" in learner-centered classrooms and more traditional or teacher-focused classrooms. Use the two figures as guides for thinking about how power relationships are alike and different in the classrooms described in this chapter.

- Chapter 8 lists the seven instructional adjustments Dwyer (1995) identifies as key to shifting away from traditional, teacher-centered classrooms and toward learner-centered ones. Do you feel like all three teachers in this chapter have made the transformations in all of the instructional elements? If so, what evidence can you point to? If not, think about which elements still seem in transition (realizing that a brief capsule of a classroom's operation may not capture all that goes on within it).

• What do you see in any of these examples that affirms your work? What next steps do you aspire to as you read and reflect on these examples? What questions about learner-centered teaching remain unanswered for you, and how might you gain greater clarity about those issues?

• Make a note here (or somewhere else that would be more accessible to you) of your four most important takeaways from the book.

• For future reference, write down at least three specific steps you plan to take in order to continue growing as a learner-centered teacher.

A Final Look Ahead

Dylan Wiliam (2011c) reflects that schools tend to function as talent refineries. That is, when they see talent, they provide opportunities to extend it. So, for example, students who exhibit high academic ability are likely to be accorded the chance to take advanced classes, or they are identified to participate in programs for "gifted" students. Schools sort students into layers (which I sadly heard a small group of educators refer to as "the definitlies," "the maybes," and "the no-hopes"). The maybes and the no-hopes are seldom pushed to excel. They can opt out of classes that don't seem to be "their thing."

As Wiliam points out, coaches don't have that luxury. They have to win games with whoever is on the team. They can't say, "The quarterback is weak this year, so we won't play." It's a coach's job to make the quarterback the best he can be—perhaps better than either of them thought he could be. Coaches can't just identify and refine talent; they must incubate it, nurture it, and bring it forward.

To commit to learner-centered teaching is to commit to making the classroom a talent incubator—to commit to ensuring that each student in the class has expectations, opportunity, and support to extend their intellectual, affective, and social capacity every day. A learner-centered teacher doesn't begin by saying, "Let me see who is smart, talented, and creative so I can make sure those students are challenged." Rather, that teacher begins by saying, "Each student who comes into my classroom has far more potential than is visible to them or to me. Let me provide the opportunity and support to elicit that capacity." Student-centeredness, rightly understood and implemented, seeks to uplift the humanity of each young person, to place the welfare of each young person at the center of all decisions, and to equip each young person not just to survive in school and in life, but to matter and to thrive (Love, 2020).

My colleague Chad Prather is as good a learner-centered teacher as I have ever known. Chad frames his responsibility and opportunity as a teacher with four verbs: *embrace, guard, nourish,* and *lead* (Witmer, 2010). These are the actions of incubating talent. They are the actions of student-focused teaching—*embracing* not only through invitational learning environments, but also through invitational curriculum and meaningful peer collaboration; *nourishing* not only through meaning-rich curriculum, but also through learning environments that give rise to a student's voice and assessment that enables students to increasingly pilot their own success; *guarding* through assessment that makes sure instruction is just a step ahead of a learner so that discouragement does not drain energy away from learning; and *leading* not only by commending and modeling the attributes that bring the best in human beings to the surface, but also by pointing the way to habits of mind, work, and interaction that build to success and quality. Again, each element, each action in a classroom universe, is connected to every other one. Each, for better or worse, moves with the student from the classroom to the world outside.

To be very clear, teaching and learning driven by test prep and test scores do not and cannot embrace, guard, nourish, and lead students. However, neither can the "next new thing." I read many articles on education, and a good number of them call passionately on educators to rethink teaching and learning. I too feel passionately about the need for this transformation. Many of the articles are compellingly written, and many introduce me to strategies and technologies that sound promising and that I am excited to learn about. In nearly all of the articles, however, I detect a certain reductivism. Invariably, the argument seems to be that if we just adopted this set of apps or inquiry learning or problem-based learning or project-based learning or flexible schedules or flipped classrooms or community-based learning or personalization or standards-based learning or hybrid learning that combines technology and in-person meetings or any one of several dozen other "solutions," we would see education revitalized. We have no reason, based on research or experience, to conclude that is the case. There is limited inherent power to transform student lives in any of those approaches unless they are understood, implemented, and assessed in the context of the following:

• An **invitational learning environment** that clearly represents, commends, and supports equity, excellence, and empathy; persistently builds trust between the teacher and each student; builds community among students; supports students in learning to be good citizens of the environments they inhabit; and provides a balance of predictability and flexibility necessary for student-centered learning.

• A **curriculum** that centers on the critical knowledge, big ideas, and skills of the discipline; is relevant to the range of experiences represented in the classroom; is designed to engage the interest, curiosity, and motivation of each learner; focuses learners on making sense and meaning of the content; and is developed as a catalyst for in-depth learning.

• An **assessment approach** that is tightly aligned with the knowledge, understandings, and skills specified as critical in the curriculum design and that is designed to guide the teacher to teach more effectively in order to maximize the growth of each learner and guide the learner to develop the habits of mind and work necessary to successfully take charge of his or her own learning success.

• A set of **teaching and learning practices** that are tightly aligned with the knowledge, understanding, and skills specified as critical in the curriculum design and that respond to and dignify the learner intellectually, affectively, and socially while responding to and dignifying the disciplines the student is exploring.

Every one of the strategies or "solutions" collected in this book can be transformational for students—*if* they are used as means to enact the elements of environment, curriculum, assessment, and instruction capsuled in the bulleted list above. Every one of those strategies or "solutions" can become passing fads in the absence of attention to ensure that the four classroom elements reflect our best knowledge of teaching and learning—the knowledge that stems from ongoing research and analytical classroom experience. Instructional strategies or "solutions" are "buckets to carry the goods"; "the goods" are foundational to successful learning and teaching. Know "the goods" first. Then select a bucket or buckets that will deliver them well to the students you serve, in the place you serve them, and at the time you serve them.

What learner-centeredness asks of teachers is hard, but as teachers often say to students, "You can do hard things"—and doing them makes you a stronger, more empathetic, and wiser human being.

To paraphrase Berger (2003), this work is harder than it's possible to properly explain. Doing it well on a consistent basis takes a unique stamina. For anyone with talent and options, choosing to enter teaching and take on the stress of trying to do what learner-centeredness asks you to do is crazy... *unless* you feel that this is what you are intended for, unless you know that this is your way to share the best of what you have to give to the world. If that's you, then by all means, answer the call. Take one step at a time. When you feel lost or uncertain, remember that discouragement is the disequilibrium that is a precursor to growth (Steele, 2009)—and this is as true for you as it is for your students. Tertullian, an early philosopher from Carthage, wrote that hope is patience with the lamp lit. Be patient with yourself, but keep the lamp lit within you.

Frank Herbert, author of the science fiction novel *Dune*, writes, "There is no real ending. It's just where you stop the story." This is the end of a long period of disequilibrium for me in discovering and putting on paper the "story" in this book. And yet, I hope that for me and for you, the story will continue to be written through the work we continue to do, what we learn from that work, and how we fold that learning into the work going forward. I hope you accept the challenge to embrace, guard, nourish, and lead each young person—and all the young people—in your care.

 G3 CR G3

Afterword . . . and Onward

I began this book with a dedication to people who have been my teachers—those who taught me, taught with me, taught me through the books I read (and now reread) for insight and inspiration, and taught me by being my students. Since my first day in this profession, it's students who have taught me the most—with humor and pathos, with blunt honesty, and even through deceit. They have helped me create images of the classroom I wanted to lead and have given me energy and a sense of urgency to keep trying.

Chad Prather was a student of mine when I was still learning how to teach at a university and still having separation pains from my middle school life. He had the most amazing shock of hair I have ever seen and a tonic combination of creativity, empathy, humor, vision, and passion for the work. Chad made me want to be a better teacher every time he spoke in class, every time I read his work, and every time we had a conversation. He still makes me want to be a better teacher.

I watched Chad in his first role as a high school history teacher, when he asked to teach the students no one else was clamoring for, and I kept up with him after he moved from the town we shared in Virginia to Nashville, Tennessee, to teach in a school that seemed to enroll all the world's children. He ultimately applied to and was hired at Pearl-Cohn High School—the lowest-performing school in the city. I have now watched him champion his students in a hundred ways and cry with them when tragedy diminishes their hope and will. And always, as I watch, I learn.

I want to end this book with a reflection from Chad (whom his students, with deep affection, call "Prather") because his writing brings the book full circle. Not only does it demonstrate just about every ideal the book commends, it shows us what equity and excellence look like. It illustrates how a teacher's dogged determination unites with young hope and laughter and discouragement and despair to create a place that teaches and heals—and holds kids tight when teaching and healing are not enough. Chad's work is rooted in the science of teaching, but it always reminds me that teaching also can be a high art.

Chad has, at the writing of this book, taught for 16 years—the last six at Pearl-Cohn High School, where his "unteachable" students engage and learn deeply every day and he, in turn, learns from and through them. This is how it is in a learner-centered classroom. Let me let Chad take you there.

C3 C3 C3

Serving the Children of the Black Diamond

Most of my 10th graders at Pearl-Cohn High School grew up right here in North Nashville. To begin to know them well requires an accepting knowledge of the place that formed them.

The cultural geography of this neighborhood is vibrant and deep-rooted. Just a block from the school is the Jefferson Street corridor, at one time a true Harlem in the South. Its history sings of Black joy and flourishing: the creative genius of musicians, artists, and poets; the intellect of Fisk professors and students; the nerve of freedom fighters; and the prosperity of doctors, lawyers, and business owners. One of the historic clubs on Jefferson Street was called the Black Diamond, and the whole neighborhood around Pearl was every bit a jewel. It sparkled with voice, pride, and courage.

My students have inherited this empowering spirit. Whether they know it or not, they carry its potential into our classroom. But they also carry the heavy weight of trauma wrought by a long train of abuses and usurpations. Decades of Jim Crow, intimidation, redlining, gentrification, injustice, and over-policing have had impoverishing consequences for the neighborhood. Longtime residents have been displaced and businesses have been shuttered. The physical Black Diamond is long gone. Crime, addiction, death, and incarceration have torn families apart. Neighborhood schools have struggled to retain staff, and students have struggled to achieve. Alongside the hurt has been a constant pressure to stay on guard. This pressure has left this neighborhood exhausted, and many of my students have inherited this fatigue. They bring its manifestations into our classroom: apathy, distrust, anger, self-doubt, preoccupation, fear, agitation, anxiety, explosivity. The weight is heavy.

Still, these are the children of the Black Diamond! To serve them well, I have to tap the spirit within them. I also have to remember the words of Tupac Shakur, as taught to me by my students: "Long live the rose that grew from concrete." Hard experiences may surround these students, but those experiences have not stopped them. These Pearl-Cohn Firebirds come with a wisdom I do not have, a wisdom borne *out* of the weight. Their wisdom is my starting place.

What's Your Code?

It's the beginning of class, and I've projected directions on the screen along with a photo of El-Hajj Malik El-Shabazz:

Prior knowledge check: List up to 5 facts or ideas you already know about Malcolm X, and write 3 questions about the man you would like to have answered.

In a classroom full of students who identify as Black, I think this might be a decent place to start. Two or three kids engage, but otherwise the pens go down, the phones come out, hallway conversations start back up, and Malcolm X is left alone. That my students walked in and saw someone who looked like them—that is not nothing. By my task only engages two small groups: those who already know something of Malcolm and those with interest or curiosity about him. I am unable to get anything going after this start. I try to force a Malcolm X text into the atmosphere. No takers.

Not every student comes with prior knowledge *of* the content, but every student comes with knowledge prior *to* the content. They come with opinions and perspectives shaped by lived experiences. It has taken me some time to realize that if I want to welcome young people to the table, I need to set it with essential questions—ones that burrow into the essence of their existing insight.

It's the beginning of the next day's class and up on the screen is a photo of two characters from HBO's *The Wire*: "Bunk" Moreland, a Baltimore City police detective, and Omar Little, a stick-up man who makes a living robbing drug dealers. I play a short clip from an episode. Detective Bunk implies that Omar is behind the murder of a state's witness. (Students are engrossed.) Omar rebuts the notion; his affairs do not extend to folk outside "the game." Aware of Omar's occupation, the detective is incredulous. Omar looks directly at Bunk. "A man's got to have a code," he says.

I advance the screen so that it fills with a question: "WHAT'S YOUR CODE?" I invite students to spend seven minutes expressing their personal codes on paper. They can do it in prose, in poetry, through art—however they wish. They will not have to share it with others if they prefer not to, nor will I read what they produce unless I am invited. I put on some jazz. I step back, giving them space.

Almost immediately, every single kid is writing. We get to seven minutes. "More time, Prather," someone requests.

A student who has finished walks up to me. His name is Eric, and he has not engaged in an assignment in weeks. He is always here, but he's seldom *present*— a quiet kid, but confrontational if pressed into work. Eric hands me two single-spaced pages of writing. He wrote *two full pages in seven minutes!* "Will you read this?" he asks. "You want me to?" He nods, and I do. It's two full pages about trust and loyalty—specifically about the danger of trust and the rarity of loyalty. It's deeply personal and intense. I tell Eric I appreciate his sharing this with me.

Soon the writing stops and flows into discussion. It's honest, authentic, and respectful. No one is talking over anyone this time. I stay quiet and listen. When the conversation subsides, I advance the screen. It's Malcolm X again, but this time with a new prompt: "What's *his* code?" After we watch a short biographical clip, I tell the class we are going to annotate some excerpts from one of Malcolm's speeches. Our purpose is to get a sense of the man's code (his code at the time of this speech, that is; codes can change, I say). We also want to observe whether Malcom's code aligns at all with our codes. We annotate the first paragraphs together, and I increasingly shift the thinking from myself to the students. Eventually, I invite them to continue on their own, in pairs, or with me. Eric comes over to my table. He is all in.

We close the lesson with a piece of spoken-word poetry called "Bullet Cry" by Louis Reyes Rivera. The classroom floods with new questions about Malcolm X's murder.

Today has been a Black Diamond day. From start to finish, every student connected with this lesson. Maybe they see themselves in some aspect of Bunk or Omar, or in the claims of Malcolm X, or in the flow of Rivera's voice. I think mostly they find personal value in "What's your code?" They can engage with the question safely, significantly, and successfully. Once inside it, understanding the question fully, they feel they can tackle it as it applies to someone else, even someone as complex as El-Hajj Malik El-Shabazz. This is deep thinking, I tell them, this code-constructing from another's perspective. They believe me. More important, I sense they trust me. Even Eric.

How Do You Know They Love You?

Trust is cultivated over time; it does not just happen. The start matters, though. Week 1 is a big deal. I go into it every year wanting to lay the groundwork for some serious trust building, and I tend to feel really good about it... right up to the moment when we get to the "Rules and Management" slide.

I struggle every year with this slide. There's something fundamentally awkward about saying, "I am trying to build trust, *but* I am going to manage you, and here are rules for you to follow." I recover quickly, though, because I'm confident that what has happened in the past will probably happen again: somewhere along the line, something in most of my students will click toward me, and I will click toward them, and eventually most of us will be clicking together.

But I want more. I want my students, all of them, to start our time together feeling that they're on the cusp of something different. That in this classroom, they do not need to feel policed or compelled into compliance with more rules. I want them to get that this classroom will be a place of co-ownership and mutual accountability—a place of agreements, not rules, and a place where the norms won't only be normative to me. I want them to see that I'm not asking for obedience but partnership. (This may feel awkward, too, because how often have they felt like partners with their teachers? But this will be a different kind of awkward, more hopeful and inviting.)

How do I invite students into partnership with me? They hardly know me. And let's be honest: I look like lots of the people who haven't had their backs in the past. Despite 16 years as a teacher, I am still struggling to know how to do this—how to shift from rule giving to agreement making. Fortunately, I have a colleague who does this work beautifully, and I have learned over time that asking for help is liberating. At the invitation of my co-teacher, David Roney, Rasheedat Fetuga comes to our classroom. Rasheedat is a former elementary school teacher, local community activist, "mother" to many from the Black Diamond, and restorative justice partner at Pearl.

She asks our 34 students to pull their chairs out from behind the desks and form a large circle. Roney and I join the circle as well. Rasheedat begins with some affirmation and appreciation of the students. She acknowledges that the process ahead might feel strange, might trigger vulnerability and spark doubt. Rasheedat asks for presence, open-mindedness, and a degree of participation. She tells the students they will have opportunities to speak, though they can pass when their turn comes around. Ultimately, though, we will all be voting to adopt some agreements that we will be constructing together, and we will all be signing our names to those agreements.

Rasheedat issues a request: "I want you to think of someone in your life who has cared for you, someone now or in the past. And don't just think of someone who cared *about* you. Think of someone who has cared *for* you, someone who has *loved* you, as you understand the meaning of love in *your* mind. You don't have to share who the person is. That's up to you. But when the 'talking doll' [we called him Little Cletus] gets passed your way to indicate it's your turn, I invite you to share your proof of the care you're remembering. What's your evidence? How do you *know* they love you?"

After some quiet time for thinking, Rasheedat gets the process started by modeling it—sharing an example of the care her person had provided, then passing Little Cletus to a student. As the doll moves around the circle, some kids do pass, but most engage. They share short accounts of the men and women in their lives who have cared for them. As they share, Rasheedat listens for phrases at the heart of their evidence and writes them on the board.

Quickly, we all see that we had very different understandings, experiences, and values of care. Tatiana talks about her grandma: "She's old-school, and she gets in my face. She tells me exactly what I need to hear even if I don't want to listen. She draws a line and calls me out if I cross it. She's doing the most, but I low-key need that line. For real. She irks my soul sometimes, but I know she's just trying to protect me." A few seats later, Damion says this: "My mom lets me do whatever I want. I don't do well with rules. She knows that and trusts me to figure it out on my own. If I screw up, I screw up. She knows I'll learn." I make notes in my mind: *Tatiana values the line. Damion values independence.* I realize that *my* rules would have completely alienated at least one of these students.

We've gone around the circle once, and Rasheedat invites anyone who previously passed to share out, then she draws attention to the different values of care she's written on the board. She affirms the realness of these values. She says we are going to work outwardly from these values to create agreements, and these agreements will guide our time together in this course. She presents four questions: "How should teachers treat students? How should students treat teachers? How should students treat each other? How should everyone treat the space?"

We begin with the first question. Rasheedat asks for a courageous volunteer to suggest a guideline that might frame the way teachers should treat students. Jeremiah raises his hand. Someone throws him Little Cletus.

"Teachers shouldn't just kick kids out for no reason," Jeremiah says. Rasheedat leans in: "Say more." Jeremiah describes situations where teachers have dismissed students and written referrals simply because the students got angry about something. "We might get hot about a matter completely outside the class. You don't know, but y'all just send us out for no reason." Other students are nodding. Rasheedat writes on the board: "Teachers will not dismiss students from class for getting angry."

She tells the group we are going to go around the circle again. When Little Cletus comes our way, we can choose to agree with the guideline as written or suggest a modification. If we disagree, Rasheedat will press us to justify our disagreement and suggest a change to the statement. If after significant discussion we cannot come to unanimous agreement, then we will table it and move on to a new guideline.

About 10 minutes later we have a refined agreement in place: "Teachers will not judge students for their emotions. They will try to understand what is going on and create opportunities for upset students to re-engage. If the students can't or choose not to, then they will be respectfully dismissed." Everyone accepts it. Within this one agreement, the voices and values of the Tatianas, Damions, Jeremiahs, Prathers, and Roneys are all represented.

This agreement making moves more like an aircraft carrier than a jet ski. It advances slowly, and when it needs to turn, a whole lot has to happen. We take a full week to tackle all four questions. In the end, we have a small but powerful set of co-created agreements. We have signed our names on them, and we will come back to them throughout the year, individually and communally, as the needs arise. Thanks to Roney's suggestion and Rasheedat's expertise, my students and I are now partners in this work, and I feel equipped to roll out this process in my other classes. There is a different feel to this start, a different vibe, and it is good.

The Lessons of Civilization

A few years back I stumbled onto this rhetorical question: *You have one year left in the classroom, and this will be your students' only experience with the subject or discipline you teach. What will you do?*

I want to teach from the inside out. I want to leverage the skills my students are already honing on their own. I listen to them talk about their lives and realize they are strategizing and evaluating and innovating all the time (no one will ever convince me that kids are not practiced at deep, critical thinking). They may not realize it, but these Firebirds are engaging with their world through highly specialized lenses: *economically*, as they measure the costs and benefits of personal decisions; *sociologically*, as they talk about the impact of Nashville's systems and institutions on their families; *politically*, as they argue about the rights and responsibilities they do or do not bear; *psychologically*, as they unpack gossip and the manipulating effects of teen drama.

As their teacher, I owe my students an experience that will focus their lenses and equip them to be the designers of a changing world. Instead of positioning them to be textbook readers observing the history makers inside our curriculum, they will become the subjects of our curriculum. They will be the heads of state, the generals, the artists, the innovators, the diplomats, the activists, the agitators, the saboteurs, the economists, the refugees, the state makers, and the empire builders. They will study history, of course, but more than that they will *do* history.

Enter CIVGAME. Inspired by the World Peace Game, the brilliant creation of longtime elementary school educator and master teacher John Hunter, CIVGAME remains an organic, ever-shifting, far-from-completely-structured, and fairly unpackageable simulation experience. The game weaves in and out of our exploration of history. Self-constructed civilization teams across all six of my classes confront a driving challenge: *Build and maintain a successful state.* They are told that judges at year's end will evaluate all the existing states and offer a significant prize to the one they deem most "successful," however they choose to define the term.

"How will we know what they think is success?" a student asks. "You won't," I reply. "You'll need to determine that for yourself. What makes a state successful? Is it size and power, the accumulation of land and wealth, the growth of a far-reaching empire? Is it military might, wins in war, perhaps the conquest of enemies? Is it a set of systems that meet the needs of small populations? Or perhaps a record of humanitarianism and service to other states? You decide."

At the heart of CIVGAME are essential questions: *What does it take to get ahead? Where do good ideas come from? How do you keep from crumbling? What matters more: where you end up, or how you get there? Is there anything worth the sacrifice of everything? What drives people forward? What holds people back?* Students explore these questions over time, sometimes directly, but often in the background of the work.

Twenty-six teams form, initially ranging from one to five members. I'll focus here on three of those teams: Madaki, Krapollo, and Ix-Zamna.

The state of Madaki comprises three male students, all good friends and athletes. They are kind, lighthearted, and fun (sometimes too fun for the classroom).

Two of the three have IEPs and require significant accommodations. They do not exude a lot of academic confidence, yet they are intrigued because this course sounds like a video game. They will play it well through strategic alliances, thoughtful infrastructural investments, and outside-the-box thinking to shake things up.

The state of Krapollo begins with four students but ultimately balloons into 16 across two class periods. Krapollo is a loud mix of male and female students with very different personalities. This team has more academic horsepower than most, at least by traditional metrics (higher state test scores and reading lexiles, for instance). On paper they look smarter, and they know it. But they neglect the off-the-paper wisdom of their peers, and this ignorance will burn them from time to time. Still, Krapollo is a team of innovation and after-hours grit. No other state spends as much of its lunchtime in my classroom, scheming and worst-case scenarioing. Where others are playing with caution and restraint—playing to *not lose*—Krapollo is playing to win. Halfway into the simulation, they decide, "We lost the moral high ground long ago. The only way we win is if we conquer them all." It's a strong team. And win they might. But not if they fail to overcome their hubris, their internal conflicts and power-grabbing corruption, and a one-man coup attempt.

Finally, there is the quiet and overlooked state of Ix-Zamna. Co-led by two young women, one from Brazil and the other from Guatemala, this team does not speak much English, but that will not matter (in fact, their fluency in Portuguese and Spanish will give them a competitive advantage). Ix-Zamna has a plan from the start: *principles over profit*. She will not enslave; she will not colonize; she will not violate indigenous lands with the construction of the Keystone XL pipeline; she will send troops to stop the genocide in Rwanda; and she will invest significant capital to effect a peaceful two-state solution in Palestine. Ix-Zamna will push forward always in the direction of her Ethical North. That will have consequences.

As far as gameplay goes, CIVGAME kicks off 10,000 years in the past. Peoples are emerging from the nomadic lifestyle of the Old Stone Age and just beginning to develop agricultural settlements that will transform into advanced civilizations as teams build economies and form governments. First, teams choose their civilization's location, bearing in mind that the goal is to build a successful state. Then they identify their first non-negotiable. ("Food," the teams all say.)

Over the next week, teams create Geographic Information Systems (GIS). This involves overlaying two sets of data: the origin sites of 10 high-yield, surplus-producing crops, and the origin sites of 13 species of agriculturally useful, domesticable animals. A number of teams move through this process quickly—some because they're just plain fast, but most simply because they distribute the work efficiently among team members. Eager to move forward, these teams add a third data set to their research: high-vulnerability natural disaster zones, which they want to avoid. Any natural disasters that happen in the world outside the game will happen inside it, too, and will be costly.

As teams overlay their base maps, they see which areas of the globe have the highest asset values at the dawn of the agricultural age. All but a handful place their dots in one of the historic "cradles of civilization" (this is very fun to watch; no one has gained this information from a textbook or Google; they have nailed it through their GIS analyses). Madaki settles along the Nile in Northeast Africa, Krapollo settles in Mesoamerica, and Ix-Zamna settles in Southwest Asia between the Tigris and Euphrates.

Assessment day arrives. There are two assessments, actually. One is a short literacy test focused on the content of the Agricultural Revolution. It's nothing special: a straightforward exercise that approximates the state exam students will take in May. The second assessment focuses on the students' GIS work. It has three sections: Knowledge, Understanding, and Wisdom. I tell students the sections require different depths of comprehension. I also tell them, "You don't *have* to take the whole test." They look at me, disbelieving. "Look," I say, "if you crush the Wisdom section, then I know you've already mastered everything below it. You can't beat the top floor without using the terms and skills of the floors underneath. Crush the Wisdom section, and you'll get an A on the whole thing, even if you don't attempt the Knowledge or Understanding sections." Students seem to think this is cool—like I have bestowed some great gift upon them.

The coolness breaks when one of them asks, "What if I bomb the Wisdom section and didn't do the other two?" Everyone turns to me, suddenly less confident. "Well," I say, "my plan is to look at the steepest section first. That's the Wisdom section. If you don't attempt it, or if you fail to meet the success criteria of the rubric, then I'll evaluate the next-steepest section. That would be the Understanding section. If you're successful there, then you'll earn a *B* or *C* for the whole test, depending on the amount of success you have. But if you come up short there, too, or if you don't attempt the Understanding section, then I'll grade the vocabulary part—the Knowledge section. If you do well there but nowhere else, then your grade for the whole test will be a *D*."

A different student speaks: "So if we only do the hard section and mess up, then we'll get an *F* on the whole thing because you won't have anything else to grade. Is that right?" "Boom," I say, nodding. "So we should do the lower sections just in case," another student adds. "Bigger boom," I say.

The Knowledge section will ask students to demonstrate accurate awareness of the academic terms and specialized concepts of our work (i.e., analysis, evaluation, GIS, base map, asset value). The Understanding section requires students to analyze and evaluate a new geographic location (not the site of their state) relative to food production. I give students an absolute location. They have to use thematic maps (the same texts they employed in their teams) to discern the presence or absence of our 10 focus crops and 13 animal species. Then they have to explain whether the site is likely to have significant, moderate, or limited agricultural success, based on its plant and animal assets. Above that, at the Wisdom level, students are invited to transfer their understanding. They are told they are living in Miami, Florida. First, they have to identify a business they want to establish. Then they have to answer this question: *How will you figure out where to put your business?* Students have to justify the inclusion of at least four base maps in their GIS and then explain how the system will help them solve their site-selection problem.

Derrick, one of my exceptional-education students and the point-man for the state of Madaki, has signed up to do the Wisdom section as an interview. (I have arranged for a colleague to monitor my class while I pull individuals like Derrick into the hall and listen to them share their answers.) I start by asking Derrick to identify a business he would like to open. "A nightclub, Prather," he says. I stare at him. Derrick smiles. "For real, Prather. You know how much money people spend at the club?" I tell him I do not. He tells me he will not make me pay any cover charges at Club Derrick. I am grateful.

"How will you figure out where to put Club Derrick?" "First," he says, "I need a map of all the nightclubs in the city. I want to know where the hot spots are. At first I thought maybe I shouldn't put my club near another one. Too much competition. But now I think it makes sense to put the club in a spot where people are already going." Smart. Derrick proceeds to tell me he wants a map of all the burglaries in Miami, a map of all the hotels, and a map of all the Waffle Houses. (He says everyone he knows winds up at Waffle House at 3 a.m. after clubbing.) Derrick justifies each map with similar precision. He explains he will put all four maps on top of each other. "My GIS will help me see the safe spots in the city near hotels and Waffle Houses where people are already looking to party.

It'll squish all my little maps together, and I'll be able to see which places in the city have more of the assets I want."

Derrick dominates this test. I smile and push him lightly against the wall as I move past him back into the classroom. "Get out the way, genius." He laughs and follows me in. "Long live Madaki!" he says.

Capital points (CPs) are the currency of CIVGAME. Every decision a team makes requires an expenditure of capital. Transporting troops, fighting wars, establishing colonies, buying resources, building health systems—all of it costs. A state earns most of its CPs through team averages on summative assessments: 40 CPs for a good-try *F*, 80 points for a *D*, 120 for a *C*, 160 for a *B*, and 200 points for an *A*.

There are some other ways by which a state may gain capital points. Notably, there is the occasional blessing of Lord Prather, aligned with positive developments somewhere in history. For example: "The invention of the steam engine fuels the Industrial Revolution. Any states located in present-day England acquire 100 CPs." Of course, just as Lord Prather may giveth, so too may he taketh away: "The deadliest earthquake in history kills over 800,000 in Shaanxi, China. Any state present in the modern province of Shaanxi loses one-third of its capital."

While some capital losses do boil down to historical misfortune, teams nevertheless have the power to protect themselves from careless losses. The more a team prioritizes organization and accountability, the less likely it is to incur fines and penalties, which come in the form of "economic sanctions." Teams receive a "fatberg fine" (–10 CPs) if they leave their workspaces with a waste-like mess for me to clean up. Similarly, a "corruption penalty" (–10 CPs) is levied if I inspect a student's binder and find it disastrously disorganized. "Recession hits" (–20 CPs) are imposed when teams are woefully unproductive or stagnant in their workflow. Lastly, teams are hit with "addiction fines" (–10) and "pollution penalties" (–3) when individuals are either overconsuming their phones or filling our gentle airspace with profanity. Losing capital hurts. Winning CPs is much more fun. Derrick's *A* on the assessment is good news for Madaki, especially since his two teammates both earned *D*s. As their collective average is a *C*, the team receives 120 capital points. (I should mention that both of Derrick's teammates attend a help session and ultimately retake the test. John earns a *C*, demonstrating proficiency but not mastery on the Understanding section. Antwan earns an *A* after he walks me through the process of picking a site in Baltimore where he and I will invest in the development of a community center for kids.) The states of Krapollo and Ix-Zamna both receive 200 capital points for their A averages on the GIS assessment.

The game continues and escalates through self-inflicted loss of capital points, through bargaining for resources and protection, through health disasters, through development of modern infrastructure and creation of systems of education, health services, and technology. Modernization is both expensive and the ultimate aim of CIVGAME. After a terrorist attack in Madaki costs Derrick, John, and Antwan 40 percent of their capital points and rumors of war-hungry Krapollo and advancing Ebola set them further on edge, they find themselves arguing about the best path toward viability—is it investing in defense or health? Stockpiling uranium or phosphorous? Then the men of Madaki notice on the Natural Resources Reserves Chart that one state in their class has a lot of phosphorus, rare earth minerals, uranium—and a ton of capital points. That state is the two-woman state of Ix-Zamna.

Derrick, John, and Antwan walk over to Catalina and Fernanda. (I am very confident this is the first time these two groups of students have ever acknowledged one another's presence, let alone attempted a conversation.) The guys look nervous. Fernanda says something in Portuguese to them. (She is just messing with them. Her English, though limited, is strong enough to host a simple conversation.) Nervousness now looks like terror. Derrick starts to speak. "Do you want to be partners with us?" Fernanda turns to Catalina: "Quieren formar una alianza." Fernanda understands, but the boys don't know that. "Wait a minute," they say, confused and getting up to walk over to me. I see the girls behind them smiling and shaking their heads. Antwan explains that Madaki wants to propose an alliance with Ix-Zamna, but Catalina and Fernanda don't speak any English. Instead of correcting him, I just say, "Well then, you guys better figure out how to speak Spanish."

John grabs a laptop from the cart, and the boys go back to Catalina and Fernanda. They open up Google Translate and begin typing. The girls look at me like, "Wait, you're making *them* communicate in *our* language?" (Catalina will tell me later that it felt good not having to do all the communication work for once, that it was nice for other students to see what she experiences.)

The boys propose a fairly lopsided deal. In exchange for 10 units each of phosphorus, rare metals, and uranium, *and* 60 capital points, the state of Madaki will help Catalina and Fernanda if any teams attack Ix-Zamna in the future. What the boys mean by "help" could not be less defined. Catalina and Fernanda have many options: ask them to be more specific, modify the terms of the proposal, or just decline the offer. But I think they are feeling empowered by the request—and not just in the context of the game. I think Catalina and Fernanda feel seen and valued by their classmates, and that matters. Also, the state of Ix-Zamna has a compelling humanitarian code, and Madaki is clearly a state in need. So the principled young women agree. Both sides draft an alliance contract in Spanish and in English and sign it. I make official the transfer of CPs and resources, and Madaki immediately takes its health infrastructure from level 2 to level 3. That means better protection against Ebola. The defense systems they are also hoping to develop will have to wait.

Whatever Adele Said…

CIVGAME has worked for many of my students. It has appealed to present-oriented minds, who like the challenge of an immediate hustle. It has appealed to ones with future-oriented minds, who like the challenge of a slow-burning, competitive contest.

But there are plenty of students who hate it. Denise was one. I take owner-ship of her disengagement. She basically opted out of CIVGAME early on, exist-ing now only as a nomad. I do try to engage her as an occasional saboteur. I invite her to stir the pot and cause drama behind the scenes. She passes.

I wish I had created something wholly different for Denise—created it *with* her—so that she might have felt a deeper connection to the course as a whole. But I have not had the bandwidth to do more than I am doing. Today's legislative session, for instance, gives some indication of the work this simulation requires. During this lesson, teams have to make foreign policy decisions relative to the Saudi government's involvement in the death of Jamal Khashoggi, the human-itarian plight of the Rohingya in Myanmar, the advance of Ebola across the Congo, and the civil war in Yemen. So much goes into this one lesson—materi-als, differentiation, and language supports, among others. Denise may very well do the work today, but it will not energize her the way it will her classmates.

I hope to do better, but for now, I just have to trust that other facets of my pedagogy have created some sweet spots for this young woman. Essential ques-tions seem to animate her; she has very strong opinions, and she has come alive when given the opportunities to express them. Test days have never been her best days, but I do think Denise respects the availability of assessment options that have catered to her creative side. Even if she has not always chosen them, she knows I have taken the time to make them for her. She also knows that I have given her permission to express a full range of emotions in class, that I have honored the agreements we established in August, that I have not dismissed her for being sad or frustrated or exhausted or furious, that her profanity has not brought forth an automatic referral, or that her ripping up assignments has not led me to cancel her. I think she appreciates that I have invited her to start again each day.

In fact, I know she does. Having learned yesterday that I will be taking a break from the classroom to support teacher development, Denise comes in teary-eyed and hands me a note. She tells me not to read it right then, so I put it aside. She gives me a hug and leaves.

I open the note.

Dear Mr. Prather,
    I'm going to miss you so much. I can't believe you're really leaving me. I can't believe I'm actually crying either. Don't tell nobody, but I really love you as a teacher. Don't forget me... or you'll die. Or whatever Adele said.

I do not know what Adele said. But I am proud to know that for all our hard moments, and in spite of a curriculum that poured so much into me and Madaki and Krapollo and Ix-Zamna but very little into her, Denise knows that I have her back. She knows that I see and respect her. How can I not when I know where she comes from?

She is a child of the Black Diamond.

෴ ෴ ෴

References

Aldric, A. (2018, November 4). Average SAT scores over time: 1972–2018 [Blog post]. Retrieved from https://blog.prepscholar.com/average-sat-scores-over-time

Allen, J., Gregory, A., Mikami, A., Lun, J., Hamre, B., & Pianta, R. (n.d.). Predicting adolescent achievement with the CLASS™-S observation tool. Retrieved from https://curry.virginia.edu/sites/default/files/uploads/resourceLibrary/Research_brief_CLASS-S4.pdf

Ayres, W. (2010). *To teach: The journey of a teacher* (3rd ed.). New York: Columbia University Press.

Bain, K. (2004). *What the best college teachers do.* Cambridge, MA: Harvard University Press.

Balingit, M., & Van Dam, A. (2019, December 3). U.S. students continue to lag behind peers in East Asia and Europe in reading, math, and science, exams show. *Washington Post.* Retrieved from https://www.washingtonpost.com/local/education/us-students-continue-to-lag-behind-peers-in-east-asia-and-europe-in-reading-math-and-science-exams-show/2019/12/02/e9e3b37c-153d-11ea-9110-3b34ce1d92b1_story.html

Barnum, M. (2019, April). Nearly a decade later, did the Common Core work? New research offers clues. Retrieved from https://www.chalkbeat.org/posts/us/2019/04/29/common-core-work-research/

Barshay, J. (2019, December 16). What 2018 PISA international rankings tell us about U.S. schools. Retrieved from https://hechingerreport.org/what-2018-pisa-international-rankings-tell-us-about-u-s-schools/

Berger, R. (2003). *An ethic of excellence: Building a culture of craftsmanship with students.* Portsmouth, NH: Heinemann.

Berger, R. (2015, April 30). What it really takes to inspire students to perform well (It's not test scores) [Blog post]. Retrieved from https://eleducation.org/news/what-it-really-takes-inspire-students-perform-well-it-s-not-test-scores

Berger, R., Rugen, L., & Woodfin, L. (2014). *Leaders of their own learning: Transforming schools through student-engaged assessment.* San Francisco: Jossey-Bass.

Black, P., & Wiliam, D. (1998, October 1). Inside the black box: Raising standards through classroom assessment. *Phi Delta Kappan.* Retrieved from https://kappanonline.org/inside-the-black-box-raising-standards-through-classroom-assessment/

Bloom, B. (1985). *Developing talent in young people.* New York: Ballantine Books.

Brimijoin, K., Marquissee, E., & Tomlinson, C. A. (2003, February). Using data to improve student achievement. *Educational Leadership, 60*(5), 70–73.

Brookhart, S., Guskey, T., McTighe, J., & Wiliam, D. (2020, September). Eight essential principles for improving grading. *Educational Leadership, 78*(1). Retrieved from http://www.ascd.org/publications/educational-leadership/sept20/vol78/num01/Eight-Essential-Principles-for-Improving-Grading.aspx

Bryner, J. (2007, February 28). Most students bored at school. Retrieved from https://www.livescience.com/1308-students-bored-school.html

Calkins, L. (1983). *Lessons from a child: On the teaching and learning of writing.* Portsmouth, NH: Heinemann.

Clifton, D. (2021). How to improve student and educator wellbeing. Retrieved from https://www.gallup.com/education/316709/how-to-improve-wellbeing-in-education.aspx

Collaboration for Academic, Social, and Emotional Learning [CASEL]. (2019). CASEL competencies. Retrieved from https://casel.org/sel-framework/

Collins, M. (1992). *Ordinary children, extraordinary teachers.* Norfolk, VA: Hampton Roads.

Costa, A., & Kallick, B. (2008). *Learning and leading with habits of mind: 16 essential characteristics for success.* Alexandria, VA: ASCD.

Coté, M. (2019, November). Differentiation: Beyond blue birds and red birds. *News You Can Use: The CPM Educational Program Newsletter.* Retrieved from https://pdfs.cpm.org/newsletters/CPM_NL_Nov_2019.pdf

Darling-Hammond, L., & Bransford, J. (2007). *Preparing teachers for a changing world: What teachers should learn and be able to do.* San Francisco: Jossey-Bass.

DC Design. (2017, August 14). What is human-centered design? Retrieved from https://medium.com/dc-design/what-is-human-centered-design-6711c09e2779

Dillard, A. (1987). *An American childhood.* New York: HarperCollins.

DiSalvo, D. (2013, August 26). To the human brain, "me" is "we." Retrieved from https://www.forbes.com/sites/daviddisalvo/2013/08/22/study-to-the-human-brain-me-is-we

Drum, K. (2011, November 20). Student achievement over the past 20 years. Raw data in *Mother Jones.* Retrieved from https://www.motherjones.com/kevin-drum/2011/11/raw-data-student-achievement-over-past-20-years/

Duckworth, A. (2020, May 18). What students need before perseverance [Blog post]. Retrieved from https://www.edweek.org/education/opinion-what-students-need-before-perseverance/2020/05

Dweck, C. (2006). *Mindset: The new psychology of success.* New York: Random House.

Dwyer, D. (1994, April). Apple Classrooms of Tomorrow: What we've learned. *Educational Leadership, 51*(7), 4–10. Retrieved from http://www.ascd.org/publications/educational-leadership/apr94/vol51/num07/Apple-Classrooms-of-Tomorrow@-What-We%27ve-Learned.aspx

Dwyer, D. (1995). *Changing the conversation about teaching, learning, and technology: A Report on 10 years of ACOT research.* Retrieved from https://saidnazulfiqar.files.wordpress.com/2014/10/changing-the-conversation-about-ict-in-learning-10-years-of-acot.pdf

Earl, L. (2003). *Assessment as learning: Using classroom assessment to maximize student learning.* Thousand Oaks, CA: Corwin.

Earl, L., & Cousins, J. (1995). *Classroom assessment: Changing the face, facing the change.* Toronto, Canada: OPSTF.

Erickson, H., Lanning, L., & French, R. (2017). *Concept-based curriculum and instruction for the thinking classroom* (2nd ed.). Thousand Oaks, CA: Corwin.

Flood, A. (2011, April 14). Getting more from George RR Martin [Blog post]. Retrieved from https://www.theguardian.com/books/booksblog/2011/apr/14/more-george-r-r-martin

France, P. (2020). *Reclaiming personalized learning: A pedagogy for restoring equity and humanity in our classrooms*. Thousand Oaks, CA: Corwin.

Fullan, M., Quinn, J., & McEachen, J. (2018). *Deep learning: Engage the world. Change the world*. Thousand Oaks, CA: Corwin.

Gall, M., Gall, J., Jacobsen, D., & Bullock, T. (1990). *Tools for learning: A guide to teaching study skills*. Alexandria, VA: ASCD.

Gay, G. (2018). *Culturally responsive teaching: Theory, research and practice* (3rd ed.). New York: Teachers College Press.

Graff, L. (2015). *Absolutely almost*. New York: Puffin Books.

Greene, B. (2005, May 30). This I believe: Science nourishes the mind and soul [Web audio]. *All Things Considered*. Washington, DC: National Public Radio. Retrieved from https://www.npr.org/templates/story/story.php?storyId=4666334

Guskey, T. (1994, October). Making the grade: What benefits students? *Educational Leadership, 52*(2), 14–20.

Guskey, T. (2019, October 28). Grades versus comments: Research on student feedback. *Phi Delta Kappan*. Retrieved from https://kappanonline.org/grades-versus-comments-research-student-feedback-guskey/

Guskey, T. (2020, September). Breaking up the grade. *Educational Leadership, 78*(1), 40–46.

Hansen, M., Levesque, E., Quintero, D., & Valant, J. (2018, April 17). Have we made progress on achievement gaps? Looking at evidence from the new NAEP results [Blog post]. Retrieved from https://www.brookings.edu/blog/brown-center-chalkboard/2018/04/17/have-we-made-progress-on-achievement-gaps-looking-at-evidence-from-the-new-naep-results/

Hattie, J. (2009). *Visible learning: A synthesis of 800+ meta-analyses on achievement*. New York: Routledge.

Hattie, J. (2012). *Visible learning for teachers: Maximizing impact on learning*. New York: Routledge.

Hattie, J., & Yates, G. (2014). *Visible learning and the science of how we learn*. New York: Routledge.

Hayden, R. (1984). *Collected prose*. Ann Arbor: University of Michigan Press.

Heick, T. (2018, November 26). 12 things that will disappear from classrooms in the next 12 years. Retrieved from https://www.teachthought.com/the-future-of-learning/things-that-will-disappear-from-classrooms-in-the-next-12-years/

Heritage, M. (2010). *Formative assessment and next generation assessment systems: Are we losing an opportunity?* A paper prepared for the Council of Chief State School Officers [CCSSO]. Retrieved from https://files.eric.ed.gov/fulltext/ED543063.pdf

Hodin, R. (2013, September 4). 33 authors on why they write. Retrieved from https://thoughtcatalog.com/rachel-hodin/2013/09/31-authors-on-why-they-write/

Jackson, A., & Kiersz, A. (2016, December 6). The latest ranking of top countries in math, reading, and science is out—and the US didn't crack the top 10. Retrieved from https://www.businessinsider.com/pisa-worldwide-ranking-of-math-science-reading-skills-2016-12

K–12 Academics. (n.d.). Standardized testing. Retrieved from https://www.k12academics.com/standardized-testing

Layton, L. (2015, October 24). Study says standardized testing is overwhelming nation's public schools. Retrieved from https://www.washingtonpost.com/local/education/study-says-standardized-testing-is-overwhelming-nations-public-schools/2015/10/24/8a22092c-79ae-11e5-a958-d889faf561dc_story.html

Levy, S. (1996). *Starting from scratch: One classroom builds its own curriculum*. Portsmouth, NH: Heinemann.

Littky, D., & Grabelle, S. (2004). *The big picture: Education is everyone's business*. Alexandria, VA: ASCD.

Lough, C. (2020, April 28). Dylan Wiliam: "Immoral" to teach "too full" curriculum. *Tes.com*. Retrieved from https://www.tes.com/news/dylan-wiliam-immoral-teach-too-full-curriculum

Love, B. (2020). *We want to do more than survive: Abolitionist teaching and the pursuit of educational freedom*. Boston: Beacon.

McKibben, S. (2018, October). Grit and the greater good. A conversation with Angela Duckworth. *Educational Leadership, 76*(2), 40–45. Retrieved from http://www.ascd.org/publications/educational-leadership/oct18/vol76/num02/Grit-and-the-Greater-Good@-A-Conversation-with-Angela-Duckworth.aspx

Moss, C., & Brookhart, S. (2009). *Advancing formative assessment in every classroom*. Alexandria, VA: ASCD.

Moss, C., & Brookhart, S. (2019). *Advancing formative assessment in every classroom* (2nd ed.). Alexandria, VA: ASCD.

National Academies of Science, Engineering, and Medicine. (2018). *How people learn II: Learners, contexts, and cultures*. Washington, DC: National Academies Press.

National Center for Education Statistics. (2019). SAT mean scores of high school seniors taking the SAT by sex, race/ethnicity in 2018. *FastFacts*. Retrieved from https://nces.ed.gov/fastfacts/display.asp?id=171

National Center for Fair & Open Testing. (2019, September 24). 2019 SAT scores: Gaps between demographic groups grows larger. Retrieved from https://www.fairtest.org/2019-sat-scores-gaps-between-demographic-groups-gr

National Commission on Excellence in Education. (1983). *A nation at risk: The imperative for educational reform*. Washington, DC: U.S. Office of Education.

National Research Council. (2000). *How people learn: Brain, mind, experience, and school* (Expanded edition). Washington, DC: National Academies Press.

The Nation's Report Card. (n.d.). How did U.S. students perform on the most recent assessments? Washington, DC: U.S. Office of Education and the National Center for Educational Statistics. Retrieved from https://www.nationsreportcard.gov/

Noddings, N. (2005). *The challenge to care in schools*. New York: Teachers College Press.

O'Connor, K. (2009). *How to grade for learning* (3rd ed.). Thousand Oaks, CA: Corwin.

O'Connor, K. (2010). *A repair kit for grading: Fifteen fixes for broken grades* (2nd ed.). New York: Pearson.

OECD. (2019). *PISA 2018 Results (Volume I): What students know and can do*. Paris: OECD Publishing.

Pate, A. (2020). *The innocent classroom: Dismantling racial bias to support students of color*. Alexandria, VA: ASCD.

Perkins, D. N. (1991, October). Educating for insight. *Educational Leadership, 49*(2), 4–8.

Phenix, P. (1964). *Realms of meaning: A philosophy of the curriculum for general education.* New York: McGraw-Hill.

Policy Studies Associates. (1992). *Relevant research for school decisions: Academic challenge for the children of poverty.* Washington, DC: U.S. Office of Education.

Reeves, D. (2017, Spring). Busting myths about grading. *All Things PLC.* Retrieved from https://issuu.com/mm905/docs/atplc_magazine__spring_2017_look-in

Rimm-Kaufman, S. (2020). *SEL from the start: Building skills in K–5.* New York: Norton.

Ruby Garage. (2017, July 17). A guide to human-centered design methodology and process [Blog post]. Retrieved from https://rubygarage.org/blog/human-centered-design

Ryan, J. (2018, October 19). Read President Jim Ryan's inaugural address: "Faith in the unfinished project." Retrieved from https://news.virginia.edu/content/read-president-jim-ryans-inaugural-address-faith-unfinished-project

Sawchuk, S., & Sparks, S. D. (2020, April 23). 8th graders don't know much about history, national exam shows. *Education Week.* Retrieved from https://www.edweek.org/teaching-learning/8th-graders-dont-know-much-about-history-national-exam-shows/2020/04

Schlechty, P. (2011). *Engaging students: The next level of working on the work.* San Francisco: Wiley.

Schneider, D. (Producer). (2011, November 27). Freeman Hrabowski [Television interview]. *60 Minutes.* New York: CBS.

Sinek, S. (2009). *Start with why: How great leaders inspire everyone to take action.* New York: Penguin.

Sloan, W. (2012, July). What is the purpose of education? *ASCD Education Update, 54*(7). Retrieved from http://www.ascd.org/publications/newsletters/education-update/jul12/vol54/num07/What-Is-the-Purpose-of-Education%C2%A2.aspx

Sondheim, S., & Lapine, J. (2000). Sunday in the park with George. In S. Sondheim, H. Wheeler, J. Lapine, B. Shevelove, & L. Gelbert, *Four by Sondheim, Wheeler, Lapine, Shevelove, and Gelbart* (pp. 561–742). New York: Applause Books.

Sousa, D., & Tomlinson, C. (2018). *Differentiation and the brain: How neuroscience supports the learner-friendly classroom* (2nd ed.). Bloomington, IN: Solution Tree.

Sparks, S. (2019, December 3). U.S. students gain ground against global peers. But that's not saying much. *Education Week.* Retrieved from https://www.edweek.org/ew/articles/2019/12/03/us-students-gain-ground-against-global-peers.html

Sparks, S. (2020, February 25). Hidden segregation within schools is tracked in new study. *Education Week.* Retrieved from https://www.edweek.org/ew/articles/2020/02/26/hidden-segregation-within-schools-is-tracked-in.html

Steele, C. (2009). *The inspired teacher: How to know one, grow one, or be one.* Alexandria, VA: ASCD.

Stiggins, R. (2004). *Student-involved assessment for learning.* Boston: Pearson.

Stringer, S. (2019, January 16). Bored in class: A national survey finds nearly 1 in 3 teens are bored "most or all of the time" in school, and a majority report high levels of stress. *The 74 Newsletter.* Retrieved from https://www.the74million.org/bored-in-class-a-national-survey-finds-nearly-1-in-3-teens-are-bored-most-or-all-of-the-time-in-school-and-a-majority-report-high-levels-of-stress/

TIMSS & PIRLS International Study Center. (2019). TIMSS 2015 international report. Retrieved from http://timss2015.org/timss-2015/mathematics/student-achievement/

Tomlinson, C. A. (2014). *The differentiated classroom: Responding to the needs of all learners* (2nd ed.). Alexandria, VA: ASCD.

Tomlinson, C. A. (2017). *How to differentiate instruction in academically diverse classrooms* (3rd ed.). Alexandria, VA: ASCD.

Tomlinson, C. A., & Javius, E. (2012, February). Teach up for excellence. *Educational Leadership, 69*(5), 28–33.

Tomlinson, C. A., Kaplan, S., Renzulli, J., Purcell, J., Leppien, J., Burns, D., Strickland, C., & Imbeau, M. (2009). *The parallel curriculum* (2nd ed.). Thousand Oaks, CA: Corwin.

Tomlinson, C. A., & Moon, T. (2013). *Assessment and student success in a differentiated classroom*. Alexandria, VA: ASCD.

Toth, M., & Sousa, D. (2019). *The power of student teams*. West Palm Beach, FL: Learning Sciences International.

van Manen, M. (1991). *The tact of teaching: Toward a pedagogy of thoughtfulness*. Albany, NY: State University of New York.

von Oech, R. (1986). *A kick in the seat of the pants: Using your explorer, artist, judge, and warrior to be more creative*. New York: Harper & Row.

Weir, P. (Director). (1989). *Dead poets society* [Motion picture]. United States: Touchstone Pictures.

Weiss, E. (2013, September 12). Mismatches in Race to the Top limit educational improvement: Lack of time, resources, and tools to address opportunity gaps puts lofty state goals out of reach. *Economic Policy Institute*. Retrieved from https://www.epi.org/publication/race-to-the-top-goals/

West, D. (1995). *The richer, the poorer*. New York: Random House.

Wiggins, G., & McTighe, J. (2005). *Understanding by design* (2nd ed.). Alexandria, VA: ASCD.

Wiliam, D. (2010). Teacher quality: Why it matters and how to get more of it. University of London, Institute of Education, Spectator "Schools Revolution Conference." Retrieved from http://dylanwiliam.org/Dylan_Wiliams_website/Papers_files/Spectator%20talk.doc

Wiliam, D. (2011a). *Embedded formative assessment*. Bloomington, IN: Solution Tree.

Wiliam, D. (2011b). *How do we prepare students for a world we cannot imagine?* Retrieved from https://www.dylanwiliam.org/Dylan_Wiliams_website/Papers_files/Salzburg%20Seminar%20talk.doc

Wiliam, D. (2011c, September 16). What assessment can—and cannot—do. Retrieved from http://dylanwiliam.org/Dylan_Wiliams_website/Papers_files/Pedagogiska%20magasinet%20article.docx

Witmer, T. (2010). *The shepherd leader: Achieving effective shepherding in your church*. Philipsburg, NJ: P&R Publishing.

World Bank. (2005). *World development report: Equity and development*. Retrieved from http://documents.worldbank.org/curated/en/435331468127174418/pdf/322040World0Development0Report02006.pdf

Zhao, Y. (2019). Foreword. In J. McTighe & G. Curtis (Eds.), *Leading modern learning: A blueprint for vision-driven schools* (2nd ed., pp. xv–xvii). Bloomington, IN: Solution Tree.

Index

Page references followed by an italicized *f* indicate information contained in figures.

About the Author

Carol Ann Tomlinson began her career in education as a public school teacher and spent 21 years in the classroom and in administrative roles. During that time, she taught high school, preschool, and middle school students in the content areas of English/language arts, history, and German. She also served as the district director of programs for advanced and struggling learners and as school community relations coordinator. While a teacher in the Fauquier County (Virginia) Public Schools, she received recognition as Outstanding Teacher at Warrenton Junior High School, Jaycees Outstanding Young Educator, American Legion Outstanding Educator, and the Soroptimist Distinguished Women in Education Award. She was named Virginia's Teacher of the Year in 1974.

Tomlinson is William Clay Parrish, Jr., Professor Emeritus at the University of Virginia's School of Education and Human Development. She was named Outstanding Professor in 2004 and received an All-University Teaching Award in 2008. In 2020, *Education Week*'s Edu-Scholar Public Influence Rankings placed Tomlinson 12th on its list of the United States' most influential higher education faculty members in terms of shaping dialogue about education and 4th in the field of educational psychology.

Tomlinson is the author of more than 300 books, book chapters, articles, and other educational materials including (for ASCD) *How to Differentiate Instruction in Academically Diverse Classrooms, The Differentiated Classroom: Responding to the Needs of All Learners, Fulfilling the Promise of the Differentiated Classroom: Strategies and Tools for Responsive Teaching, Integrating*

Differentiated Instruction and Understanding by Design: Connecting Content and Kids (with Jay McTighe), *The Differentiated School: Making Revolutionary Changes in Teaching and Learning* (with Kay Brimijoin and Lane Narvaez), *Leading and Managing a Differentiated Classroom* (with Marcia Imbeau), *Leading for Differentiation: Growing Teachers Who Grow Kids* (with Michael Murphy), and *Assessment and Student Success in a Differentiated Classroom* (with Tonya Moon). Her ASCD books have been translated into 13 languages.

She works regularly throughout the United States and internationally with educators who seek to create classrooms that are more effective with academically diverse student populations. She can be reached by email at cat3y@virginia.edu.

Cℛℭℛℭℛ

Related ASCD Resources: Teaching

At the time of publication, the following resources were available (ASCD stock numbers in parentheses):

Better Learning Through Structured Teaching: A Framework for the Gradual Release of Responsibility, 3rd Ed. by Douglas Fisher and Nancy Frey (#121031)

The Differentiated Classroom: Responding to the Needs of All Learners, 2nd Ed. by Carol Ann Tomlinson (#108029)

Differentiation in Middle and High School: Strategies to Engage All Learners by Kristina J. Doubet & Jessica A. Hockett (#115008)

Differentiation in the Elementary Grades: Strategies to Engage and Equip All Learners by Kristina J. Doubet & Jessica A. Hockett (#117014)

The Highly Effective Teacher: 7 Classroom-Tested Practices That Foster Student Success by Jeff Marshall (#117001)

How to Differentiate Instruction in Academically Diverse Classrooms, 3rd Ed. by Carol Ann Tomlinson (# 117032)

The Innocent Classroom: Dismantling Racial Bias to Support Students of Color by Alexs Pate (#120025)

Never Work Harder Than Your Students and Other Principles of Great Teaching, 2nd Ed. by Robyn R. Jackson (#1180340)

Qualities of Effective Teachers, 3rd Ed. by James H. Stronge (#118042)

Students at the Center: Personalized Learning with Habits of Mind by Bena Kallick & Allison Zmuda (#117015)

Teaching for Deeper Learning: Tools to Engage Students in Meaning Making by Jay McTighe and Harvey F. Silver (#120022)

Teaching with Empathy: How to Transform Your Practice by Understanding Your Learners by Lisa Westman (#121027)

Teach, Reflect, Learn: Building Your Capacity for Success in the Classroom by Pete Hall & Alisa Simeral (#115040)

Understanding Differentiated Instruction (Quick Reference Guide) by Carol Ann Tomlinson (#QRG117094)

For up-to-date information about ASCD resources, go to www.ascd.org. You can search the complete archives of Educational Leadership at www.ascd.org/el.

For more information, send an email to member@ascd.org; call 1-800-933-2723 or 703-578-9600; send a fax to 703-575-5400; or write to Information Services, ASCD, 1703 N. Beauregard St., Alexandria, VA 22311-1714 USA.

WHOLE CHILD
TENETS

The ASCD Whole Child approach is an effort to transition from a focus on narrowly defined academic achievement to one that promotes the long-term development and success of all children. Through this approach, ASCD supports educators, families, community members, and policymakers as they move from a vision about educating the whole child to sustainable, collaborative actions.

So Each May Soar relates to the **safe, engaged, supported,** and **challenged** tenets. *For more about the ASCD Whole Child approach, visit* **www.ascd.org/wholechild.**

1   HEALTHY
Each student enters school healthy and learns about and practices a healthy lifestyle.

2   SAFE
Each student learns in an environment that is physically and emotionally **safe** for students and adults.

3   ENGAGED
Each student is actively engaged in learning and is connected to the school and broader community.

4   SUPPORTED
Each student has access to personalized learning and is supported by qualified, caring adults.

5   CHALLENGED
Each student is challenged academically and prepared for success in college or further study and for employment and participation in a global environment.

Become an ASCD member today!
Go to www.ascd.org/joinascd
or call toll-free: 800-933-ASCD (2723)

ascd

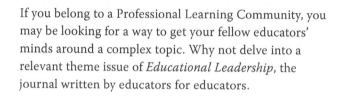